John Reading's Diary

Diary page, June 1747. Courtesy: Alexander Library
Special Collections Department, Rutgers University.

John Reading's Diary

Transcribed and Edited

By

David R. Reading

From Original Transcriptions

By

Dorothy A. Stratford

The Mount Amwell Project
Alexandria, Virginia, 22314
2010

Acknowledgments

Dorothy A. Stratford
Union, New Jersey

Fred Sisser III
Brick, New Jersey

The Hunterdon County Historical Society
Flemington, New Jersey

The Genealogical Society of New Jersey
Trenton, New Jersey

Printed in the United States of America

IBSN 978-0-615-37098-9

Published by

The Mount Amwell Project Inc., Alexandria, Virginia, 22314
www.mtamwell.org.

Dedicated to my mother, Roberta T. Reading,
whose interest in the family history inspired this book.

And

To my brother, Allan T. Reading, Secretatry/Treasurer of the The
Mount Amwell Project from the beginning. He lost his life while
training for a charity bicycle event on May 6, 2010.

David R. Reading, Editor.

CONTENTS

PREFACE .... **IX**

Introduction IX
Provenance XI
Transcription Rules XI
Acknowledgments XIII

JOHN READING'S DIARY **1**

1746/7 1
1747/8 22
1748/9 39
1749/50 51
1750/1 64
1752 75
1753 86
1754 91
1755 103
1756 113
1757 121
1758 131
1759 139
1760 148
1761 155
1762 160
1763 164
1764 168
1765 171
1766 174
1767 177

BIBILOGRAPHY **181**

INDEX **187**

PREFACE

Introduction

John Reading was an American-born official of the British Government in colonial New Jersey, serving as a member of the Governor's Privy Council from 1722 to 1758. He was President of the council for twelve years due to his longevity and seniority and twice acting Governor. Probably Hunterdon County's wealthiest resident, John Reading owned numerous properties in Hunterdon, Burlington, Sussex, Morris, and Warren Counties, most of which he inherited from his father, Col. John Reading.

Col. John, a West New Jersey proprietor,[1] had settled in the Quaker colony at Gloucester prior to 1684. For many years, he was clerk to the council of proprietors[2] and was appointed to the Royal Governor's Privy Council in 1712 serving until his death in 1717. Gov. Robert Hunter nominated his son, John Reading, to take his place in 1720. He would take his seat on the Council in 1722 and hold it continuously until he retired in 1758 due to poor health. He was appointed president judge of the court of common pleas for Hunterdon County in February 1727, and later that year was commissioned surrogate for Hunterdon and Somerset counties. As president of the council, a position which he attained in 1746, John Reading assumed the role of acting Governor and Commander-in-Chief of the province upon the death of then acting Governor John Hamilton in 1747. He would be the first American-born person to hold that high office and was required to assumed that role for a second time in 1757 on the death of Gov. Jonathon Belcher, albeit reluctantly.

John Reading was born in Gloucester in 1686 and reputedly traveled to England for his education with his mother, his sister Elsie, and possibly his uncle Daniel around 1691. The family relocated from

---

[1] A proprietor is someone granted ownership of a colony and full prerogatives of establishing a government and distributing land. http:// www.merriam-webster.com/dictionary/proprietor (August 18, 2010).

[2] The Council Proprietors of West New Jersey was established on September 6, 1688 to "record proprietary rights to the soil, supervise the distribution of dividends, issue warrants of survey, and have charge of unappropriated lands." John E. Pomfret. *The Province of West New Jersey 1609-1702* (Princeton, New Jersey: Princeton University Press, 1956) 157.

Gloucester to the Stockton area after their return and established an estate named Mount Amwell. As Col. John's only son, it is assumed that John Reading worked closely with his father during his young adulthood: managing the plantations, perfecting his deed writing skills and learning the art and science of surveying. Evidence of his growing reputation as a surveyor and administrator is demonstrated by his appointment as Surveyor General for the Council of Proprietors in 1712 when he was 26.[3]

He accompanied his father on a trip through northwestern New Jersey in the summer of 1715 to survey lands for the proprietors and their clients. In 1719, he was appointed by Gov. Robert Hunter as one of the commissioners to determine the north boundary line between New Jersey and New York and in the summer of 1719, embarked on a second trip to the upper Delaware River through the Delaware Water Gap to complete the survey. He recorded his adventures on both of these surveying trips in a journal which has survived.[4]

On the 1715 trip, he and his father visited George Ryerson. It is likely that this is when John Reading met George Ryerson's daughter and his future wife, 19 year old Maritje (Mary). They would marry five years later, settle on land near Flemington and join the newly formed Dutch Reformed Church (Mary Ryerson was a third-generation Dutch-American) where all of their future eleven children would be baptized.[5] For the next twenty-five years, he and Mary raised their children, managed their business affairs, and generally established themselves in the growing settlement of Hunterdon County while he continued his official duties as a councilor and judge.

John Reading would begin to keep a record of his daily financial transactions in January 1747, twenty-five years after the birth of his first child and eight months before taking on the role of acting governor for the first time. He records nearly everything: expenses paid when traveling, loans made and repaid, accounts reconciled and balanced, agricultural products sold, money collected for surveying and writing services, purchases of goods, tradesmen and laborers paid, slaves and indentured servants bought, taxes paid, charity given, support to the

---

[3] John E. Pomfret, *The New Jersey Proprietors and Their lands* (Princeton, New Jersey: D. Van Nostrand, 1964) 101.

[4] "Journal of John Reading," *Proceedings of the New Jersey Historical Society* 10 (January-October 1915) 95.

[5] Beulah Gangaware. "Baptisms of Readington Reformed Church 1720-1837, Readington, Hunterdon County, New Jersey." Typescript digital images, *Raub and More*. http:// raub-and more.com/ readingtonbap (16 Dec 2008).

local church, subscriptions to the Pennsylvania Gazette, books purchased, doctors and school teachers paid. Most importantly, he records the names of over 1,500 men and women with whom he transacted business. John Reading lived at the center of political, religious, and economic life in colonial New Jersey and his remarkable diary encompassing the last two decades of his life is a unique and valuable record for both historians and genealogists. John Reading made his final diary entry on November 4, 1767, one day before his death.

Provenance

The original diary consists of two "books" held by the Special Collections Department of the Alexander Library at Rutgers University in New Brunswick, New Jersey, and a third set of pages covering the first six months of 1753 held by the Hunterdon County Historical Society (HCHS) in Flemington, New Jersey. The 1753 manuscript was given to the HCHS as part of the Capner Papers in 1978. Sarah Matilda Capner, daughter of Hugh Capner Esq., married William Reading (1822-1897) a great-great grandson of John Reading in 1845. This marriage is the only circumstantial evidence known regarding the ownership history of the diary. The two books at the Alexander library were also probably part of the Capner Papers. It is unknown how the diary "books" landed at Rutgers. No matter how sketchy the provenance, to our knowledge, no one has disputed the authenticity of the diary and it should be considered a valid historical source document.

Transcription Rules

It is ironic that the John Reading Diary is not called a "journal" and the surveying journal is not referred to as a "Diary" as the diary entries look more like an accounting journal and the surveying journal reads more like a diary. The Diary records daily business transactions and expenses. John Reading's purpose was, presumably, to keep a record of his private affairs. Writing to himself as audience, he uses contractions extensively and at times they become ambiguous when taken out of context. For example, D'r and Dr in context can mean Debtor, Daughter, or Doctor. His spelling is inconsistent. His abbreviations for units of measure are inconsistent, for example bushel is written as bu, bul, b'l, b'll, and bush'l. His punctuation, capitalization, and grammar are typical of 18th century writing. The thorn (y is used for th, as in "y^e" for "the"), double f, superscripted abbreviations and the occasional Latin word or phrase appear throughout.

The Diary contains a wealth of important historical and genealogical information for the modern audience. Our goal is to render Reading's inscriptions both *readable* by the general reader and *accurate*. The document is made readable by liberally emending the source text to modernize the 18th century forms, thorns, etc., expanding the contractions, and updating some punctuation. Accuracy is maintained by not correcting spelling, guessing the meaning of unclear spelling or abbreviations, or changing the semantics of his entries.

Dorothy Stratford transcribed the original documents literally, that is, she copied the text as written, thorns and all. Regrettably, she did not transcribe all the monetary entries. These were considered of little interest to genealogists.[6]

The editors at the Genealogical Society of New Jersey minimally emended her work, bringing down to the line superscripted contractions and abbreviations and little else when they published the diary years 1747-1752 in the 1980's.[7] Our work presents a more liberally expanded transcription.[8] Headings and entries are standardized with the dates reproduced as written, and aligned to the left. The month and year headings are standardized and the spelling corrected. Proper name spelling is not corrected. Other spelling is not corrected unless obscure, then corrected within brackets. John Reading occasionally used the Latin *et*. It is replaced with *and*. Capital letters are retained as written. The first word of sentences is always capitalized.

Erratic punctuation is standardized, *e.g.*, missing periods, etc. Brackets in the original text are replaced with parentheses. Colons used at end of sentences are replaced by periods. Blank spaces are not retained. Missing or illegible words are shown with underlines. An editorial addition (supply), *e.g.,* "[an amount]", was occasionally inserted

---

[6] Dorothy A Stratford, telephone conversation with the editor, 11 June 2009.

[7] Dorothy A Stratford, "John's Reading Diary," *The Genealogical Magazine of New Jersey* 62.1 (January 1987): 1-8; 62.2 (May 1987): 83-88; 62.3 (September 1987): 128-134; 63.1 (January 1988): 40-48; 63.2 (May 1988): 91-96; 63.3 (September 1988): 133-138; 64.1 (January 1989): 19-24; 64.2 (May 1989): 73-80.

[8] The rules governing this transcription were based on guidance given by Michael E. Stevens and Steven B. Burg, *Editing Historical Documents, A Handbook of Practice* (Walnut Creek, Wisconsin: Altamira Press, 1997) and Mary-Jo Kline, *A Guide to Documentary Editing*, 2nd ed. (Baltimore, Maryland: Johns Hopkins University Press, 1987, 1998).

for missing monetary values when required to maintain semantic continuity. Monetary value forms are retained as written in the original transcriptions. The tailed p is replaced with per, pre, or pro as appropriate. Et cetera shown as &c is transcribed to *etc. Dᵒ* is expanded to *Ditto*.

Abbreviations for units of measure are not expanded because the full meaning of an abbreviated unit is not always apparent. Therefore, rather than introduce an error due to a false interpretation, the abbreviated units are left as originally written. Reading uses the symbol -0- extensively, usually for hay sales. It is believed that this symbol represents a hundred-weight, or one hundred pounds. Contractions are silently expanded; *Pay'd* becomes *Payed*, etc. Superscripts are moved down and the entire word spelled out, *e.g., Surᵍ* becomes *Surveying*. Thorns are replaced with *th*. Double *f*'s are replaced with *F*. Crossed out passages are retained and enclosed with brackets: [ ]. Open brackets are also used to clarify an obscure meaning. If the meaning of a word or phase is clarified by an editorial conjecture, a question mark is inserted inside the brackets [word?]. Abbreviations of people's names are left as written, *e.g., Bro: Luke, son D'l*.

Surnames are spelled inconsistently and given names are heavily abbreviated, and in some cases omitted entirely. The first name of men considered "gentleman" was frequently omitted, for example Mr. Hude or Mr. Antill. Full names, correctly spelled, are provided in the index if they could be determined with an acceptable degree of certainty. For example, Mr. Hude and Mr. Antill are clearly James Hude and Edward Antill, members of the Privy Council.

Acknowledgments

The collection and publication of the John Reading diary into a single indexed volume could not have been possible without the support of many individuals, both from the institutions and organizations holding the material to the people who helped me directly.

The Genealogical Society of New Jersey granted permission to publish parts of the diary previously published in their Society's magazine. The Hunterdon County Historical Society in Flemington, New Jersey allowed us to publish the 1753 transcription.

Fred Sisser III a member of both of these organizations provided a great deal of support and encouragement. Fred Sisser also helped to verify the manuscript against the Stratford transcriptions and researched the accuracy of the names in the index. Fred had also assisted Dorothy Stratford with the original transcriptions.

Bill Luken alerted me to the existence of the diary that started us on this endeavor. Eugenia Klein volunteered to edit the introduction and provided me with important comments and suggestions. Janet Riemer provided the photocopy of the original diary page and Rick Hayes-Roth contributed a final review.

Lastly, this publication is based in its entirety on the work done by Dorothy A. Stratford. Ms. Stratford, without hesitation, graciously provided me copies of her invaluable transcriptions and has given us permission to use them. I am grateful for her original work and for her support during the editing process.

Finally, I was not always able to find clarifying information or understand the meaning of a contraction. I also may have made some mistakes. The work may be imperfect, but the responsibility is entirely mine.

JOHN READING'S DIARY

1746/7

January 1746/7

1   Payed Mr. Ringo[9] for 35 lb sugar. And arrived at home that _____ Pen[nsylvani]a about noon.

2nd   This last night toward day was taken very ill with bad W[?] and some giddiness in my head. Took a vomit.

3   Continued sick sent for a Doctor who blood let me

4   Sent to the Docter for a purge who sent me one.

5th   I took the same in the morning _____.

6   The giddiness was not yet wholey removed but I grew better.
Alex'n Hunter left on Jas Martins account [money].
Got some of the wheat out of the barrall.

7   Winnowed up to 52 lb wheat being the last in the barn.

8   Sent for a wood slead from Benj Stout.

9   Reconed with Robt Calcut and paid him the Balance and at the same time lent him [money].

10   Reconed with Mary Kinny and paid her.

12   Sent Daniel for Mrs. Lee.

13   Payed Mr Wm Montgomerie for 2 gall of ___; for 13 gals melasses; for pewter.

14   Daniel returned with Mrs. Lee.

---

[9] PHILIP RINGO (1682-1757). Hunterdon County Judge, tavern owner, and father of Albartus and John. David Leer Ringo, Jr., "What Ever Happened to the Ringoes?" (Hunterdon County Historical Society meeting, Ringoes, New Jersey. October 21, 1967).

15   Sent by Tho Marton to Burlington with 5 returns; one for Ruloff
      Skank enough for payment thereof to the Surveyor Generall and
      Wooley: ___ Eliz: Pain; Chal'd Remersey.
      Recorded ILiffs last deed being lodged with Mr. Sam'l Harrison[10]
      and the first with Mr. DeCow[11] at Burlington. Wrote to S'l
      Harrison to send the last up and exchanged.
      Let Wm Force have 6 bu of wheat upon these conditions, either
      to give me credit for it with Godfrey Van Duren, or else to work
      it out in harvist as usual.

16   Lay'd out at Lawrence Williamses for Earthenware Expenses at
      Mr Ringoes.
      Spoke for a side Sadle and _[flax] reeds at Behtelsimer.
      Acknowledged a deed from Peter Middagh[12] to Derrick ___.
      Received for said deed to said Derrick.
      ___t lb Mr. Franklin[13] for the newspapers to Co___.
      Accompted with Martin Shefley & paid him the balance.

18   Cash Payed to Valentine the Peddlar.
      Received from John Deal Berg for a Deed (acknowledged).
      Mr Wm Montgomerie _____
      T ___ tons account the sum of [money].

---

[10] SAMUEL HARRISON (d. 1762). High Sheriff of Gloucester County. At a Council held at Perth Amboy the 23rd day of November 1739, Samuel Harrison is recognized officially as the "Sherrif [Sheriff] of Gloucester County." In a Council held at Burlington May 30th, 1740 with John Reading in attendance, he is referred to as "Samuel Harrison high Sherrif of the County of Gloucester..." Frederick W. Ricord and William Nelson, eds. *Documents Relating to the Colonial History of New Jersey,* Vol. XV: *Journal of the Governor and Council 1738-1748* (Trenton, New Jersey: The John l. Murphy Publishing Co., 1891. Rpt. PDF NJA1153A, Morristown, NJ: Digital Antiquarria, 2006), 64, 85.

[11] ISAAC DECOW, ESQ. (1673-1751). Surveyor General of the Western Division of New Jersey. Surveyor general offices were established in Burlington and Amboy under the same act in 1719 that authorized the expedition to establish the boundary between New Jersey and New York. Ella S. DeCou and John Allen DeCou, compilers. *The Genealogy of the DeCou Family* (Trenton, NJ, 1910), 69.

[12] PETER MIDDAGH (b. 1685?), d. after 1755). Elected to the Assembly in 1754. Owned land on the Raritan River. William A Whitehead, ed. *Archives of the State of New Jersey: Documents Relating to the Colonial History of New Jersey,* Vol. VIII: *Governors 1751-1757* (Newark, New Jersey: Daily Advertiser Printing House, 1885. PDF NJA1081A, Morristown, NJ: Digital Antiquarria, 2005), 401.

[13] BENJAMIN FRANKLIN (1706-90). Presumedly for the Pennsylvania Gazette. In 1747 Franklin was planning to retire from his printing business which he did in 1748, turning it over to his foremen David Hall. Walter Isaacson. *Benjamin Franklin, An American Life* (New York: Simon & Shuster, 2003), 233.

Peter Hay by C ___ (not paid)
Wrote to Henry Lane by A'r Louzier to send by him the
Balance of our account ____ was better than 19 in gold or silver.
Take his Receipt with a promise to deliver it.

February 1746/7

2d   At the request of Sam'l Green by Jos'r Opdike I sent him a Draft
and Field works of Benj: Severns & his land and of the divisions
thereof that the said Green might be enabled to settle the affair
between them. To which Draft and Fieldworks[14] he gave me 2/6.
At the same time wrote a letter to said Green.

3   Received from Ann Kitchin for a deed.

4   Benj: Severns obtained from me a certificate in the affair between
him and Opdike containing as underneath vizt: these may certify
that I have been employed as a surveyor by Benj: Severns and
Jos'p Opdike to run round the lines of their Plantations in
Amwell conveyed to them by Sam'l Green their Father in Law
and divide by protraction of Courses and Distances if I miss not
to contain in the whole 495 A's strict measure. And also that I
ran the Dividing line between them and find that there is
contained in Benjs: lines 37 more than in Jos'as.

Feb the 4th 1746 [signed]

John Reading

Johan Yerie Behtelsimer bought two reeds which came to 10s
which with one other and a flax reed came to [an amount].
Received from Robt Large for two Deeds.
Sent letters to Mr Jno Coxe[15] and Zach'y Blornersfelt and Corn's
Bowman.
Received an answer from Mr Wm Coxe and Corn's Bow[man].
Went up to Bethlehem. Surveyed 5 Acres of Swamp of Robt
Large. Charged for same.

---

14 A Draft is hand a drawn map. Fieldworks are the record of the measurements made in
the field. John Love, *Geodaesia: or, the Art of Measuring Land, etc., 8th ed.* (London: 1768.
Springfield, Missouri: Gingery, 1984), 56, 61, 68.

15 JOHN COXE (1712?-62). Son of Col. Daniel Coxe. Rev. Henry Miller Cox, *The Cox
Family in America* (Somerville, New Jersey, 1912), 212.

9   Surveyed 5 Acres for Adrian Hege[man].

12   Received from Jno Jewell in full of a _____.
        Peter Rockefeller had his deed sign[ed].
        Went to Burial of Jeromus Van Est.
        Sent down to the Landing to Ishmael Shipen who I had engaged
        to finish John's house.

20th   Sent up to Bethlehem James Willson Deed per Pennington.
        Went to survey Phil Phelps plantation in Amwell.

21   Went to Divide the same and surveyed a vacancy.

23   Went towards the Landing in order to speak with and hasten the
        joyner to finish Joseph house. Met with him in the Road. Came
        back that night. Expenses in the journey and a pair of Sizars
        bought.

24th   Received from Thomas Logan in full for a pair of leases.
        At the request or Jno Robbins C'trn[?] a Commission for laying
        out of Roads. Met at Vanboskirks in order to lay out a Road but
        the people not meeting nor concluding on the same deferred to
        another time.
        Brought from Godfey Van Durens Beetle rings and a wedge
        made out of our own Iron, wt 61 lb.[?]

29   Winowed up 21 bu Rye out of the lesser stack.
        Received from Godfrey Peters for a Deed from Jno Quick to the
        daughters of Ad: Albertse and survey a lott of land.

March 1746/7

2d   Robert Calcut entered his month's service at 30s per month.
        Went down to Trenton on an arbitration Acknowledged a deed at
        Pennytown (Received the pay). Arrived there in the afternoon.
        Took several Depositions on the affair Adjudged to Pennytown
        30th.
        Paid John Yard for 2 hatts one beaver, one castor. Paid Wm
        Seman the Brewer for Bro: Ryerson.
        Left with Phillip Weller's wife on Benj: Stouts account. _____ at
        Wm Yards and expenses on the Road.
        Payed for _____ of _____ 5 shaloon and Almanack.

The breadth of the Front of an angular cupboard ought to be at least 4 ½ feet of a clothes press 4 foot 4 Tiers of shelves to slide with drawers under to front the outside.

Ishmael Shippen sent up his apprentice whoe began on the 6th.

6th   Went to the Tryall of Negroes. Rent at Wal: Harney's ____.
Payed Dr. Van Waggoner in full.

7th   Continued the Tryall. Sentenced Harry, Tom, Pigg and Priamus to be whipped.
Lent Godfrey Van Duren [money].
Robt lost ½ of a day this week.

9   Joh's Bossenberg Payed towards the Exchange of land. Robt Calcut had 2 bu Rye.

10   Went with John Van Nest to view the Mss Coxes Land in Bethlehem. Wrote to Mr John Coxe on the same account.
Went to Town Meeting.
Lay'd out upon fish bought by my wife.
Received in full from James Martin the sum of [money].
This day in the morning Ishmael Shippen went to work upon John's house having come up the night before.

12th   Mrs. Lee went home. Had for her service [an amount].
Went to survey some of Mr Coxes land sold to D'd Kinny, Wm Flocker and others.
Mrs. Lee had 2 bu wheat. Paid for same.

13th   Went to survey t[he land] supra. Daniel returned from carrying Mrs. Lee home.

14th   Went upon the above surveys.
Received with Benj: Stout upon the woodwork of John's house cupboard and slead and paid him the balance.
Gone to Bethlehem on surveying of several persons lands.
____ the Division between Aaron Seyoe and his son. I charged 7s. Received Barclay Tract and charged 5s.
_____ lines of Samuel Johnson ___ affair charges 15s
_____Thatcher Received from Jas ____ for a deed ___ and began to survey 1000 Acres from the B_____.

19th   Proceeded in said survey and division of the 1000 Acres. Finished the same charged 20s.
Went to Jere Thatcher and Thos Curtis's ran round and divided

some lands for them.

Bought from Thos Thatcher 2 Deer skins being a pair of charges for surveying, making a Draft sent to Phila.

21   Came home.

22   Gave to a Charitable Use.

23   Received from Henry Lane by Ishmael Shippen light money.[16]

24   Acknowledged a deed for Wm Exceen (not paid). Agreed with Wm Force for some land bought from Bosenberg.

25   Began to plant [son] Johns orchard at the Royall Oak.

Continued planting. Tab, T. Woolverton's carter, brought up 400 foot of boards the carting to pay for the boards.

27   Peter Romine paid 12/8 in part of Rent.

Sent Benj: Howell[17] with Eliz: Harney to carry her part of the way to Mr Beatty's.[18]

28   Returned from and expenses Sent [cash] by John for lime.

30   Went to Pennytown on the affair between Wm Snowden and all and Corn's Ringo[19] and his wife. Expenses on the road.

April 1747

1   Payed Helena Johnson in part for spinning.

2nd   Surveyed 8 Acres of Land for Jas Baird and about 7 Acres for Wm Taylor.

3rd   John brought home from Wm Montgomerie's a barrell of Pork Sent to the Sadlers for a side Sadle and bridle.

Ran out and Divided some Land between Joh's Bossenberg and

---

[16] New Jersey light money was valued 1/6 value below New Jersey proclamation money. Alvin Rabushka, *Taxation in Colonial America* (Princeton, New Jersey: Princeton University Press, 2008), 370.

[17] BENJAMIN HOWELL (b. 1724?). Son of Capt. Daniel Howell. Married Agnes Wooliver. Josiah Granville Leach, *Genealogical and Biographical Memorials of the Reading, Howell, Yerkes, Watts, Latham, and Elkins Families* (Philadelphia, 1898), 158.

[18] CHARLES BEATTY (1715-72). Born in Ireland, he came to America and eventually came under the influence of the Rev. William Tennent and was licenced to preach in 1742. He was appointed a trustee of The College of New Jersey in 1763 and married Ann Reading, John Reading's oldest daughter in 1746. Charles C. Beatty. *Record of the Family of Charles Beatty* (Steubenville, Ohio, 1873), 9-26.

[19] CORNELIUS RINGO (1695-1768). Brother of Philip. Died in Maidenhead (Lawenceville), New Jersey. Ringo, "What Ever Happened to the Ringoes?"

Robert Barns in Amwell. Charged [an amount].

Payed Tab for bringing home the Boards.

7th   Set out for Burlington and Phila. Called at Trenton. Went to Bristol.

8th   Proceeded in my Journey to Phila arrived there about 10 of the Clock.

Left with George Plumly £70 to be paid Mr. Edward Shippen[20] for the use of Mr. Alford[21] out of which money I kept back (but paid other money) 2 Ducats[22] paid to me for 16s a piece but they are current for no more than 14s. Lodged at Poquessing. Lay'd out and expended sum of [money].

9th   Came to Bristol. Breakfasted there. Went to Burlington. Paid the Board money for 11 Returns.

Payed to the Sec'ys office for Recording several deeds. Gave Sec'y Read[23] a Pistole[24] for part of fee for a Patent which I left in the Sec'ys office to be Recorded. Payed the Clerk of the Coun'l of Prop's for 3 warrants of Resurvey.

10   Returned homewards. Expenses at Bristol and Ferrys etc.

11   Went and made a Survey upon more Land near Francis Quick's

---

[20] EDWARD SHIPPEN, III (1703-81). A wealthy merchant and government official in Philadelphia, Pennsylvania. He and John Reading were on the board of trustees of the College of New Jersey (Princeton). His grand-daughter, Margaret Shippen, was the second wife of Benedict Arnold. http://en.wikipedia.org/wiki/Edward_Shippen_III. (July 23, 2010).

[21] JOHN ALFORD (1685-1761). Of Charlestown, Mass. He was a member of the Ancient and Honorable Artillery Company in 1714; was one of the King's Councillors, and was distinguished as founder of the Alford Prof, of Nat. Theology, at Harvard, and for giving a large sum to the Society for Propagating the Gospel among the Indians in North America. John Alford purchased several land tracts in Hunterdon County in 1714. See Stanton D. Hammond, *Hunterdon County Maps with Name Index*, (Genealogical Society of New Jersey, 1965) for land listed in his name and William Allen, *An American Biographical and Historical Dictionary*. 2nd ed., (Boston: Hyde, 1832). 18.

[22] A gold or silver coin minted in Europe John J. McCusker, *Money & Exchange in Europe & America, 1600-1775, A Handbook* (Williamburg, Virginia: Institute of Early American History and Culture, 1978) 11.

[23] CHARLES READ (1713-74). Colonel Charles Read, collector of the port of Burlington, mayor, a justice of the Supreme Court, and sometime chief-justice of the Province, many years secretary to the Provincial Council, and a Colonel in the service of New Jersey prior to the Revolution. Whitehead, *Colonial History of New Jersey*, Vol. VIII, 408.

[24] A Spanish gold coin equal to two escudos or 28 shillings McCusker, *Money & Exchange in Europe & America, 1600-1775*, 11.

in Amwell and tried A Line of Hen: Oxley's Survey. Came to Mr. Ringoes. Met with F. Quick who agreed if the land Supposed to be a vacancy proved to be to let me have the Timber of Two acres next adjoyning up to that taken up in satisfaction on for what he has destroyed upon that. I had taken up Mart: Ryerson[25] and Phil: Ringo Evidences.

13   Went to Trenton on the Arbritration formerly mentioned but two Evidences taken.

Charges at Wm Yard's.

14th   Wine and Expenses left unpaid when went to Burlington. To a pair of shoes and sundry's bought at Mr Reeds.

Left a Return of H: Oxley's 50 Acres to be sent to Burlington. Tho: Martin Payed me in cash sent from Sam'l Furman.

15th   Bought an horse from the Widdow Nuel Forster. Paid her in hand £1.9.4. Gave my note for the remainder payable on the 16th of Nov'r next. She in the meantime is to prove her late husbands will and performe the office of an Executrix.

16   Went over to Jno Quicks Plantation to run out a piece of Land bought from Daniel Collin now sold to Daniel Kinney [?].

17   Received from Wm Anderson the balance of our Accounts.

Went with Jno Van Nest upon an alteration of _____ To be _____ Trouble not _____.

20   Acknowledged a Deed for Jos'a Opdike. He paid.

Mich'l Short paid the Interest of a Bond for £25.

Paid to son John[26] on Sarah Thomas's account for Mr Mart: [Ryerson].

21   Went to Trenton. Came back to Mr Ringos that night.

22   Jos Bossenberg paid towards the exchange for Land.

23rd   Gave Jere: Wright and Jos: Mott leave to plant an old Field at

---

[25] MARTIN RYERSON (1698-1767). John Reading's brother-in-law. Brother of Lucas, Blandina, Mary, and George. He married Catherine Coxe. Martin was a judge in Hunterdon County. Phyllis A. Ryerson and Thomas A. Ryerson, *The Ryerse-Ryerson Family 1574-1994* (Ingersoll, Ontario: T.A. Ryerson & Son, 1994, 1996) 18.

[26] JOHN READING (1722-66). John Reading's first son. Married Isabella Montgomery. Father of Valiant John, a revolutionary war soldier, who was father of Joseph who was father of Hon. James Newell, John Grandin, Joseph Hankinson and Phillip Grandin Reading, all leading citizens of Hunterdon County in the 19th century. Leach, *Memorials*, 41.

Paquaess they makeing and mending the fence round the same substantially with railes made from the dead trees in the field. Corn's Weycoff paid the Remainder of his Bond with light money.

25   Went to Mr Joseph Stouts on account of the monies.
      Robert Calcot had 2 bls of Rye.
27th Went with Mich'l Henry to trye the lines of his son Daniels plantation bought from Geo: Lesley.[27] Charged _____. Since paid.
28   Wrote a deed for Wm Taylor.
29   Set out for Trenton. Acknowledged a deed for Jos: Boss. Received from Go'd: Peters and Pet: Rockefeller for the Recording of 2 Deeds by me Sent to Burlington.
30th Bought severall thumb latches and nails. Paid for a pair of shoes for Margt Youngblood.

May 1747

2nd   Came home. Spent at Mr Ringoes coming and going.
      Payed Benj: Stout for mending the wagon.
      Payed Margaret Youngblood for spinning.
      Payed Helena Johnson for Ditto. Payed Eliz: Robert for Ditto in cash and sunries per account.
4th   John Garrison paid in part of a Bond.
5th   Went to Amboy to Council pursuant to a Summons by the Presidents[28] orders.
6th   Sat in Council.
7   Still in Amboy waiting on the Assembly.
8th   The Assembly passed a bill for a further provision of the Troops at Albany.
9   President Signed the bill and gave leave to the Assembly to adjourne themselves to the 25th of [this month?] instant. That day came home.

---

[27] GEORGE LESLEY (d. 1751). Inherited land from his uncle George Willocks, one of the twenty-four Proprietors of East New Jersey. Sold land in 1742 or 1743. Whitehead, *Colonial History of New Jersey*, Vol. VIII, 401.

[28] JOHN HAMILTON (d. 1747), President of the Privy Council, who was the acting Governor. Whitehead, *Colonial History of New Jersey*, Vol. VI, 435.

Payed for my board vizt: Lodgings and Breakfast. To Mrs
Serjeant for dinners, horse and Expenses. Expended on the other
accounts at Amboy and on the Journey.

To Corn's Bogart for Expenses by son John's cart's of wheat. To
John Brown in bringing some boards from the Landing.

Corn's Ringo gave me 7:6 to bear my expenses at the time of the
Arbitration.

11   Son Daniel[29] brought from Henry Lane in part of pay for last
years crop.

13   Went to Trenton paid for 3 small screws for 4 locks, 3 bolts, for 3
skins of parchment.

14   Mr Phil: Ringo assumed the payment of 3s upon Wm Exeens
account. Since paid.

Payed Godfry Van Duren the Balance of our accounts and took
his Receipt.

15th   Vincent Robert had 2 bll wheat.

Tho: Deremus Paid in cash 78:01 which together with a Bond
from his two sons for £18:2:8:1 completed the pay for 727 acres
of Land at the Bog Meadow. A third part of which is mine. I. had
14:00:6 of the cash and took the Bond which made my share of
the same.

Sent by Wm Anderson to buy two bottle of British Oil.

Ishmael Shippy finished Johns House and A Cupboard.

Delivered to Peter Horner a Bond from the Messrs Kirkbrides to
him for a Title to Land.

16   Payed Sarah Thomas.

18   Received from George Schamp jur for a deed.

16   Sent to the Landing to buy Hinges.

Received from Henry Lane the balance of our account.

18th   Left with son Daniel 10s Light money to buy 2 b'l salt.

19   Set out on a journey in Quest of a Mineral Spring in Penna.
Lodged at Pohohatcong that night.

20   Proceeded on our Journey. Arrived there and returned back as far

---

[29] DANIEL READING (1727-68). Married Euphemia Reid. His great grandson Daniel
K. Reading left funds to establish Reading Academy on Bonnell Street in Flemington.
Leach, *Memorials,* 49.

as _____. Lodged there that night.

21   Proceed in our Journey homewards. Came over the ferry went up Delaware above the Marble Mountain and viewed and took the course of the River of some land above the Ladds, Wetherills and Decows. Went to Prickets and lodged there that night.

22d   Run out forth of Mrs. Helby's Tract above Pohohatcong for Walter Cohoon 400 acres. The same day went to Rich'd Stouts at Muskonetcong to Run the lines of a tract of land formerly surveyed to John Bray. Began that night.

23   Finished and Returned home. Received for my Trouble [an amount]. In my absence there was paid to Nancy Calcot [money]. from Dennis Woolverton in Balance of Accounts.

Received from John Reading the sum of Twenty six pounds fifteen shillings being in full of all accounts and demands to this date [signed] Ishmael Shippy.

27   Received from Wm Voreheise for a deed (in my absence left the pay).

Martin Ryerson borrowed of me 46s.

29   John Lindsley jur left with me £ 3:13:7 on Mr. Alfords account, which with a Receipt from Messrs Sergeant and Bonnells pays off the Principal and Interest due upon Bond to said Mr Alford.

Richard was to set out this morning from Jos: Kings[?] for the Minnerall Spring in Pensilv'a.

30   Payed the Schoolmaster Rich'd Weeks for a 12 Months Scholeing of 4 Children and 2s over upon brother Martins account. Bought a horse from Albertus Ringo[30] for £15. Payed him in part. Went to Tunis Quicks to Resurvey his Plantation.

June 1747

1st   Received from Corn's Johnson on James Chain's Account.

2   Gave Master Jas Weeks for services don to George.

Surveyed And: Heaths plantation and lands adjacent charged [an amount]. Agreed with said Heath to let him have so much

---

[30] ALBARTES RINGO (1722-1800). Son of Philip. Lived in Hopewell, New Jersey. Ringo, "What Ever Happened to the Ringoes?"

Proprietary Right to cover the overplus included in his survey at the rate of 10 per 100 Acres payable the next Fall.

3 Payed James Bradbury the cooper for well bucket 2 pails and piggins 7s and six pence over towards the flour cask.

Martin Ryerson borrowed from me to pay the Schoolmaster Richard Weeks the sum of £ 3:3:8.

Mr. Wm Coxe gave a Receipt upon back side of David Kinnys Bond.

4th Went to Tunis Quicks to finish the lines of his and Mart: Hardins's Plantations. Staked off the Division Line between them to the doing of which he had consented on 30th of last month and upon a Resurvey if there was found so much land in his tract as to allow said Quick to have his 60 chains he would allow it but when on this day I came he would by no means be brought to Establish the said line but never tbe less he assisted to fix the same which was from an oak stump near the brook to a post by the Road at the distance of 60 chains South from the corner white oak. Received from said Quick for my often attendance and service therein and for Resurvey. On the same day went to John Williamson's and Jacobus Whittaker's in order to Resurvey their Plantations. Measured several lines of the same.

5th Finished the same and ordered by both of them to sell them a Proprietary Right to lay upon the Overplus. John Williamson gave me 30s to pay (for the Returning of his Part) to the Surveyor General charges for said service 15s besides Returning. Johannes Yerg Binder had 1 bl of wheat and Ditto of Rye.

9 Received of Antho Lousier for the Hair Cloath 9 yds. Coenradt Shafer had 2 bus of wheat.

10 Said Coenradt made up 10 dys work at 2/6 per day. Surveyed a lot of land for Hen: Landis. Received from Daniel Carlin for Surveying.

11 Acompted with Tho: Marting and Rosts to pay for son Johns House (all other accounts Balanced). No allowance to be made for 3/6 upon Widdo Kitchens account.

12 Set out for the Mineral Spring in Penna in company with son

George.[31] Gave him £ 4:1:3. Left with my wife to send to New York £:1:16 Went as far as John Andersons near the Forks that night.

13   Went to Joseph Pettys and agreed for son Georges Diet, Washing and Lodgings at 3/6 per week. Horse pasture Joseph asked 9s per week. Lodged there that night.

14   Set homeward where I arrived at night. Expenses _____
      In my absence fetched 4 galls of Rum @5/6 per gall from Mr. Ringoes.

15   David Connagh began to mow grass.

17   Received by Express the news of Presidents [John Hamilton] death. Wrote to Mr Antill[32] and Mr Hude[33] acquainting them that I intend for Amboy next day.

18   Agreed with Walter Harney to go to Trenton for 5s the Journey. Wrote by him to Mr [John] Coxe, Mr Rodman[34] and Mr Smith.[35] Set out for Amboy. Lodged at Mr Antills that night.
      Robt Calcot came this day and began his month @ 50s per mo.

19   Proceeded in our Journey and arrived at Amboy about 8 in the morning. Was qualified[36]. Went to the funeral of the late

---

[31] GEORGE READING (1725-92). Married Rebecca Mullen. After she died in childbirth in 1781, George resettled near Ft. Ligonier, Pennsylvania where he was a Revolutionary War officer. George and sons then moved to Bourbon County, Kentucky and later to Missouri. Leach, *Memorials,* 44.

[32] EDWARD ANTILL (1699-1770). The son of a prominent New York City merchant Appointed to the Governors's council in 1745 and reappointed to serve in Gov. Belcher's council in 1746. In 1754 he gave £1800 towards founding Columbia College in the interest of the Episcopal Church. Whitehead, *Colonial History of New Jersey*, Vol. VIII, 378.

[33] JAMES HUDE (1695-1762). A merchant in New Brunswick, 1726; first recorder of the city of New Brunswick, judge of the court of common pleas, 1732-48, member of the provincial assembly, 1738, member of the governor's council 1738-46, 1761-63, trustee of Rutgers College, master in chancery, and mayor of New Brunswick. "Hude, James". *The Twentieth Century Biographical Dictionary of Notable Americans* (Vol. V, 1904) N. pag.

[34] JOHN RODMAN (1679-1755). He was, like his father, a prominent physician and a member of the Society of Friends. He was a member of provincial assembly 1727-9, member of governor's council 1738-55. William W.H. Davis, A.M., *History of Bucks County Pennsylvania.* Vol III, (New York, Chicago: The Lewis Publishing Co., 1905) 162.

[35] RICHARD SMITH (1699-1751). He was one of two representatives from Burlington in the Assembly 1730-48. Whitehead, *Colonial History of New Jersey*, Vol. VIII, 416.

[36] Sworn in as President of the Council and acting Governor. Whitehead, *Colonial History of New Jersey, Vol. VI*, 462.

President.

20   The Instructions and Papers relating to the affairs of Govt were delivered to me.

Mr Peter Kimble[37] was qualified for one of his Maj's Council.

Expenses this journey out and in.

21   Came home this day about 1 of the clock My wife in my absence let son John have [money] to pay T. Collins.

22   Lent to Martin Shifly 0:15.

Sent to Auditors in Jno Huff case and Returned from them on account of the dividend of goods attached the sum of 2:05:10.

Payed the said Auditors (by son John) for wheat in stack, and for sundries bought at the vendue.

23   Bought from Walter Harney 1 gall rum.

24   Martin Shifly paid back the 0:15.

25   Sent son Joseph[38] to plow Mart: Shiflys Indian Corn.

Received two paquets from the Agent in England.

26   Son John gave me from Sam'l Fleming upon account of wheat formerly John Huffs the sum of [money].

27   Robert Calcot absent upon account of his wifes indisposition.

29   Robt came again. Vincent Robert had 2 bu'll wheat.

    John Thatcher 27s in part of 30s for mowing gras.

July 1747

1st   Sent down by Sam'l Wynes to Burlington, Sam'l Greens Return for 275 Acres on the North at the Great Meadows.

Said Wynes also left with me 29 s for the use of said Green.

2   John Hofmans wife bot for us at York a watering pot at 7s and 10 lb loaf sugar at 1/6 per lb.

5   David Connagh for mowing grass 11 ½ day cradling Rye and

---

[37] PETER KEMBLE (1704-89). Kemble settled at New Brunswick, New Jersey, where he entered into a successful business and resided for several years. *Collections of the New Jersey Historical Society Vol IX,* (Newark, New Jersey: New Jersey Historical Society, 1916) 150-152.

[38] JOSEPH READING (1728-1806). Hunterdon County Judge and patriot. Served on Gov. Livingston's council during Revolutionary War. Married Amy Pierson and lived on farm near Stockton. Leach, *Memorials,* 50.

helping to bind the same (6s over his wages).

This day at night George returned from the Spring.

8   Payed a Pedlar upon Robert Calcots account. Payed to Ditto upon my own account.

9   Received from Robt Large for a deed and Survey.

10 Payed an Indian Woeman for pulling flax.

12 Gave to a Charitable Use.

13 Received a letter from Sherif of Middlesex per _____ Reed.

14 Answered the same.

15 Went to Trenton. Paid Dr Cadwalader[39] his share of Thos: Deremus's money being the last payment for land.

16 Payed John Yard for a hat. Returned home. Expenses. Sticks of sealing wax.

    Son George went 2d time to the Minerall Spring with Richard.

17 Accompted with William Force for mowing making a cradle and some other work. And rested due to balance.

18 Payed David Connagh for three days and half cradling of wheat. Martin Ryerson paid towards money borrowed.

21 Set out in the afternoon for Amboy. Proved Rainy towards night. Lodged at Mr Van Hornes.[40]

22 Proceeded on the journey. Called upon Mr Antill who went along with me arrived there before noon. Sat in Council the afternoon.

23 Sat again in Council upon the affairs of the Rioters.

24 Set out for home where I arrived a little after 1 of the clock. Expenses in and out.

    My wife Received in my absence 12s left to pay for a deed to be made for Benj: Severns.

    Daniel Received from Aaron Mattison for 2 bus'l barley.

---

[39] THOMAS CADWALADER (1707-79). Born in Philadelphia, educated at the French Academy, Philadelphia and received a medical and surgical education in London. Moved to Trenton and named its first Burgess when it was chartered in 1746. He was a member of the Governor's council of Pennsylvania. Whitehead, *Colonial History of New Jersey*, Vol. VIII, 388.

[40] ABRAHAM VAN HORN (1699-1759). In 1722 Abraham purchased 490 acres of land in Readington Township, Hunterdon Co., New Jersey. Here he developed a grist mill and saw mill on the banks of Rockaway Creek which ran through the property. Van Horn built the first tavern in the area on the road from Clinton to Somerville where it crossed Rockaway Creek (now Route 22). Whitehead, *Colonial History of New Jersey*, Vol. VIII, 421.

27   Payed Joh's Binder for 7 days raking and binding. Joh's left
        unpaid for a bus'l of wheat and a bus'l of Rye.

28   Sent 9 casks of flower to the Landing.

30   Sent 12 casks of flower and 20 of Middlings and 4 bus'l of wheat
        (to make up 200 lbs) to Henry Lanes at the Landing. Cash laid
        out for Salt Molasses etc Light money. Received from John Clook
        15s in full of all accounts This day John Clook brought 2 letters
        from Gov. Sherley.[41]

31   This day Hermanus Simoness the Currier finished his currying
        and it was said he earned 12s 3p but he went away in the morning
        before I was up so that I did not pay him out of which said sum
        he is to discompt 8s light money upon Andreis Tenykes account
        it being 6:10:1 Prock.[42]
        Payed Benj: Stout for Axle Treeing the bigg wagon and the
        making of an Harrow.

August 1747

1   Mr Joseph Stout[43] left in my keeping a Bond of Indian Philips
        from Thomas Botner.

3   Sent Richard up to Pohohatcong on Mr Ch's Reeds account.
        Received from Will: Bishop for the writing of a Bond. Received
        from John Opdyke in full excepting what was due for services
        done about the Land bought from the Rawly[?]. Received from
        Wm Taylor for a Deed and part of Surveying.

4   Set off for a journey to Burlington. On the Road Nicholas
        Albertson paid me for Acknowledging two Deeds. Went to

---

[41] WILLIAM SHIRLEY (1694-1771). Twice Governor of Massachusetts 1741-1749 and 1753-1756. Governor of the Bahamas between 1761 and 1766. Served as temporary Commander-in-Chief, North America during the French-Indian War in 1755-56. William M. Fowler, Jr. *Empires at War – The French and Indian War and the Struggle for North America 1754-1763* (New York: Walker & Company, 2005) xix, 87-91.

[42] Proclamation money or New Jersey proclamation money valued at approximately £170 per £100 sterling between 1747 and 1767. Money in colonies was set at 133% value over sterling by Quenn Anne's proclamation in 1704, but this valuation was generally disregarded in the colonies. Rabushka, *Taxation in Colonial America*, 370-371.

[43] JOSEPH STOUT (1686-1766). He was a colonel in the New Jersey Militia and made several campaigns against the Indians. Lived in Hopewell, New Jersey. *History of an American Family*, http://www.branches-n-twigs.com/genealogy (July 23, 2010).

Mahlon Kirkbrides paid him his share of Tho: Deremus's money being £32:03 being the last Payment for Land sold in Partnership. Lodged there that night.

5　　Got to Burlington. Met the Council of Proprietors.

6　　Payed Mr. Richard Smith 30p for Tho: Martin took his Receipt whereof was due to said Martin for building of Johns house.
Paid Jas Hancock for a Whig.
Payed Mrs. Bickley Share of Expenses.
Left unpaid at Mrs. Hunlokes 3 and 8p. Since paid.
Paid Wm Yard for Expences and Shoeing of my Horse.
Got a writ of Resurvey for all or any of my Lands and got one from the Council of Proprietors for the Bray's. Payed for it.
Paid for a pair of shoes to Ed: Paxtons plus 1/6 over.

8　　Received by an Express the news of Govr Belchers[44] Arrival at Amboy. Paid P'r Savery 15s for a former Express on the Notice of the late Presidents Death and now 7/6 more for going to Trenton.

9th　After dinner set out for Amboy. Lodged at Mr Antills.

10　　Set out in company with Mr Antill arrived at Amboy about 9 of the clock.
Waited upon His Excell'y who's Commission was published about 3 of the clock with great Expressions of Joy.

11th　The Next day Stayed at Amboy till about 4 of the clock then set out homewards. Lodged at Mr Antills.

12　　Arrived at home about 12 of the clock. Expenses in and out and Lodgings.
On this day I ordered Henry Lane to sell my wheat and flower and to get me spanish pieces for the pay.

14　　My wife set off to see her daughter.

15　　Went to Justus Gans to survey two acres bought from J. Porter and paid said Porter for 2 shoes and a remove. Reconed with Robert Calcot paid him the Balance being [an amount].

---

[44] JONATHON BELCHER (1682-1757). Colonial governor of Massachusetts, New Hampshire, and New Jersey. Born in Cambridge, Massachusetts, he attended Harvard University. Governor of the Province of New Jersey, from 1747-57, played important role in the founding of the College of New Jersey. http:// www.belcherfoundation.org/ governor_jonathan_belcher.htm (July 23, 2010).

Received from Peter Lauseet for a deed.

18th   Set out for Burlington. Lodged at Trenton. Payed the Shoemaker for a pair of Mens Shoes and 6p over.

19th   Went to over to Burlington.

20th   Payed the Treasurer the Interest money for the Year 1746.

21   Stayed at Burlington.

22   Payed Issac Decow for some Returns of my own and other persons. Payed Mrs Hunlock for Dinners and Clubs. Set out homewards. Left unpaid my Lodging and Breakfasting. Paid since. Horse Pasturing and Expenses upon my Journey and at Trenton.

27   Payed David Connagh for mowing of grass 8 days and for cradling of oats left unpaid heretofore.

28   Rich'd Stephens came to put up an aple mill which he made.

29   Sold 15 sheep to John Wills for £ 4 for which he gave Bond. Paid Richard Stephens for Apple Mill.

31   Payed Mr Beatty for 3 books vizt: 2 Vol of the Xth History 17s and Charitable Plea for Infant Baptism[45].

September 1747

1   Payed Abraham Delameter for 101 lb of beef and a hide wt 55 lb.

3   George returned home from the Spring. Returned me back out of the money I gave him when he went away.

5th   Received from Godfrey Peters for half a Deed and Bond. Received from Charles Morrey for one Deed.

7th   Payed Sarah Moor for Spinning light money.

8   Payed Wm McMollen for weaving. Received from Bro: Ryerson for leather (left unpaid 6p).

9th   Sent for from Wm Montgomeries nails, sugar etc.

11th   Sent to Trenton by Jno Lawrence to buy Jesuit Bark.[46]

14th   John Hawkins paid for some Leather formerly had by a hide and

---

[45] Probably *A charitable plea for the speechless: or, The right of believers-infants to baptism vindicated: and the mode of it by pouring or sprinkling justified* by Samuel Finley published in 1746, Printed by W. Bradford, at the Sign-of-the-Bible in Second-Street. (Philadelphia).

[46] The bark of the cinchonaor chinchona tree. The active constituent of Jesuit's Bark is quinine. http://www.websters-online-dictionary.org (July, 23, 2010).

cash. Bought a part of a Hog of Jon's Hill for 7/6 paid it him.

17th   Wm Montgomerie sent ___ of Kersey[47] and Trimming.

22d   Received from Isaac Bodine for a deed ½ over which I pay to Bro: Reyerson.

Went to Volkert Douw to write his Will. Reconed with Vincent Robert. Remained in his debt.

25   David Kinny left in my hands towards his Charges for Survey.

26th   Payed Benj: Stout for helping tbe Cider Mill.

30   Payed Matte Coursen for Spinning.

October 1747

1   Sent down to the Landing 20 b'ls of wheat and a 15 t [?] Bill Received for said wheat being 4-3 per bus'l light money. Light money which is 3-12:1 Proc. Layed out and expended so that I Received back in Prock Money 3:12.

2   Payed Hermanus Simones 7s Proclamacon being 6p over and above his due.

5th   Set out with And'w: Bray for Muskonetcong.

6   Resurveyed the Brays Tract of Land. Lodged at Jo'h Pickels.

7   Rained in the afternoon held up went in company with Henry Stewart and viewed some Lines of said Prick't and Panc't.

8   Ran some lines of said [William?]Pancoast, Martin and Pricket fixed said Stewarts Norwest corner went up to Joseph Warfords surveyed 50 Acres of Land for him and lodged there that night he giving me 15s in part of the charge of a return for some land on the North side of the Pohohatcong.

9   Went up to Tho: Scot's in order to Run the line of a Tract of Land he lives on but not finding some of them we left off sought for one of the Corners (supposed to be) by the Tract of Land surveyed for Mr Logan[48] but not finding it. Lodged at Wm Henry's that night.

10   Went to Dan'l Bates in order to make an Addition to his Tract of

---

[47]A kind of coarse, woolen cloth, usually ribbed, woven from wool of long staple. http://www.websters-online-dictionary.org (August 2, 2010).

[48] JAMES LOGAN (1674-1751). Prominent Philadelphia Quaker and gentleman. Isaacson, *Benjamin Franklin, An American Life*, 498.

Land. But he not being at home prevented it. (expended in said journey). Came home.

12th   Payed Tho: Brown the Schoolmaster for one Quarters Schooling.

13th   My wife set off for New York by whom I sent in cash £26, Sent down to Brunswick 30 b'l Barley at 3s per bu's. Bought at the Landing 1000 of oysters paid for them. Expenses in the journey. On the same day Payed Mr Henry for the support of the Gosp'l Colledge. [49]

12th   Subscribed towards the building of a Colledge £10. Lent Mr Davenport Mr Herberts and Capt Rogers Voyag's [50].

17th   Received from Jas Kinny for writing and Surveying. Payed Margaret Youngblood for Spinning.

21   Bought a Deerskin.

22   Sent down to the Landing 20 bl of wheat and 40 bl Barley. Johannes Bossenberg paid toward Exchange of Land. Received in cash for said Barley and wheat _____ wheat at 4/3 Barley 2/6. Paid for sundry goods bought and Expenses (but not made out).

24th   Wm Fonger paid for 3 Bonds 4s part of Surveying 4s. Isaac Bogart had six sheep to the hire of 1 lb of wool per year. Old ones to be made up and Returned.

26th   Received from Sam'l Fleming for 7 bus'l of flax seed.

30   Gave son John to pay the Sadlar.

November 1747

1   Payed Dr Nause for something for my wife.

2   Gave Walter Harney in part of account between himself and I.

3   Walter Returned from Trenton. Gave him out of the Loan Office [51] Money's 2 and 3s and 9p of my own money and he having renewed his mortgage and is now for £19:13: 9.

4   Agreed with Giles Lawrence for a black Walnut desk for 21 5s more than the pay for a black walnut tree lying near

---

[49] College of New Jersey (Princeton).

[50] Woodes Rogers, *A Crusing Voyage Round the World* (London 1712).

[51] Loan offices were established in each County to make mortgage backed loans in an attempt to solve the colony's shorage of hard currency. The borrowers were required to pay back loans on an annual basis with interest. Rabushka, *Taxation in Colonial America*, 7.

Penunagactong[52] and 20s which he is indebted to me. The desk to be cased and sent up to Trenton this month.

6   Sent £9 to Dr Witt at Germantown for Medicine's for his mother.

7th   Returned with the same with our daughter Ann[53] and her Husband. Medicines cost 17s besides Expenses.

10th   Mr Beaty returned home this day my wife was taken extremely ill was despaired of her life. Towards evening something better. Payed Mr Beaty for a Book being an Answer to Mr Finly's Charitable Plea for Infant Bap'm etc.[54]

12   Received from James Abbit in part of 3 Acknowledgements. Indebted for one still which he is to leave at Mr Ringoes. Paid John Hofman 30s in part for 3 Hides (as he says) at 2 ½ lb. The Hides weighed 184 if as above I must pay him 8:9 more. Bought oysters, Madera Wine Claret etc.

20   Adam Teets Payed for a Deed. Payed to Tho: Atkinson for 21 casks 1/6 per cask per Brad:

24th   Received from Richard Crook for acknowledging a Deed. Payed said Crook for fulling and dying 116 yds of Cloath.

26   Received from Tho: Silverthorn for 4 Bonds. Received from Nich's Heiglut (by L. Ryerson) due a Bill.

28   Lent Mart: Shiftly 141 light money.

30   Payed Tho: Coat for weaving of 30 yds of Parragon.

December 1747

[52] Near Belvidere in White Township, Warren County. From The N.Y. Mercury Aug 4, 1755 advertising a land sale; "A tract of land lying about two miles form the Delaware River, at a hill called Penunganchong, and about 4 miles from Oxford furnace, containing 1500 acres; the whole being well timber'd, part of which is black walnut, a branch of the Pophaneunk river [Pophandusing Brook] called Beaver Dam Branch, runs through said tract." William Nelson, ed., *Documents Relating to the Colonial History of the State of New Jersey*, Vol. XIX, *1751-1755* (Paterson, N.J.: The Press Printing and Publishing Co., 1897), 521.

[53] ANN READING (1723-68). John Reading's oldest daughter. She married Rev. Charles Beatty in 1746. Leach, *Memorials*, 41.

[54] *Anti-Paedo-Rantism, or, Mr. Samuel Finley's Charitable Plea for the Speechless Examined and Refuted: The Baptism of Believers Maintain'd and the Mode of It, by Immersion, Vindicated*, by Abel Morgan, Middleton, East Jersey, 174 pp., printed in Philadelphia, by Benjamin Franklin, in 1747.

1   Tho: Collins had a Hog W'd 116 lb @2 ½ per Lb.
3d   Bought from Sam'l F1eming 2 dz of buttons and 2 sticks of Moorhair.
4   Received for a Deed for Joh's Behtelsiemer.
5   Ordered Vincent Robert to take 2 bls of Wheat from the Mill.
7   Let Martin Shifley have a Barrel of Sider.
        Received from Paul Coul for a Recording and Acknowedgment of a Deed. Reconed with Mr Wm Montgomerie and paid him the balance.
9   Peter Rockefeller Jur paid for 2 Deeds and Bond (Survey not paid).
10   Had a Quarter of Venison. Weigh'd 21 lb from B: Stout.
11   Bought fish from Corn's Weycoff paid him.
12   Paid Tho: Marshall for 15 ½ and 1/8 of Wheat at 3/10.
15th   Bought a Quarter of Venison from Benj: Stout by son John.
24th   Bought a gall of Rum at Mr. Ringoes.
26   Payed Sarah Moore 17:6 light Money. Remains to pay for her work 6/6.
29   Martin Shifley had a bush'l of Indian Corne.
30   Delivered and account with Joseph Yard [?] for that share of the Loan Office Money which I had Received and tooke Receipt for the same.
        Sold to Adam Poke half a barrel of Cider. He paid for it.

1747/8

January 1747/8

4th   William Force finished a Peleasure Slead. For his pay he agreed to have 2 lbs Rye and 9 bls of Oats.
8th   Vincent Robert had 2 bl of Wheat.

10th   Payed Mr Beatty for a bottle of Elixer Proprietatis.[55]

14th   Payed Alburtus Ringo the Remainder for the Horse bought from him.

15th   Vincent Robert had 2 b'usl of Oats at 1/6.

24   Went to Delaware paid for a Bottle of Rum.

25   Vincent Robert had 2 bl of Rye. Wm Wertegen paid for a Deed. Jacob Quick paid for a Confirmation and other trouble about his Deed.

26th   Received from Henry Lane by Jeromus Van Eote the balance. For the W[hea]t and flour.

27   Set out for Burlington. My Horse falling sick occasioned

28   My stay all night. Proceeded in my Journey dined at Trenton. Arrived at Burlington. Expenses on my Journey.

29   At Burlington.

30   At Burlington.

31   At Burlington.

February 1747/8

1   Remained at Burlington and so Continued till the

19th. Set out homewards dined at Trenton. Lodged at Mr Ringoes. Expenses homewards at Trenton and Ringoes. Paid John Yard for a new hat and dressing [Gown?].
       Expenses and layed out for some necessaries, for Accomedations and my horse at Mrs Bickleys. At Mr Hunlokes for dinners and Club. A pair of shoes for self. A pair for my wife. To Sundries at Joseph Hollingsheads. To the Recording of 4 Deeds at the Secretary Office (not paid). To Dr Shaw for Bloodletting and Physick brought home.

20th   Accompted with Mr P. Ringo and Payed the Balance of our accounts. Received Ed: Millers Loan Office Money for 1747

---

[55] A concoction made of saffron, aloes, and myrrh said to be particularly a remedy for the *Gout.* Harvey Wickes Felter, M.D. and John Uri Lloyd, Phr. M., Ph.D. *King's American Dispensatory* Nineteenth Edition. Third revision. In two volumes. Vol. I. (Cincinnati: The Ohio Valley Company, 317—321 Race Street. 1905) I: 695.

being 5:05. Mr Ringo accompted for an Acknowledgment of Wm Exceens.

In my Absence Mart: Shifly had 2 b'lls Oats. Vin't Robert 2 Bus'ls of Oats. J's Yery Binder 1 Bus'l of Rye and 1 bus'l of Oats (should be 2 b'l of Rye).

23   David Stout paid for his Release and Surveying don.

24th   John Opdicke paid the balance due for Work on Writings made for the land bought from Wm Rawles Executor which was besides 16s by Tho: Thatcher in 2 Deer Skins.

The charges besides James and Jere: Thatchers, Barracaloes and Arrions sent to Rich'd Green 6s being Balance due to him on account of Return.

Vin't Robert had 2 b'ls of Oats. Now about paid Jos: Hankinson[56] for Bricks.

25   Mart: Ryerson paid for a Return and for a pair of Dividers.

27   Payed Dr. Van Wagoner in full of accounts (and 2 pence over).

March 1747/8

4th   Martin Shiftly had 2 Bus'l of Oats. Payed Sarah Thomas upon Mr. Beaties Account.

6   Received from Stephen Ganoe towards a Barrel of Cider. James Pharoe, Debtor to ½ Bar'l of Cider.

7th   Sent by Mr Beatty to Phila Tho: Van Etta's and Mc Murteries money. Reconed with John Johnson due to him 14s for which he is to have 5 ½ B'lls of Oats.

8   Paid off the Scholemaster Tho: Brown. Bought the Seaman's Calendar. Went to the Town meeting where I acknowledged a Deed for Brush[?]. Andrew Trimmer paid for a Deed and Bond. Godfrey Peters paid for the Recording of his Deed. Paid off a note for £5:15 to the widow Forster for a Horse.

10th   Received from the Brandenburgers for 15 bll Oats. Received from Joh's Hull for his share of Surveying and 2 Bonds.

---

[56] JOSEPH HANKINSON (1712-83). His daughter Elizabeth (1748-1817) married John Reading's Grandson John in 1772. Leach, *Memorials*, 55.

11   Payed Wm Anderson 4 shillings for a British Oil 1 shill for Charge.

12   Handeel Burg paid for Recording of a Deed by Peter Foin.

14th   Went over to Delaware River in order to Divide the Tract of Land designed for Joseph and Richard.[57] Whilst I was out Acknowledged 4 Deeds one for Cotton one for Waterhouse (paid for these two) and 2 for Js'h Quinby.
Bought a small toothed Comb.
Agreed with Tho: West for a Tennant for 5 Winter crops to be taken from Richards or the lowermost share (not complyed with).

21   Signed a bond with my son John for the sum of Seventy pounds current lawful money of the Province of New York[58] payable to John Vander Spegel on the 6th of March next with lawful Interest for the use of Margt Rutgers of the City of New York. Bond bears date the 7th of March (I think). On the same day went to John Lamberts in order to Survey part of Lands formerly Dr Dindsdales.[59] Now sold by Rich'd Smith to said Lambert. Stayed with the Surveyor being Jno Watson who had been formerly spoke to on said occasion (The bond is altered by son John's taking up the money elsewhere).

22nd   Received from said Lambert by Daniel Howell[60] for my service in the above affair. Ran out some of the Courses of Wachcchiok Brook.

20   Agreed with Ab: Honey as a Tenant for Penunganchong, the lower part of it for 6 winter Crops. He to give me after 2 first Winter Crop's from the Lowland, the third part of what is produced therefrom to clear fit for an Orchard as much ground as will plant 150 Apple trees in such part as we shall agree upon

---

[57] The original draft of this survey is dated 1744, but this entry suggests that may be an error. Hunterdon County Land Drafts, MSC 163 F1, (Spruance Library, Bucks County Historical Society, Doylestown, Pennsylvania).

[58] New York currency in 1748 was worth about 3% less than New Jersey Proclamantion money. McCusker, *Money & Exchange in Europe & America, 1600-1775*, 165.

[59] DR. ROBERT DIMSDALE (d. 1718). A West New Jersey proprietor. Dr. John R. Stevenson, "Physicians in the Colonization of New Jersey," *The Jerseyman*, Vol. 11, No. 4 (April 1905): 23.

[60] DANIEL HOWELL (d. 1790). Son of Capt. Daniel Howell. Married Julia Ann Holcombe. Leach, *Memorials*, 155-156.

said Honey what buildings he makes to be well and good of the sort fences to be good lawful rail fence not bound to clear any certain quantity of the Upland but what he clears he is not to take any Winter Crops from the same oftener than every third year but may make a Sommer Crop on the New Land stuble If he builds from the River or any natural stream of water. If not too Chargeable I am to be at the Cost of getting water if it suits me as to scituacium. (Abraham Hone lives upon the Terms agreed for John Allison to have the opperp'l [opportunity?] on said terms).

21   Condescended that Wm Scholays son Rich'd should be as a Tenant upon that Tract of Land which lies near the heads of South Branch of Rariton Containing in the whole 500 and odd Acres such part of it as lies contiguous to some meadow where said Scholey has and now doth mow. Said Rich'd to Settle and Clear in such part of it where the timber is not of the best: he to clear principally meadow and so much ground as will plant an 100 Aple trees at least and to be in such part as we shall agree upon the buildings to made well and good as such kind as they shall think fit. The fences to be made good and lawful for 6 winter Crops and not oftener than every third year after the two first crops one of which is to be a summer Crop and at the Expiration of the Term to give and surrender up the peacable possession in good tenantable repair. (Not complied with).

25   Went to Derr'k Hogelands to Divide a Tract of Land which himself, his son John [Hogeland] and Jos: Boss had bought from Mr Tho: Leonard[61] containing 200 Acres.

26   Tunis Hobbagh paid me for a Deed. Proceeded to Run out some land forth of a Tract of Land now Rich'd Smith's for Tho: Martin and Derrick Hogeland but finding not to Answer according to the Course and distance given and directed in the Draft it left off but spent a day therin and running out a small piece of wheat ground for D'k Hogeland.

In my absence Tho: Collins had a b'll of Oats.

---

[61] THOMAS LEONARD (d. 1759). Served as a member of the colonial legislature between 1723 and 1744. He was appointed to a seat on the Council in 1745 and one of the first trustees of Princeton College. Donated land for the Princeton college cemetery. Whitehead, *Colonial History of New Jersey*, Vol. VIII, 400.

28th   Vinc't Robert had a b'll of Oats. John Johnson had 2 b'll of Oats.

29th   Went to the Tract of Land formerly Mrs Eastaughs to divide some of their Lotts. Received 8s from Christ: Coel.

30th   Went to Nich's Sines, Rich'd Rounsavalls to run out 50 As and to certify and find out a supposed mistake in the dividing line between him and J: Taylor. Received from Peter Kase for surveying said 50 Acres.

31   Sold 1 Barrell Cider to Nixson. Sold 1 hog[shea]d to Jacob Maurer supposing it to be 88 Gall's for 27s and he to return the Hogshead or else for 30s and a barrel which I kept and he is to keep the Hogshead Received fro[m] said Maurer.

April 1748

2   Went to Joh's Borts and Jos Cocks a Surveying.

4   Received from Lewis Chamberlain for a Deed.

6   Paid Sarah Thomas in part for Kniting. Paid Ad: Aten for Smith's work to this day.

7   Wills Force had one bus of Oats.

8   Set out for Burlington. Called at Trenton. Expenses and ferriage. Received from Henry Oxley for Surveying at _____ Return and Surveyor General fees. Payed Mr And'w Reed for one years publick papers of Mr. Franklin.

9   Went to Burlington Expenses and ferriage. Payed for a ___ of Resurvey for Francis Quick. Paid it back.

11   Received from Matth's Sharpenstien for his Will.

12   Received from D'd and Tho: Van Horn for 1 days Surveying.

13   Reconed with Yery Behtelsimer in full. Reconed with Coenradt Sever and work which he had don for me was due to him 1:15 Against which we set 2 bu wheat and living in the house and other Conveniences.

14th   Paulus Botner had 2 b'ls of Oats. William Force had 2 b'ls of Oats.
    Received from Mich'l Short for Interest of £20.
    Received from Jno Vansicklen for Surveying and Writing.

16   Mart: Shiftley had 2 b'ls of Rye.

18   Philip Young paid for a Deed. I believe I have Received the greatest part. Sold to Ab: Delameter and Tho: Marshal 10 b'lls of Oats.

19   Went to Trenton. Acknowledged a Deed for Ch: DeRosel. Accounted with James Pharoe. Paid him the balance.

20   Returned homewards by Em'l Corials[Coryell's][62] where was some time spent in endeavouring to accommodate the affair between him and Rich'd Holcomb[63] but to no effort.

21   Went up to Bethlehem to run round the lines of P'r Smok's plantation formerly Richd Heaths. John Parke to pay for the charges (he marryed the Widdow Heath).

23   Accompted with Tho: Collins for grubbing and paid him the balance Paid Jno Coursen for work for his Negro. Paid Richard Long for weaving.

25   Set off for Trenton: Acknowledged 2 Deeds: Expenses in and out. Payed Edward Paxton the Shoemaker for 2 pair of woemens shoes.

30   David Connor finished the Ditching being 144 Rod at 7 yds per Rod. Received from Henry Tilding for writing and Surveying. Mart: Shifly had 2 b'lls wheat.

May 1748

2   Received from Derrick Hogeland for a Deed and Surveying Received from John Hogeland[64] for a Deed and Surveying. Received from Jos: Boss for a Deed and Surveying. Received

---

[62] JOHN EMANUEL CORYELL (1704?-1749). He secured a patent in 1732 from King George II to operate a ferry in the vicinity of what is now Lambertville, New Jersey. Alfred G. Petrie, *Lambertville New Jersey from the beginning as Coryell's Ferry*. (Lambertville, New Jersey, 1949) 10.

[63] RICHARD HOLCOMBE (1726-83). Son of John Holcomb Jr. (1682-1743) who purchased 350 acres north of the first survey line, the Old Bull Line in 1705 and generally regarded as the the first resident of Lambertville. Alfred G. Petrie, *Lambertville New Jersey from the beginning as Coryell's Ferry*. (Lambertville, New Jersey, 1949) 13 and http://freepages.genealogy.rootsweb.ancestry.com   /~jonkh/RegJohnHolcombe.htm (July 28, 2010).

[64] JOHN HOAGLAND (1712-77).   Member of the New Jersey Assembly. He purchased 176 acres in Somerset County in 1745. Whitehead, *Colonial History of New Jersey*, Vol. VIII, 397.

from Sam'l Fleming for 300 lbs Hay. Lent Henry Dildine upon bill. Sent to New York by Eliz: Harney. Paid Molly Harney in part.

3   Received from Ab: Carmer for Acknowledging a Deed. Set out for Burlington. Acknowledged a Deed from Jos Cheek to Peter Young. Dined at Trenton. Went over to Burlington.

4   Stayed at Burlington. Paid Isaac DeCow for Surveying fees.

5   Came up from Burlington to Trenton that night.

6   Came home in the afternoon an Acknowledged two Deeds one of them for P'r Young the other for the Widdow Dawles. Expenses in and out. Bought at Trenton 12 lb sixpenny nails.

9   Reconed with Wm: Jewell on act of cutting Lambs and calves.

10   Set out for Burlington and Trenton: Arrived at Trenton. Paid Saml Furman for his daughter's combing of wersted.

11   Met the Freeholders and Justices. Cancelled the Prime on the 20,000.[65] 182:4:6 one deficiencies. Cancelled also the 40,000[66] defeciencies likewise. Cancelled a defenciency on 2:07:0 in the year 1746.

12   Went to Burlington to the Privy Council.[67] The Govr present. Came back to Trenton that night.

13   Set off homewards where I arrived in the afternoon. Received from Edwd Milner in my journey at Mr Ringoes 13s/ and 5s to be accd which I kept of J: Swallows charge for Writing and a Surveying.
Received at the same time at Pennytown for 2 Acknowledgments.
Received at Richard Reeds for the acknowledgement of his Deed at Trenton.
Acknowledged a Deed for P'r Young - not paid for it.
Acknowledged a Deed from Jno Mullen to Johannes Backer.

---

[65] Refers to the bills of credit (£20,000) issued under the second loan-offfice act of 1730. The first loans were made in 1733 and were supposed to be paid back in 16 years. Bernard Bush, compiler, *New Jersey Archives, Third Series, Vol. II, Laws of the Royal Colony of New Jersey 1703-1745* (Trenton, New Jersey: New Jersey State Library, Archives and History Bureau, 1977) 427.

[66] The third loan-office act passed in 1735 for £40,000. The first loan was made in 1737. Bush, *New Jersey Archives, Third Series, Vol. II*, 474.

[67] An advisory council to the Royal governor. Also referred to herein as the governor's council or his Majesties council.

Took the Acknowledgments of David Bertrons Deed from the Coxes.

14 Went to Walter Harney's upon a Reference from the Supreme Court inter[?] Benj: Rounsavell, Archibald Morrison, Mart: Rierson, Mr Henry and Self Ref[erees']s.

16 Went to Nich's Williamsons on the Peters affair.
Payed towards his freedom 5 of Mr Isaac Sharps[68] money and 20s of my own.
Payed the Sadler 40s.
Let Henry Dildine have 31s 6 towards a larger sum.

17 Gave son George when he went to Trenton [amount].
Let out upon Bond by land Security £19:18:6 to Henry Dildine which with £4:11:6 which he formerly had makes the sum of 24:10 to be paid this time 2 years with Interest. Received from Henry Dildine for writings on the above account.

19 Payed for Parchment ½ A doz. Gave to a Charitable Use. Raised son John's Barn.

20 Paid David Connagh for Ditching.
Received for the Acknowledgmemt of a release from Jas Hutchins to Crawf'd.
Received from David Wright for a Deed.

23rd Went up into the country as far as Pennongachong.

24th Began the Survey of Tho: Scott's place sold by Mr Kirkbride P_____ the same. Received for my trouble from said Kirkbride at this and former time.

26 Went with Jos: Stout to survey over against Hunters ferry.[69]
Surveyed some lands and went to Jas Harkers.

27 Finished the Survey. Came home that night.

28th Received from the son of Tho: Deremus on account of Land.

30 My wife set out for her Daughters in Pennsylvania.

---

[68] ISAAC SHARP (d. 1770). Judge of Salem County Court, appointed by King George II in 1741. http://en.wikipedia.org/wiki/Isaac_Sharp (July 23, 2010).
[69] ALEXANDER HUNTER (?). A Presbyterian from the north of Ireland arrived in the Forks of Delaware (Easton) with about 30 families in 1730. He took up 300 acres of land on the North Branch, near the mouth of Hunter's (or Allegheny creek) creek, where he established a ferry. W. W. H. Davis, A. M., *The History of Bucks County, Pennsylvania, From the Discovery of the Delaware to the Present Time* (Doylestown, Pa.: Democrat Book and Job Office Print. 1876), 589.

Acknowledged a Deed for Wm Wertegen.

Endeavored to settle the affair of Mr Byerlys Land in order to return it into the Court of Chancery. This day gave leave to _____ Howe to settle the upper part of Penungachong land on the same terms as Ab: Howe. He is to have the Libertie to sow about 6 or 8 Acres of winter grain this fall and it is to be no part of the account of Rent. (Note: who never went on the place to settle).

June 1748

3d	Received from George Behtelsiemer for a Mortgage, a Bill and an Acknowledgement to a Deed.
	Payed Molly Emley for Hay making etc.
4	Robt Calcut had a bu'l of Indian Corn by his wife.
	Payed Mr Wm Montgomerie for 6 skins of Parchment.
	Received from Dennis Woolverton on account of a Right to 24 Acres of Land Surveying and Surveyors General fees.
	Received from P'r Romine for Rent.
6th	Run out the Joh's Shavers 7 Acres. Received pay for same.
	Gave to a Charitable Use.
8th	Went to Muskonetcong to run out some lines for Tho: Hunt.
9th	Ran out 52 ½ Acres for Marens Hulings.
11th	Received from John Alburtus towards the one half of Jacob Johnson's resurvey Return and Warrant.
17th	Payed Tho: Rugnion on Luke Ryerson's[70] account.
18th	James Bradbury paid for a Deed.
	Jos: Hill Jur paid for a Deed.
21th	Sent to Buy Rum and Salt at Wm Montgomeries.
23	P'r Hofman, Hen'y Winter and Wm Kase paid for their deeds 12s each.
25	Received from Wm Briton for 7 bll of Oats.
	Paid David Conner for 4 ½ days mowing of Grass.

---

[70] LUCAS RYERSON (1704?-64). John Reading's brother-in-law. He married Elizabeth Howell in 1736. She died in 1745 and he married Susanna Van der Linden. Susanna died during childbirth in 1747. He then married Johanna Van de Hoff in 1750. Ryerson, *The Ryerse-Ryerson Family,* 25.

July 1748

1st   Payed David Burk for Combing Worsted in cash and a Deed for the Lot of Land.

2d   Payed David Conner for 2 Days Cradling.

9th   Allowed David Kinny for 2 Days Cradling.

11th Received from Wm Black for 2 bonds.
      Paid for 2 lb of shingle Nails at Saml Flemings.

15   Gave leave to Calab Horton of Roxbury to Mow some of the Meadow at Paquaess. (not interfering with others who have had leave heretofore) until he is repremanded. (I think this made use of by some others).

16   James Farrow Debtor to 2 Bonds.
      Received from William Black for One Bond.

19   Received from David Barton for a Deed Surveying and a will.

20th Set out near night for Burlington. Lodged at Mr Ringoes.

21   Arrived at Burlington about noon. No Council. Mr Leonard sent for.

22d   Mr Leonard came in the afternoon. No Council.

23d   The Govr held a Council. A Charter Granted for the Erection of a Colledge in the Jerseys. Set out homewards near one of the Clock and arrived there in safety about 8.

25th Payed Robt Calcot by his wife 1 bu Indian Corn.

26   Lent son John 12s and paid 4s I borrowed from him for a Charitable Use.

28   Agreed with Jos: Howell[71] for the Land belonging to the 5th Dividend of an eighth part of Proprietary for £11 Procla. to be paid him at the signing of the Deed.

30th Payed David Conner for 5 days mowing of grass and helping to cut Oats which with sixpence overpaid in July 1747 came to [amount].

August 1748

1   Benjamin Stout borrowed in cash and paid back again.

---

[71] JOSEPH HOWELL (d. 1776). Brother of Capt. Daniel Howell. Lived in Kingwood, Hunterdon County. Leach, *Memorials*, 152.

2nd   Set out for Burlington. Lodged at Trenton. Received from Jo:
      Yard.

3rd   Went to Burlington in the Morning. Payed into the Treasury.

4th   Council of Proprietors Adjourned. Payed Jos: Hollingshead for
      mending my wives Buli___[?].

5th   Set out in the morning for home where I arrived in the afternoon.
      Paid for a girth. Expenses in and out.

6th   William Force had 2 bus'ls of Wheat.

13th Received from Executors of John Hofman for his Will.
      Received from Joh's Bosenberg 2 D'blloons[72] at £5:8.
      Received from George Saxton for taking 2 Affidavits of Jac'b
      Johnson and his wife and riding to their House.
      Payed John Chandler for weaving 38 Ells[73] of ticking [yards
      written over the word Ells]. Lent him light money.

15th Johannes Binder had six shills Proc. Paid by my wife.

17th Payed to a Charitable Use.

18th Payed Matte Coursen.
      Layed out with Valentine the Pedlar.

20th Payed Cath: Jones for spinning etc.

23   Benj: Stout paid back the 12s he borrowed.

24   William Force had 2 bus'ls of Wheat.

25   Wm Barns for a Deed paid by Tho: Thatcher and Thos Curtis.

24th Jeromus Wolf paid for a Surveying and Bond for a Title.

26   Layed out for Melasses, shot and paper.

29   Went to Wm Hepburns on the affair of the Lottery. This Month
      Eliz: Harney had 2 bus of seed Wheat.

September 1748

5th   Proved a Deed for Joh's Melegh he paid for it. Payed Margaret
      Cock for Spinning. Bought from Joh's Binder ____ of Beef.

---

[72] A Spanish gold coin equal to £1.66 sterling or £2.822 New Jersey currency. http://blindkat.hegewisch.net/pirates/money.html (July 23, 2010).

[73] "A measure for cloth, now rarely used. It is of different lengths in different countries; the English ell being 45 inches." http://www.websters-online-dictionary.org/definitions (August 2, 2010).

10   Agreed with James Martin and George Beatty for a tract of Land lying upon the Muskonatcong River in Morris country containing 284 Acres for 60 lb per 100 Acres Proc In three Payments. The first payment (without interest) sometime before Christmas the day for the two next payments to be the first day of Aprill from which day Aprill next they are to pay Interest for the Remainder Second Payment to be on said day in the year 1750 the next 1751 upon the first payment they are to give Bonds for the money and I am to give Bond for Title upon the payment of the Carried money. I am to make it up 300 Acres by Land which lyes vacant on the N side of the River for which quantity they are to pay according to the above Rate. Gorg Beatty, James I/J Martin, Jno Reading. Complyed with.

12th   Set out for Burlington. Lodged at Trenton. Paid for a pair of shoes at Trenton for Sarah Moor. Expenses at Trenton and shoeing of my horse.

13th   Set out from Trenton for Burlington. Dined at Bristol.
Went over to Burlington. Waited on the Govr in Council in the Evening. The Charter for the building of a colledge was New Engrossed with some alterations. Consented that the seal should be fixed thereto.

14th   Set out in the morning homewards. Expenses at Bristol on the Road and ferriages. Gave (AD Edificat: Ecclasit[?] in Trenton).
Received from Isaac Davis for 2 Indentures.
Sold a sheep to Timothy Toy.

19th   Received from Jno Arrison[74] and Yacus Barraloe for 2 Deeds.
Sold a sheep to J. Chandler. Son George bargained with him.

20th   Gave to George when he went to his Grandfathers.
Received for acknowledging two Deeds at 3s per Deed J's and G'e Willson.
Went over to Musknoetcong.
Received from Jno Coat for Cider.

21   Lay'd out some Land on Muskonetcong Hills.

22d   Lay'd out some Land on Pohohatcong hills.

---

[74] JOHN ARRISON (b. 1680?). Bought 3000 acres in Basking Ridge in 1717. Also known as Jan Aertsen. Whitehead, *Colonial History of New Jersey*, Vol. VIII, 402.

23rd   Lay'd out some Land on the North side of said Hills and bought deers leather from Jos: Warford 6 skins.

24th   Came home by Dan'l Bates's.
        Payed Matte Coursen for spinning.

27   Payed Johannes Binder 1:15:11 Lt. money being Balance due for Harvist work and 38 lb Beef.
        George Returned of the money when he went to his Grand Fathers.

29   Paid Elenor Koel for spining.
        Paid Molly Harney for work formerly don.
        Received from Benj: Low for writing his Will 5:6 to pay him back for taking up the Canoe.
        Received from Will: Bate for a Deed.

October 1748

1st   Went to Trenton.
        Wm Force had 2 bl of Wheat.

3d   Sent by my wife to New York £27 Proc, To 22s: Daniel 7: wife and Daniel for expenses 7s.

8th   To the Balance of an account with Arch'd Morrison.

12th   Paid Tho: Coat for weaving 43 yds Paragon.
        My wife came home from York.

13th   Payed Wm Montgomerie the balance of all accounts.
        Deposited in Wm Rightinghouses[75] hand 2 D'blloons for the use of Joseph Howell to be paid him (upon consideration of a Parcell of unlocated land bought from him per a former entry) when I obtain a Warrant to take up the same. He has Received 4s being the whole Consideration.

15   Sent 4s for the dressing of 4 Deerskins.

17th   Acknowledged a Deed for Sam'l ___ton to Daniel Bailes

20   William Force helped to make a Gate from 10 to about sunset.

---

[75] WILLIAM RITTENHOUSE (1695-1767). Married Capt. Daniel Howell's sister Catherine. Leach, *Memorials,* 146 and Daniel K. Cassel, *Genea-Biographical History of the Rittenhouse Family,* (Philadelphia, Pa. 1893), 101-104.

21   Agreed with Martin Shifly an exchange of his place for some land
      lying in the Rear of mine being 13 Acres out of the Old Tract and
      six Acres from the Coxes Tract (if I can procure the same) I am
      to buy it from them on what terms I can but the said Shifly is to
      allow me 20s per acre advanced on the same. The said Shifly is to
      live at the old place so long till he builds and gets conveniencys to
      remove to take the apple trees away if he sees cause and the old
      Building of a house if not loose Boards or any fruit trees either
      old or young. The said Shifly to move in two or three years at the
      farthest or sooner if it suits. To give each other a Title to the
      same as soon as the said Reading can get a Title from the Coxes.
      (Signed) Jno Reading / Martin Shifly [in German Script].
      Complied with.
      Bought a Smoothing Box Iron from Thos Collins for 14s in part.
      Send to the Doctors for my son Richard.[76] Had medicines.
      Sent towards Making the Wall of the Graveyard at Buckingham.
      Expenses upon the above journey by Daniel.

25th Set out for Burlington. Went no farther than Trenton.
      Philip Beven brought a Cowhide.

November 1748

1   Set out for Burlington. Arrived there that night.
2   Stayed there the next day: Lodged at Bristol that night.
3   Payed for the Returning and Recording my Resurvey.
      For Jacob Johnsons Resurvey.
      For the Returning of Edmund Wooly's Survey.
      For the Returning and Recording of John Crooks Resurvey,
      Bought a stock Buckle and Stedds. Payed for the making and
      triming to a Coat. Lent to Nicholas Albertson [an amount].

---

[76] RICHARD READING (1732-81). Married Catherine Reid, granddaughter of John
Reid (Quaker turned Anglican) an East Jersey surveyor and proprietor. Richard sold his
inheritance in Rosemont to Asher Mott in 1768, and moved to Monmouth County. He
was a Loyalist, volunteered in New York in 1776 was captured and released with sons.
His property in Monmouth was confiscated. It is thought that he was murdered in 1781
on Long Island. Richard's wife and her four youngest children went to Nova Scotia and
applied for relief for loyalist families. David R. Reading, "For Love or Loyalty?" (*The
Mount Amwell News Fall* 2010): 1-2.

John Reading's Diary

4th	Returned home.
7th	Payed Black Peter for Harvest work in full. Sent son George with Peter to his old Masters to pay him the money agreed for his time And to Enter with the Town Clark for 2 Strays.
8	Went up to Dan'l Bates surveyed for him.
9	Went to Wm Heneries. Surveyed part for said Bates and part for said Henery.
10	Surveyed Walter Cohoons Land and Protracted said Heneries.
11	Surveyed almost 100 Acres for Chris: Falkenbergen for which by a former Bargain he was to pay £20: vizt part in Nov 1747 and part in Nov 1748. Stands to said Agreement.
	Spent the Remainder of the day in an Agreement between him and his son in law Christian Sharpenstein.
12	Returned home. Paid Robt Steward for bringing up 1000 of shingles. Paid Walter Williams for carting 1000 or shingles. Reconed with Sarah More. Paid her light money. Remained in her debt 1:5 ½.
	Paid toward the support of the Ministry.
16	Tunis Hendrixse paid in full of accounts for Surveying and other trouble. Lent Sam'l Fleming 101 ft of Pine boards. Lent son John three pounds and 12 shills.
17	John Emmans paid for a Deed and his part of Surveying. Payed for a spining wheel and Expenses in fetching it.
18	Received from Lawrence Low for a Deed and Bond.
19	Let Adam Poke have a pine board - 15 feet.
21	Set out for Trenton. Lodged there that night.
22	Came home. Vincent Robert made nine pair of shoes.
23	John Hull[Null?] paid for a Deed.
24th	Paid Hermanus the Currier for work in my Debt.
26th	Philip Bevin had 2 sides of leather curried and uncurried. Weight of the soal leather 9 1/4 lbs of curried leather 3:3/4.
	Received from Matth's Housill in part of Surveying and Writing.
28th	Paid John Chandler towards his weaving.
	Sent to Wm Montgomeries for a Ream of Writing Paper.
29th	Set out for the Calf Pasture upon Raritan South branch arrived there that night. Lodged at S'l Tomkins.

30   Went up the Meadow on the head of Black River. Sought out some timber land. Came back to said Tomkins.

December 1748

1   Went from Saml'l Tomkins's to Wm Pues lodged there.

2   Surveyed a spot of Land joyning to the Mess'r Penns[77] Lot and went up to Daniel Landens in order to divide the lot of the devisces of Mr Lambert. Viewed the same and lodged at said Landens.

3   Set out for home where I arrived before night. Expenses to Daniel Landen 3/9: to Pues 1/6, Gave son Daniel when he went Phila 4/6: this day he returned and brought back with him 12s.

5   Son Daniel Received from Edmond Wooley for finding out Charges Expenses and Surveyor Generals fees for 200 Acres which think is 1:13 extraordinary.

7   Went to Ph: Bevins run forth of Tho: Kitchins Land for him 4 Acres. Took the Acknowledgment of Jos: Thatchers deed from the Penns.
Took four other Acknowledgments of Deeds vizt: Jno Forter to Neil Campbell; Neil Campbell to R'd Crook 133 Acres. Ditto to Jno Petty 100 Acres: Ditto to Daniel Bates 100 Acress. Paid to John Porter for the laying of an Axe. Lent to Yocham Van Maple a board containing 14 ft. (not returned). Payed John Edmunds for Sarah's Coffin 6s who paid it me back in part of some money hereto for borrowed. Bought fish.

10th   Received from Thomas Hunt for a Deed and Draught to the Penns.

12   Received from Crist: Coil Jur and Aller for 3 Acknowledgments.

17th   Received from Robert Colvert for 2 acknowledgments of Deeds. D'd to said Colvert a Deed from Wm Scoley and Ux: to Wm Cook.

19th   Wm Jewel had 4 1/8 1b of Leather. Indebted to the said Jewell

---

[77] William Penn's sons: JOHN PENN (1699–1746), THOMAS PENN (1702-1775), and RICHARD PENN (1706-1771). http:// en.wikipedia.org / wiki/ William_Penn (July 23, 2010) and Stanton D. Hammond, *Hunterdon County Maps, Name Index* (Genealogical Society of New Jersey, 1965), 28.

for a Calfskin.

Payed to Tho: Evans for haling ___ ft of Boards

21 James Martin and George Beaty paid £60 being the first payment towards the Land Agreed for on Sep'r last.

24 Bought 2 galls of Rum.

Received from John Williamson for 35 Acres of unlocated land. Deed for same for Resurveying his Plantation. C[harges] and fees to the Surveyor General.

Payed Jacobus Whittaker towards 2 4/10 acres (bought from him) by the sale of 13 Acres of unlocated land resurveying his Plantation. Charges to myself and fees to the Surveyor Genl.

26 Went to Mr Joseph Stouts. Received for an Acknowledgment of a Deed.

27 Finished surveying the old Place the viewing of the new.

28 Went to D'l Lakes run around the lines of his land for part of pay charged 12s.

Acknowledged a Deed for Wm Allen Jr. Not paid for.

29 Tryed the lines of some land William Allen bought for H. Farnswort.

30 William Force finished riving some pails for the garden.

Heretofor mended a waggon wheel.

1748/9

January 1748/9

2d Reed from Peter Rockefeller for two Deeds.

4th William Force had 2 ½ bus of Indian Corn.

Received from Andreis Gordenier for a Deed of Mortgage.

6th Received from Rob: Lett: Hooper on account of the Estate late

Daniel Howell.[78]

Payed Mr Beatty £50 towards towards his wives Porcons received from Ja: Martin. Received from Mich'l Short on account of a Bond. Payed Mr Beatty for a Roaster.

16th Eliz: Robert had Cloath and Tape for an Apron.

13 Mr Short paid for a Deed. Payed to Wm Force upon G. Halls Account.

16 Got the Bond from Mr. Tobias Tenyke given by Wm Force and My self for 20s Light Money having paid it off.
Tunis Quick paid me for a Prop'y writing and services.

19th Vincent Robert made 8 pairs of shoes.
Set out for Burlington. Lodged at Trenton. Daniel Leonard fell short of his Rent which I Payed to Mr. Cox. Payed in 1756.

20 Came to Burlington about 12. Sat in Council in the afternoon. Left some surveys in the Surveyor Generals office.

21 Set homewards. Came by Trenton and arrived home at night. Bought 6 ½ lbs of Jesuits Bark at Eli: Bonds.

28 Received from Michl Demot for Writings done.

30 Set out on a journey to Pahquanack. Lodged at Whippaning.

February 1748/9

4 Returned home from Paquanack.

10 Lent John Chandler fifteen shillings.

13 Received from Joh's Bussenberg towards his Pay for Land, his Receipt in the Trunk.

15th Reconced with Justus Gans and paid him the Balance.

17 Received from Mich'l Short on account of Surveying and Troubles etc. Received from John Short for Surveying and a Deed.

18 Payed Eliz: Robert toward her spining. Received from Mr Creature and And'w Abel for 2 Deeds. Lent Jos: Warford a pieces of 8.

---

[78] DANIEL HOWELL, CAPT. (1688-1733). Married John Reading's sister Elsie. Her father, Col. John Reading, gifted a large amount of land near Stockton to Daniel and Elsie as a wedding gift *ca.* 1710. Leach, *Memorials,* 22, 149.

20   Set out for Burlington. Went over the River and lodged that night at Mahlon Kirkbrides.

21   Went over the River to Burlington. Left my horse at Tho: Marriots.

Stay'd till the 4th of March then came up to Trenton and came home the next day.

Payed at Burlington for a pair of shoes. Expenses at Burlington and in and out upon my journey.

In my absence Received from several persons following: Joha's Binder for 2 bls of Rye at 4s per bul. Peter Aller and Math's Pockus for Writing and Surveying. Daniel Grigs paid for a Deed. Payed at Burlington for mending Tea Tongues, w't Knee buckle. Vincent Robert had 2 bls of Rye.

March 1748/9

4th   Payed for 2 pair of woeman's Shoes.

6th   James Farow had 3 t of hay @2s per __ [?]

7   Martin Shifley had 4 t of hay @ 2s per __ [?]

8   Set out for Burlington (dined at Trenton) arrived there at Night.

11th   Set out for Philadelphia arrived there that day. Paid Mr Edw'd Shippen for Mr Alford £ 21:12:6. Bought ½ a Doz. of parchment.

12   Bought 2 pair of silver studs.

13   Returned to Burlington. Expenses out and in.

17   Set out homewards. Lodged at Jno Kirkbrides arrived

18   At home: Expenses out and in.

8   Harmanus Simoness bought 7 __ [?] of hay @ 2s per __ [?].

9   John Smith bought 3__ [?] of hay

10   James Pharo had in Cash borrowed [amount].

17   Adam Poke bought 4 __ [?] hay

18   Sold ½ Bll flaxseed.

20   James Pharo bought 3 __ [?] hay. Stepehen Ganoe bought 3 ___ [?] hay Stephen Ganoe paid by Discompt with son John.

22d   Payed Tho: Collins for stubing 5 Acres of Land.

23   Set out for Burlington. Arrived there that night

29   Stayed there 'till the 29th. Set out homewards. Arrived there that night.

Payed for my Boarding at Mrs Pearsons. For washing; barber; expenses at Jr Thomas's for my Horse at Tho: Marriot's hay and oats. For cording the whip and ferriages. Left unpaid at Trapnals 4:6 besides the charges on the Expenses in and out.

In my absence Jno Edmonds bought 2 __ [?] hay. Timothy Toy bought ½ [?]. Walter Cain paid by himself £ 1:0:6; by son Jno 4/6 for a Deed.

Paid Henry Landies for a Bridle, Bridle bits and sadle strap.

30   Received from Henry McMullen on account of Damage don by Hoggs in my Wheat.

Henry Grove to pay 1/6.

Paid John Johnson for making Shoes, Boots etc. 10/6. Upon Matt's Smiths account for 4 boards.

31   Paid Vincent Robert on changing of a D'bl D'bl Loon.[79] Paid Mr. Ringo for 2 galls of Rum and quart of Wine.

April 1749

1   Received from Mich'l Moier for a Deed. Lent John Hoff d'bl for which he gave bond payable 1750.

3   Vincent Robert had 2 lb of Rye. Timothy Toy had ½ __ [?] of hay. John Williamson bought 1 lb of Barley. Wm Force bought one Bus'l flaxseed.

4   Jacob Woolever bought 1 bu'l of flaxseed. Eliz: Harney bought 1 bu'l of flax seed.

7   Derrick Hogeland bought 1 bll of Barley. Derrick Sutphen bought 3 pecks of Barley.

Mary Matthews Received from me for spining on my own account and son John's.

10th   Went to Pennsylvania in Bucks County. Lodged at 4 Lanes End.

11   Went to Trenton, attended the Loan Office from thence home.

---

[79] A Spanish gold coin equal to £3.32 sterling or £5.66 New Jersey Proc. which is 5 lbs 8 shillings. McCusker, *Money & Exchange in Europe & America, 1600-1775*, 172 and http://blindkat.hegewisch.net/ pirates/ money.html (July 23, 2010).

Expenses in said journey and 1/6 for fish.

12th   Agreed with Ishmael Shippy for a building 20x16 foot to be enclosed two floors layed doors and windows sides to be Clapboarded to be shingled with Cedar which I am to find for 1:8:16.

Tho: Atkinson while I was absent as above had 1 bll Barley Sam'l Stout paid for 1 bul of Barley.

Went to Ralph Smiths and from thence on _____.

13th   Tryed the Society Line[80] in Conjunction with the said Smith.

14   Tryed the outside lines and Divisions of a tract of land of Mr. Logans in the Long Valley and returned to said Smiths that night.

15th   Returned home by Jacob Tenykes in order to run the Courses of the River but did not do it.

Luke Ryerson this week had 20 bls of Barley and one bl of flaxseed.

17th   Attended this week in Cutting and Tying tickets for the Lottery.

22   Finished the Tickets and went over to John Garrisons in order to run round some land late belonging to Mr Lambert.

24th   Lent to Paul Botner Cash.

Mr Jos: Sackets son left [an amount] to pay for a Return in the Surveyor Office.

27   Went to Trenton. Received from James Baird by Mr P'p Ringo.

28   Acknowleged a Deed for Jno Corwine by Jacobus Johnson; paid for.

29th   Aaron Praul paid for a Warrant and Surveying.

May 1749

1   Attended on the Lottery all this week and finished on the 12th being Friday in the next week but met on Saturday being the 13th to examine the proceedings therin.

7th   In which time above some other affairs intervened as the selling of a strey Heifer by Tho: Hunt one of the Overseers of the Poor which my son George bought for 15s took said Hunts receipt for

---

[80] The boundary line of the West Jersey Society's "Great Tract" in northern Hunterdon County. Hammond, *Hunterdon County Maps*, Map C: A5.

the same dated May the 7th 1749.

Received from P'p Young 20s (greatest part of which was for a deed formerly wrote from John Cook to said Young). The remainder being paid for a Deed from Casper Haughinback 3s left unpaid.

Payed to Jacobus Whittaker the remained of the Consideration money for a Lott of about 2 1/4 Acres of Land.

Received from Freegift Stout 15s part of 20s for a deed from Val: End[Ent].

10th   Sent son George to Trenton to meet the Justices and Freeholders in my stead and to assist in the cancelling the money. And there was sunk in the 20,000 the sum of £185 being the whole and remaining part of that emission. The sum of £330 in the 40,000 Emissions being 40£ short which was all the Jersey money we had.

15th   Set out for Trenton. On my way took an acknowledgment of a Deed at Nath'l Parkers. Lodged at Nath't Moors.

16th   Arrived at Trenton. Took an account of the Delinquents and some other affairs in the Loan Office. Took the Proofe of a Deed for J. Rouze (not paid for) and another for a man in Cumberland County (paid for). Payed my Dividend of the charges at the Sinking of the Money and my present expenses being about 12s and set homewards where I arrived that night.

20th   Payed James Pharrow towards his account which he brought in the said day was £7:13:4 besides a share then b't home.

22d   Set out for a Journey up into the Country. Lodged at Wm Henns that night.

23d   Ran round by the lines a Tract of Land formerly surveyed to Sam'l Furnis Containing 600 Acres. Received from Amos Hains for said service. Lodged at Sam'l Tomkins that night.

24th   Mart: Ryerson came up to said Tomkins and surveyed for me at the Indian Fields and the head of the Black River 100 Acres. Lodged at Aaron Starts that night.

25th   Ran some of the lines of the Tract of 340 Acres at the Indian Field went to the Pond and lodged at P'r Degoes.

26   Went to Sam'l Greens wrote a Deed and Bond for Jonathan Pettit. Reckoned with Sam'l Green and Received the Balance.

27th   Set homewards. Lodged at Wm Pues.

28th   Arrived at home in safety about noon.

In my absence bought 9 ½ of veal 1/7 Calfskin 2s from Timothy Toy. Timothy Toy had ½ bush'l of Indian Corn. Robert Calcot had one bus'l of Indian Corn.

30   Sent by my wife to New York and ten Bush of Wheat to the Landing by son Daniel. Gave to son George 0:7:6.

Received from Joseph McMurterie upon Mr Alfords account paid by Mr Beatty.

31   Son Daniel bought 2 sythes and returned back [an amount].

Sent up to Ab Henreys at Penungauchong these creatures following vizt: an old black low mare with a small star branded with W on the far buttock and a Bow and Arrow on the Near shoulder and thigh-black horse Colt with a large star.

2). A Bay Mare 5 Years old Branded with a Bow and Arrow on the near shoulder and thigh with a brown Mare Colt a star.

3). A Chestnut Bay Mare three years old Branded as above.

4). A Black yearling Mare Colt branded as above.

5). A Red Roan Horse small yearling colt branded as above a star.

6). A Black Yearling Horse Colt a long stripe something Crooked grayish tail Branded as above.

June 1749

5th   Took the acknowledgment of a Deed for Arie Gaerdineer. Andr to pay it. My wife returned from New York.

8th   Payed to James Whittaker for 3/10 of an acre of Land being an overplus in that lot I formerly bought of him. The Deed being altered so as to include the same and new __hed and evidenced after the alteration made. James Whittaker paid me for my trouble about his affairs.

10   Sent to the Landing to buy Nails. And: Gardinier paid for the above acknowledgment and one other now took.

12   John Louks paid for a Deed.

16th   Drew a copy of a Return and Wrote to Mr Alexander[81] for which
        I Received from John Bowlby [an amount].
18th   Payed Ishmael Shippey in part for his work.
21   Payed D'd Conner in part for 18 Days Mowing Grass.
23   Daughter Eliz:[82] came home and returned back 11s [New York]
        Money.

July 1749

3d   Son George went to Burlington bought 2 skins of Parchment.
        Paid Postage of 2 Returns.
4   Payed Johannes Binder for 6 days Binding at 5s 18 in cash and a
        blanket my wife sold 12s Light Money.
        William Force cradled 6 ½ days.
5   Jacob Erwine paid for 100 bl of wheat deducting 1s for Melasses,
        Carting of Boards and short in measure of wheat sold @6/3 per
        bu.
11th   Payed Sarah Moor for wages.
12   Sent Daniel for Dr Witt and with him sent [money].
15   Son Daniel Returned and brought some Physick cost 8:2. Bought
        ½ a Doz of Parchment. Brought home from Phila ½ a Doz more
        of parchment bought by Mr Montgomerie and left at Joseph
        Woods in Phila.
        Altered the mortgage of Henry Dildine from 124 by leting have 2
        bl more which made it £60.
17   Benj: Stout and Gershom mended the shingling on the back of
        the House for which I am to pay for one days work the one half
        to each other.
        Son Daniel returned part of the money sent to Phila.
19   Robert Calcot borrowed 1 ½ a b'l of Wheat.
20   James Pharow had 2 bus'ls of Wheat.
21   Peter Dirdorf had 20 t upon Bond.
23   Gave to a Charitable Use

[81] JAMES ALEXANDER (1691-1756). Scottish born aristocrat who was surveyor general of both East and West New Jersey from 1715 until his death. http://en.wikipedia.org/wiki/James_Alexander_lawyer (July 23, 2010).
[82] ELIZABETH READING (1730-81). Married John Hackett. Leach, *Memorials*, 51.

24   Robert Calcot had one bul of Indian Corn.

25   Tho: Newman paid for a Deed; surveying the Lott.

28   James Logan by Ralph Smith for trouble on the Society Line.

29   Paid Wm Montgomerie for ½ a doz. of parchment bought as above.

August 1749

Sometime this month Robert Calcot had 1 Bu wheat and 1 Bu Indian Corn.

1st   Set out for Trenton where I arrived at night.

2d   Stayed at Trenton. Mr Byerly's share to Land in Hunterdon and Morris County being 9009 Acres besides the disputable part was sold for 3000 £ Proc.

3d   Went to Burlington by Jno Kirkbride. Met the Council of Prop's. Payed Jno Trapniel __ ahold ac'r and charges at the Proprietor dinner.

4th   Stayed at Burlington. Payed upon Sam'l Greens account for a Warrent of the Survey for Tho: Silverthorn. Left with Mr Isaac DeCow for Surveyors Generalls fees. Received Deeds out of the Secretarys Office fees [amounts].
Accompted with John Ladd[83] upon Account of 5th Dividend Land remained due from said Ladd (which he promised to send up to Trenton-Landing in Shingles).
Payed for a pair of shoes for wife and account at Wm Yards.

8th   Accompted with Thomas Atkinson and paid him in full of Grinding, Bolting, Packing and all other accounts. Paid Tho: Atkinson for James Bradbury for 21 casks Son Daniel returned from the Landing brought home 400 of Oisters for which and his journey he expended [an amount].

14   Sam'l Green paid by Mr Jos: Stout remainder of his account to

---

[83] JOHN LADD (d. 1771). John Ladd II was a surveyor and man of prominence for many years in Salem and Gloucester counties. He was elected a member of the Assembly from Gloucester in 1754. While still a member of that body, he was recommended by Governor Belcher in 1758 for a seat in the Council. In 1762 he was appointed one of the Surrogates for West Jersey. From *Collections of the New Jersey Historical Society Vol IX*, (Newark, New Jersey: New Jersey Historical Society, 1916), 155.

the Surveyor Generals Office.

18   Dear son Sam'l[84] departed this life about 6 of the clock in the morning.

Sent to buy Wine and Rum and Skrews for the Coffin.

19   Burial at the Meeting House in Amwell.

21   Sent homewards Daughter Ann. Mr Beatty met her at Jo: Howells.

22   More of the family taken sick of the sore throat whome we vomited.

23   Rich'd being sick of the feaver and Ague took the Bark Yesterday four doses; today two put the fitts by _____.

25   Daniel went to Dr Watsons medicines cost [amount] Geo: and Richard went to Tho: Lakes. Gave him 7:6 against rum.

26   Johannes Binder had a quarter of Veal.

29   Paid Peter for Wages in part for mowing. Sent by Mr Beatty to Mr Edw: Shippen Jos: McMurtrees money.

September 1749

First   Accounted with Ishmael Shippen for the House shop work and days work. Came to £14:0:6 and 2 pair of Shoes at 15s the remainder I paid him. Payed Wid: Harney in a former account and a gall of Rum.

8   Bought 74 lb of Beef from J:V: Est [Ent] @ 2d per lb. Now about Mart: Shefly had 1 bl of Indian Com.

12   Bought Gun powder ½ lb. and 4 lb shot.

14   Wm Force with Casar made a mantle Piece. Mart: Shifley had ½ bl seed wheat.

16   My wife set out for her Brother Georges [Ryerson][85] in company with her son George, Bro: Martin and Luke. Sent by her 1:0:0.

19   Robt Calcot had one Bus'l of Indian Corn.

20   Benj: Stout worked ½ of a Day at a Door Frame.

23   Molly Matthews was paid in full for her spinning.

---

[84] SAMUEL READING (1741-49). John Reading's youngest son. Leach, *Memorials*, 39.
[85] GEORGE RYERSON (1702?-92). John Reading's brother-in-law. He married Mary Duboise in 1744. Ryerson, *The Ryerse-Ryerson Family*, 21.

25   Son George Returned of the money sent by his Mother. Bought a
      bl 1/4 almost of flaxseed from Ab: Delameter.
29   Wm Henery left 1:10 to pay Mrs Biles for a Book.
30   Payed the Schoolmaster for ½ Years schooling 1/4 for two.
      Payed Jos: Bost for haling of 685 foot of boards from Mr Ringos
      (George Hall left with me to buy a pair of Buckskin gloves) [this
      in parentheses struck out.]

October 1749

2d   Sent for Boards to Mr Ringoes and for as much Rum as 7/6
      would buy. Bought a stone pot, bl of lime and Nails.
3   Bought 12 lb Nails. George Hobbagh paid for a Deed. John
      Garrison paid for a Deed. Reckoned with Benj: Stout and Payed
      him the Balance of accounts charged for work at the malthouse.
      George Hall left with me to buy a pair of Gloves.
5   Bought fish from the Pound at Delaware. At 2 other times
      bought fish from bros M and L Ryerson.
9   Peter had by Robt Calcot [amount]. John Van Est had the
      Balance for the Beef.
11   Payed Sarah Moor for wages.
13   Agreed with John Smith to sink a Well for 3/6 per foot till it
      comes to the Rock; then 4s and to wall it for the same price. Not
      to leave it untill he gets water if possible to be had. If he has
      occasion to blow to pay 5s towards the tools and bear the Cost of
      Sharpening and Upseting and Powder.
16   My wife set out for N. York by whom I sent [amount]. Wm
      Wertegen paid for a Return Recording and Acknowledged Deed.
17   Bought 15 lb of fish.
18   Received from Casper Shafer Principal and Interest of a Bond.
      Received from Anna Minor for a Power of Attorney and other
      Troubles.
19   Payed to Johannes Binder for a hide w't 25 lbs ½ by ¼ of Veal.
20   Received from broth: Mart: for Acknowledging a Deed.
21   Bought a Parcells of Oisters of son John.
25   My wife retured from New Y: having sent the money back Gave

her being Jersey Bills and got so much of Henry Lane being part of pay for wheat and flower.

27   Paid by son Daniel for 2 Horses. Bought deers leather. Payed to Arie DePue for services.

28   Bought nails at Tho: Newmans at the Landing.

31   Bought a hide from Jo: Edmonds. Payed to Tho: Martin for work done this Month.

November 1749

4th   Lent Robt Calcot [amount]

9   John Smith refused to dig any further in the Well. I paid him towards his wages vizt: 15s in cash and 6s in a pick. If he will get his work appraised I have given him leave to bring any two responsible persons used to such work and I will give him what they shall allow provided it does not do me damage in the finishing the same. At the same time paid him for filling in Robts House.

11   Mart: Shifly had a quarter of Beef.

14   Bought 2 Hides from Jac'b Gray @ 2 ½ / lb. Eliz: Harney bought 124 lb of Pork.

15   Paid Rich'd Crook in full for fulling of Cloath. Bought a Bulls Hide from H'y Grave. Sold to Sam'l Flemings 2 hogs weighed by my stilliards 311 lbs by his but 301 lb. Sold Bro: Ryerson one Hog wt 239 lb.

17   Received from Corn's Bowman for Surveying of 100 As and half of other Charges with Christ: Harshall.

20   Received from Morris Creature pay for Recording his Deed.

21   Received from Wm Waert for a Bill of Sale. Bought from __Bishop ½ Doz. of Silk Handkerchiefs.

24   Bought one hide from Ab: Delamater.

25   Bought 4 Doz of Perch.

      James Pharoe had in cash [amount].

29   Mart: Shifley had 2 bl of Rye.

December 1749

1st   Joost Habbagh paid for Deeds and Surveying.

2   Martin Shifley had 2 bl of Rye.

      Christopher Preston paid for Writings being 2 Bonds 12 Awards being one half of the whole. James Farow to pay for the other half.

6   Henry Cock paid for an Acknowledgment.

7   Bought ½ gal of Train Oil.[86]

8   Martin Shifley had 2 bls of wheat.

9   Charles Dubois paid for Writing and Surveying.

11   Paid Peter in Full of all accounts.

      Received from Willgus for a Deed. Received from James Stout for Surveying.

12   Bought 2 gals Rum and 1 ½ yds of Shalloon.[87]

14   Sam'l Fleming paid for 301 lbs Pork.

18   Fred: Hab't Fox paid for a Deed.

21   Bought a Gall of Rum. A fish weighing 12 lb. Paid John Griggs for a Pint of Oil and Botle.

23   Paid Julian Miller for Sowing.

28   Acknowledged 2 Deeds for Isaiah Quinby.

1749/50

January 1749/50

1   Bought from Arie Depue deerskins.

4   Martin Shifly had one bl of Indian Corn.

5   Received from Jos: Hill for Surveying.

---

[86] Train or whale oil, derived from any species of whale, including sperm oil from sperm whales, train oil from baleen whales, and melon oil from small toothed whales. From the 16th century through the 19th century, whale oil was used principally as lamp fuel and for producing soap. http:// www.britannica.com /EBchecked/topic/641432/whale-oil (July 23, 2010).

[87] A lightweight wool or worsted twill fabric, used chiefly for coat linings. http:// www.thefreedictionary.com/shalloon (August 2, 2010).

16   Payed Dl Laroe [an amount].

17   Payed to Jos: King order of John Johnson. Martin Shifley had 4 bl of Wheat.

18   Reckoned with Martin Shifley; remaining in his debt [amount].

20   Sold ½ bl of Barley.

22   Nancy Calcots mending of her shoes paid to John Johnson. Reckoned with J. Johnson paid him the balance.

25   John Van Esse paid the balance of his Account for Surveying and deed and trouble about the Road which together with 15s formerly paid is in full.

Henry Van Ste upon his late fathers Account

29   Martin Shifly had 4 __ of hay.

February 1749/50

1st   Peter Young paid for a Deed.

5   Set out for Burlington lodged at Mr Warnells that night. Payed Mrs Biles on Wm Howels account for a Book.

6   Went to Burlington. Stayed there till Saturday.
Set out homewards. Lodged at Mr Ringoes.

11   Arrived at home. Expenses whilst at the Councill. Other Expenses besides my Horse.
Received for Acknowledging some Deeds for Robt Pearson.

12   Benj: Stout Axeltreed the big waggon. Christ: Coil paid me for a Deed.

13   Received from ___ Robinson for Acknowledging a Deed.
Sometime in my absence Mart: Shifley had 2 bl of Ind: Corn.
Bought at Sam'l Fleming 1 ½ yds of Flanell.

14   Set out for Burlington. Arived there that night.

17   Hermanus Simonse's account for currying, Debtor to Hay etc.paid him the Remainder.

13   James Farow brought in his account which was from the 19th of April 1748 the sum of £14:18:7 at the said day. I engaged to pay M'l Henery the sum of £3 towards same.
Sometime in the beginning of this month my wife reconed with Justus Gans[?] the Cooper and paid him.

16   Came over to Bristol in order to come home.

17   Set out homewards but was much hindered by the Ice. Lodged at the Widow Corials.

18   Got home stoping at the Meeting.

21   Bought fish.

22   Surveyed at Amwell Dr Dimsdales' land.

24   Received from Gerardus Lequire for 2 Deeds and Surveying.

26   Paulus Butner paid of a Note given April last.

27   Set of for Burlington. Arrived there that night. The Assembly prorogued the day before.

28   Stayed at Burlington. Sat in the Privy Council or Council of State.

29   Sat in Council. Gave our Opinions to the Govr in Referrence to the Justices complained against by the Assembly and came to Trenton. Lodged at Mr Warrell's.

28th   Mr. Charles Read Secretary paid me in full for his fees whilst President. Paid Isaac DeCow for fees due to the Surveyor Generals Office. Paid Isaac DeCow Jur[88] for accomodations. Paid Tho: Marriot for my Horse.
Tho: Marriot paid a deficiency in the Loan Office for the last year.
Expenses besides my debts and Horse.

March 1749/50

3   Received from Joh's Yerie Binder for the lott of Land formerly bought from me now sold to Jac'b Coursen.

6   Surveyed for Jeromus Horn and P'r Rockefeller.

7&8   ___Along with Mr Will: Coxe at Mt Carmel and Lebanon.

10   Received from Mich'l Shurt due by bill and some Interest thereon. Lent Mart: Shifley 0:06:0.

16   Payed John Johnson for making one pair of Boots.

17   Payed Hezekiah Bebe for making Shoes.

21   Corn's Stevens paid for a resurvey and Return.

23   Tunis Case paid for service done this day (the running out old lot

---

[88] ISAAC DECOW, JR. (d. 1755). Son of Isaac Decow Esq. Married Hannah Nicholson. DeCou, *Decow Family*, Chart III, 78.

not paid).

26   Molly Matthews spining came to £1:5 was paid.

31   Jasper Achenbach paid for the acknowledging of a Deed.
Accompted with D'k Zutphen and paid him the balance.
Sarah Moore finished spining the 26th. Wages came to £2:5:0.

April 1750

5   Dom: Van Duchren paid for a Deed and Bonds.

8   Set out for Burlington where I arrived that night.

9   Paid to Deputy Secretarie for Recording several Deeds.

10   Set out for Trenton arrived there before Noon. Went up that night to the Widdow Corials. Payed for one years Pub. Papers to Moor Furman.[89]

Payed Joseph DeCow for 2 bl ____.

11   Arrived at home about 2 of the Clock. Expenses in and out.

12th   George Birket paid for an Acknowledgment of a Deed.

17   Went to Trenton. Paid in part to Js: Hutchinson for 400 Acres of Land and gave a Bill for the Remainder payable on the 1 of Nov. next.

Payed for 2 pair of Shoes. Expenses out and in (not being paid at Wm Yards).

21   Jacob Runk by P'r Rockefeller paid for a Deed and Surveying.
Gave my wife for New York 6 pieces of 8.

23   Went with Mr Jos: Turner[90] to the Land late Mr Tho: Byerly's.

---

[89] MOORE FURMAN (1728-1808). Prior to the Revolutionary War, Moore Furman was a highly successful merchant and public servant. In the 1750s he partnered with Andrew Reed in the mercantile business and served as High Sheriff of Hunterdon County and Postmaster of Trenton. In the mid-1760s Furman purchased a large tract of land northwest of Flemington on which he built an entire village, named Pittstown, including a nail factory, grist mill, hotel and dwelling houses. During the remainder of his lifetime, he continued to serve in a variety of other public offices, including: agent for the United States Lottery, during the war; commissioner for the construction of the first State house in Trenton, in 1791; and first mayor of Trenton, 1792. http://www.state.nj.us/ state/darm/links/guides/pfurm001.html (July 23, 2010).

[90] JOSEPH TURNER (1701-83). For many decades prior to the American Revolution, he was in business with Chief Justice William Allen; their firm, Allen & Turner, was one of the most important in the colonies. Turner entered into trade agreements and iron mining and manufacturing ventures, including the Union Iron Works in Hunterdon County, New Jersey, at present-day High Bridge, New Jersey.

24   To Run Round the lines of that share thereof which Mr Allward
      himself had Purchased. Spent most of the week therin excepting
      part of Saturday in which I finished the same and ran out of Mr
      John Coxes land.
27   For Mr David Martin 105 Acres. Received from Mr Turner for
      my service.
28   Received from Aaron Davis part of Jos: Lynns account.
      Sometimes this week Martin Shifly had 2 bls of wheat. Michael
      Short paid for a Deed in my absence.

May 1750

2   Abraham Behtelsiemer paid for a Deed.
3d   John Smith by Edw'd Milner Jur paid for a Deed. Mr Shifly had 2
      bls of Wheat.
      Edw'd Milner by his son Edw'd paid for Surveying. Ezekiel
      Bennet paid for a Deed Mortgage and Defeazance.
4   Corn's Low[91] gave his Receipt for £2:4 in full of accounts. Henry
      Lane sent up by son John for Barley.
7   Corn's Williamson his Deed and 4 Bonds come to 19s. Matth's
      Trimmer and Philip Kelse paid for 2 Deeds 14s each.
8   Went to Trenton. Received pay for the acknowledging of two
      Deeds of Nath'l Parker.
9   Cancelled before the Justices and Freeholders the sum of 300 lb;
      320 of this years Principal and an arrearage of 40 lb the last Year.
      There being a deficiency this Year of 50 lb.
10   Payed Wm Yard my Expenses this Year and for trouble about the
      Boards and Shingles in Receiving them getting them on the bank
      etc.
12   Charles Gordon paid for a Bargain and Sale[92] and Defeazance.[93]

---

http:// en.wikipedia.org/wiki/ Joseph_Turner_loyalist23 (July 23, 2010).
[91] CORNELIUS LOW (1700-77). In 1729, he married Johanna Gouveneur. They
moved to the port community of Raritan Landing near New Brunswick, where Low, a
merchant with shipping capabilities, became one of the community's most prosperous
businessmen. http:// en.wikipedia.org/ wiki/Cornelius_Low_House (July 23, 2010).
[92] A deed "for which the grantor implies to have or have had an interest in the property
but offers no warranties of title to the grantee. A *bargain and sale deed* is especially used by

Payed to the support of the Ministry.

with James Farrow and paid him the Balance of his account to the 13th of Feb: 1749.

15   George Biggs paid for a Paper Deed of Bargain and Sale. Martin Ryerson paid for the Acknowledgment of 2 Deeds.

16   James Farrow had a Deed from Henry McMullen. Jacob Erwine paid for a Deed. Wm Akers paid for a Deed.

Paid Catherine the knitter.

14   Payed Wm Montgomerie the Balance of his Account.

16   Son George Returned from Dr Dainurs in Pensylvania where had been above five Weeks.

17th   Son Richard returned from Dr Watsons with Medicines for Daniel.

19   Peter Romine paid for Rent. I gave him a Receipt for rent paid June the 4th 1750. Receipt said to be lost.

21   Payed Mich'l Henry upon Account of stock tickets for self and son John. Payed Ditto for IV Tickets taken out by James Farrow for which he gave a Note.

John Lawrence paid for a Deed.

23   Sent up into the woods 27 cattle. Daughter Eliz: went to Philadelphia by her sent for sundries.

24   Luke Ryerson paid part of my wife's Legacie Light Money.

Received for the Acknowledgment of two Deeds.

26   Daughter Eliz returned from Phila, gave back of the money sent.

Mr Montgomerie sent 1/11 an doz of Parchement not paid for.

28   Benj: Stout Accompted for a Bond being in part of pay for 1 days work at the Wagon shaft.

Received for VIII more Bonds at 1/6 per Bond.

Robert Calcot per his wife had one Bus'l of Indian Corn.

31   Mathias Trimmer paid for 1 Deed and Release.

Payed some time this month to John Cock for Riming three Waggon Wheels or 3 days work at 4s per diem.

---

local governments such as executors, and in foreclosure sales by sheriffs." http://en.wikipedia.org/wiki/Deed (July 23, 2010).

[93] A provision that voids a bond or loan when the borrower sets aside cash or bonds sufficient enough to service the borrower's debt.

http://www.investopedia.com/terms/d/defeasance.asp (August 2, 2010).

John Reading's Diary

June 1750

1   Thomas Young came from the Great Meadows who by a permission was to setle thereupon a lease for 10 years from this spring. He is to Improve no more Upland that what is just necessary for Winter grain for his family. He is to improve the Meadow and raise from thence Indian Corn and at least 10 Acres. To begin his Improvement next spring and go on yearly with it or he may improve the same immediately and is not confined to no more than 10 acres but as much as he pleases so that he ditcheth it and bring it into order. Setled according to Agreement. Is gone off.

       Received from John Arrison in part for writings (whole 1:5 and Bond).

2   Payd to Sarah Moor in part of Wages.

       Went to try some lines between D'k Hogeland and Jos: Bost. Bought a Gall of Rum cost besides 2 qts formerly short in measure.

       to Robert Farmar for Combing Wool.

5th   Set out for a journey to the Depues in Penna. Arrived there that night.

6   The next day surveyed a piece of land lying on the SE of Deleware in the Jerseys.

       The next day came to Jos: McMurteries. Divided Robt: Howe's and Robt: McMurteries land. Jos: McMurt: paid upon Mr Alfords account towards the Land.

8   Arrived at home. Sam'l Scholey by John Coat paid for Acknowledgment.

11   Mary Hayes [?] paid in part for a Bond.

13   Went to Trenton. Paid JnoYard for 3 hats. Payed the shoemaker for a pair of Woemens shoos.

14   Lent some Moravians a pieces of 8 which the stranger assured [me] I would [be repaid]. It was one of the Second Company. Paid back Sep'r the 19th 1750.

16   Wm Housel paid half the Surveying of 140 Acres.

18   Son George set out for N. York whome I gave for his own use 10 cask of flower and in cash £ 23:14:6 for other uses. Dan'l went

with him by whome I sent to buy Sundries.

19   Martin Shifly had 2 Bus'l of Wheat at Trenton.

23   Son George returned home from York.

29th Lent to David Connor which was paid to Jno Magray for Mowing. Payed John Marshal for 4 days Mowing.

30   Philip Yager paid for a Deed and Surveying. Gideon Rouser paid for a Deed and Surveying. William Allen paid for a Deed.

July 1750

1   Began the Corn Harvist. Beginning with the Rye on the ____.

2   Continued the Harvist.

3   Continued the Harvist.

4,5,6 [Illegible]

7   Finished our Corn Harvist with the help of son Jno hands.

9   Went to son Johns and helped him with our hands and Am to pay for One day ½ mowing to Jno Aller, J'o Magrau, blk Peter, Mart: Tegen for Ditto Raking and binding. Magd: Brewer 3s. Payed John Magrah for Cradling wheat 7 ½ days @ 4/6. Payed Magdalen Brewer for Raking 1 ½ day @ 2-day. I am to pay son John for 1 ½ days of Mowing by Jno Aller.

15   About Midnight son Johns Child[94] dyed.

17   Went to the burying. Received for Acknowledging a Deed.

18   Valentine End [Ent] Payed for a Deed wrote in 1745.

20   Sold a Calfskin to Arch'd Stienson.

27   Valentine End [Ent] paid for a Deed and 5 Bonds. Harman Wagoner paid for a Deed.

August 1750

2   Payed blk Peter for mowing of Grass and Corn. Valentine End paid for a Deed.

6th   Set out from home for Burlington. Lodged at Mr Ringoes.

7   Breakfasted at PennyTown. Dined at Trenton. Arrived at Burlington in the evening.

---

[94] Name and birthdate unknown.

Paid for a pair of woemens shoes at Trenton.

8 At Burlington. At the Council of Proprietrs. Will: Montgomerie Received on my account.

9 Remained at Burlington. Payed the Treasurer the full of the Interest to this Year.

10 Set out from Burlington. Came by Trenton called at the Kings Attornies. Returned a Borrowed Book. Got home in safety that night. Expenses upon the Road out and in. Expenses for Self and Horse at Burlington and Bristol besides Council fees.

11 Made Dan'l Seberings Will.

13 Received from Thomas Martin for a Deed. P'r Lawshitt paid for the writing of a Will. Jos: Sacket paid me for Surveying and Deed and c't [current] York Cur[renc]y.

14 Lent Martin Baker 22/6.

23 Gave Mr Charles Beatty a D'bl D'bl Loon to buy books and pay for Mr Henerys Annotations first Vol[95].

27 Payed to Jos: King for Plank 312 foot. To Amos Thatcher for rectifying the Aple Mill.

30 Bro: Luke had two pound of Tow[96] 10th w't he had before mad 12 lb both parcells this Month. Payed the same in fish.

31 Wm Force having worked about 3 half days at the most at Georges Barn floor charged 8s (to be enquired into) joynting the first half day 13 Plank the next day 11 more and flatted one sleeper on one side the next day layed the sleeper and put the plank down agreed to the charge of 6s.

September 1750

3d Gave Daniell for Expenses and to buy some things at the Landing. Lent to Wm Force by bill to M'l Henery.

8 Then Accompted with Mart: Tegen for clearing of Swamp 52 days at 2/6 per day and 1 ½ days of Harvist work amounting to the sum of 6:17:0.

12 Sent by Mr Wm Montgomerie to Phila to buy Linnen.

---

[95] Matthew Henry, *Commentary on the Whole Bible In 6 Volumes*, (England: 1706, 1721).

[96] Coarse broken flax or hemp fiber prepared for spinning.

13   Received from G. Biggs and Wm Kinny for 2 Bonds.

15   Mart: Tegen worked 2 days more about the Swamp. Reckoned with son George and fell in his Debt 3:13:7 [New] York Money.

17   Payed son George the above account. Sent by son George to N.Y. to buy Sundries.
        More sent by said George.

18   Ceesar had from me for Binding and Raking.
        Bought from Bro: Luke a Cowskin and paid him in leather.
        Went along with the Me'ss Yards to Survey at the Earl of Melfords[97] Tracts.
        Received from Henry Lane 26:4:4 for 100 bl of Wheat N. Y: C'r besides Charges thereon.

19   The Moravians paid back the pieces of 8.

20   Payed Isaac Hutchinson upon Bill.

21   Reconed with the Spinners. Paid Molley her Balance of £1:8. Paid Sarah Moore her Balance of £4:14:9 Paid Magd'n Brewer her Balance of 19s:6.

25th   Mr Beatty brought some Books home which he bought at Phila and some yet Remaining at his house vizt: the Universal History[98], Mr Heneries Exposit vizt: I vol and for which I have given him £15:3. The Balance in his hands is £2:15:5.
        Received from John Aller for 1 Bul of Barley 3s and 2 Bonds 2s.

27   Blk Peter borrowed since Received for in a Reconing. Bought from George Hatton 2 Calveskins.

28   Jos Binder Dyd leather for a pair of shoes. Bought 14 lb of fish. Payed Tho: Coat for Weaving.

October 1750

---

[97] MELFORT, JOHN DRUMMOND, EARL OF (1649-1714). One of 24 East Jersey Proprietors, he was granted 1000 acres in 1685. John Drummond was the younger brother of the Earl of Perth. In 1680 he was deputy governor of Edinburgh Castle. Four years later he was named Secretary of State for the Kingdom of Scotland, and raised to an Earl. John E. Pomfret, *The New Jersey Proprietors and Their lands* (Princeton, New Jersey: D. Van Nostrand, 1964) 37 and http://en.wikipedia.org/wiki/ John_Drummond, _1st_Earl_of_Melfort (July 23, 2010).

[98] *An Universal History, From The Earliest Account Of Time.* 65 Volumes. London: (1747-1765).

1st   Sent Daniel and Richard for the Cattle to Penungauchong. Gave
       them Cash.

3   Lent son Richard toward payment for a Gun. Received from Eliz:
       Harney part of a Balance of Account.

4   Received from Joh's Kener by P'r Rockefeller for a Deed. Martin
       Baker having made 12 pair of Shoes went home.

8   Martin Baker had 5 ½ lb of fish at 2/ per lb.
       Received for the Acknowledgment of Two Deeds. Lent son John
       out of the L[and]. Off[ice]: Money £6:0:0.

9   This day my wife son Joseph and Daughter Molly[99] set out for N.
       Yk. I sent by wife in cash York Money 20. By son Joseph 0:16:0
       Proc.

13   Martin Ryerson paid for an Hog wt 239 lb at 3p lb.
       Wm Force paid back the money lent to him 3d of the last month.

18   Promised a six shilling Bill towards the Building the Dutch
       Ministers house upon Rariton.

16   My wife returned from N. York.

19   Sold 5 stiers to Mr Bird for 18 lb 15s besides the hides which are
       to be returned.

22   Archib'd Stienson fetched a Sow which he bought for 12s having
       taken 9 pigs on Saturday before at 1/4 per pig. Not agreed for
       certain at the Price sold afterwards for 1/6 and 2s a piece.

24   Mr. Bird Payed for the above Stiers the sum of 18:15:0.

27   Bought a Hide from Barnet Kole w'd 4 lb at 2 ½ s.

29th   Received the above Stiers Hides. Sold to Eliz: Harney 3 Barrells
       of Cider at 10s per Bar'l.
       Arch'd Stiensons hide w'd 32 lb.

                        November 1750

1   Sold to Mart: Shilley a Fatt Cow at besides the Hide £3:05:0.

2   Accompted with John Edmonds and Balanced Accounts by two
       Hides w'd 108 ½ lb. Eliz: Harney had one other Barrel of Cider

---

[99] MARY "MOLLY" READING (1736-94). Married William Mills, Presbyterian
minister and 1765 graduate of Princeton. Leach, *Memorials*, 52-53 and Val D.
Greenwood. *The Researcher's Guide to American Genealogy*, 3rd ed. (Baltimore, Maryland:
Genealogical Publishing Co., Inc., 2000), 42.

at 10s.

3   Peter Woolever and Valentine Shultus had 12 sheep (6 each) to hire for 3 years at one pound of wool each sheep per year to be dehiered at our house and to return 12 sheep at the end of the time as good as and as young as those they then had. Job Warford paid for a Deed. Jacob Runk paid for a Deed 15s for Surveying 7-6.

5   Payed John Cock for mending a waggon wheels. David Eveland Payed for his Deed and running out his Land.

6   Set out for Burlington and arrived there that night.

7   Made a Quorum of the Council of Proprietors Sat and Adjourned.

8   Paid to Joseph Scattergood for Recording of several Deeds. Received from Rich'd Smith jur for surveying of Mart: D Hog'd and P. Fishers Lands by him with Eb: Large sold to them. Returned home Expenses in and out.

9th   Altered the Division line between J'b P'r Suiter and Fran: Passion.

10   Sold a Boar Pigg to Jno Edmunds. Tho: Atkinson bought 6 bl of Wheat at 4/4 per Bus'l. Tho: Atkinson sold a Cask of Kernel for which he paid us.

12   Went to the Vansicklens and Corn's Lane surveyed for them.

13   Went to Foxe Hill. Surveyed for Morris Creature 88 Acres He having purchased the same from me after the rate of £20 per 100 Acres he paying the Survr Genls Fees. My labor given in paid one part.

14   Dennis Woolverton paid a Bill off. Daniel Howell paid for two Deeds. Ditto Payed part of surveying in Amwell.

16   Peter Foxe paid for a Deed £1. For a Bond 4s.

17   Accompted with William Force and fell in his debt £1:4:6; £1:4 part thereof he paid for one years Interest of a Bond given to Tobias Tenike for £20 Light money.

Wm Force paid part of the above of 20£ being £9:6:8 Light money.

19   Joh's Besenberg paid off a Bond for 10£ and Interest thereon. Ditto paid for a Deed, Recording it and Surveying.

21   Surveyed in Kingwood for Jno Haff jur and Paul Coenover.

22   and for James and Jeremiah Thatcher.

23   for James Bown[e].

24   Acknowledged a Deed for Gab'l Foxe. Came home. This week in
     my absence our People killed some Hogs. The Wid: Harney had a
     half of one Hog weighed ____, she paid ____.
     John Yerie Binder had the other ½ weighed- __ at 3d per lb.
     Brother Mart: Ryerson had a Hog.
     Bought 2 Hides from Th: Marshall the other from Ad: Kurshow.

27th Went to Corn's Van Campens upon an Arbitration between Jno
     and Richd Hall. Spent therein 3 ½ days.
     In my absence our People killed the rest of the Hoggs and two
     Beeves.
     The last Week Eliz: Harney had two more bar'ls of Cider at 10s
     per Bar'l And Germans in the Long Valley on Mr Logans Land
     paid for 4 Deeds.

December 1750

2   Sent Dan'l to Dr Watsons for his Bro: John Medicines.

3   Surveyed Garret Van Campens Land. 702 Acres.

4th Surveyed Charles Coxes's Land 300 Acres. Henry Sleight left 3s
     to pay for Acknowledging a Deed.

10   Bro: Luke Ryerson paid 2:12:6 Proc: towards his sisters Legecy.

11   Peter Dilts paid for a Deed and two Bonds.

12   Sent by Wm Montgomerie to Mr Beatty for to buy cloth. Gave
     Mr Montgomerie towards his Account 3£ Ordered to buy Paper.

14   Henry Cough paid for the Recording of his Deed.

15   Payed the Remainder of the fullers account to son George. Payed
     son George for Sugar and Rum.
     Sarah Moor paid six and 40 pence Light money being Balance of
     Accounts. Corn's Low jur paid for a Deed and Bond. Johannes
     Hull paid for a Deed to be Write.

17th Wm Brewer had 2 quarters of Beef W'd 162 lb.

22   Lay'd out with Const: Oriel[?] a Pedlar.

25   Bought a Barrell of Cod fish @ 30s light money.

27   Martin Beker finished making shoes the 2d time having now

made 8 pair. The first time 12 to the best of our Remembrance. Had 2 lb of Cheese. ½ half a bushel of Apples.

1750/1

January 1750/1

3   Jacob Burdsall paid for Recording of 2 Deeds, Acknowledging one.
5   Received from Garret Van Fleet for Surveying.
6   Bought a stier from Martin Baker paid him in leather.
7   Son John Paid back the six Pounds formerly borrowed. Gave son Daniel 3s to buy Rosin. Bought rosin and some med's for Eliz:
16   Martin Baker had a side of soul leather w'd 7 lb.
23   Bro: Luke Ryerson paid in part for Barley.
25   George Beatty paid part of the consideration for Land. A mistake of £3 in this money by calling the D'bb Loon 8:8s.
28   Set out on a Journey to Burlington the Assembly Seting. Received for the Acknowledgment of a Deed at Trenton.

February 1750/1

5   James Bown[e] paid me for Surveying.
14   Bought a pair of Gloves.
     Payed to the Secretary's Office for Recording of Deeds.
     Payed to Jos: Holinshead for Gould Studs and Mending of 2 pair of Buckles (besides the old Gould Stud).
20   Martin Baker had fish. Came to [amount].
23   Returned home where I arrived at night in good health. Laus Deo.
     Payed to Moor Furman Postage of a Letter 2/6 for the cost of said Papers. For my Board and Washing at 12s per week. For my horse 25 nights @ 1/ per night.

26   Cash paid for viewing the Prospect.

In my absence there was delivered to Bro: Luke Ryerson 20 B'ls of Barley.

March 1750/1

6th   Lay'd out with Sam'l Henery per my wife.

8   Jno Van Sicklen, Corns Lane and Wm Brewer paid for 3 Deeds.

9   Gave son George for Writing.

Archibald Stienson bought leather to the value of [amount].

Gave son George to pay the Schoolmaster for Instructing in Singing.

11   Sent to Wm Montgomerie at Phila to buy Triming.

12   Aaron Praul paid for a Deed.

14   Payed to Martin Tegen his wages earned last Somer in the Swamp.

19   Thomas Martin finished Georges Cellar.

20   Went up to Penungauchong with Aple trees to Plant an Orchard.

23   Returned home. In my absence Bro: Luke paid towards his sisters Legacie.

Payed also towards her Div'd of the moveables of her fathers Estate.

26   Received from Mr Jos: Turner for Surveying.

Sent to the Landing for Nails for son George. Gave to a Pious use.

Wm Kinny paid on his late Bro: David's Account.

29   John Lambert paid for his Deed.

Bought 14 quarts of Timothy Seed.

30   Wm Allen paid upon the Estate late Ab: Slover for Writings.

This Month Bro: L: Ryerson had 16 bls of Barley and ten to malt for our own use.

April 1751

1   Archibald Stenson paid for a Sow and Piggs.

3   Bought 2 quarts of Rum.

4   Received from Jacob Housel for Recording of his Deed.
        Received from Ditto for a Draft of his Land. Received from Phil:
        Kol[Kohl?] for a Bond.

8th   Set out for Burlington. Arrived there that night. Bought 2 Calf
        skins.

9   At Burlington. Paid for 2 Writs of Resurvey and Orders thereon
        for Youngblood and Colvin.

10   Arrived at home Expenses out and in.

12   John Corial paid for an old old account of his fathers took a
        Receipt.

13   William Force mended the Waggon.

15   William Logan by Ralph Smith paid for Surveying and Surveyor
        Generals fees.

16   Set out on a Journey to the Heads of Rariton absent 'til the __.

19   Then returned Home. Expenses with a bottle of Rum about
        [amount] besides help about Surveying in Ch: Carrying.
        In my absence Patrick Nixson had a Hogshead of Cider sent by
        McMoyor[?].

23   Payed a Taylor for Making a Coat.

24   Went to Trenton. Expenses.

25   Reckoned with Sarah Moor for work don and paid her.
        Bought 20 Bus'lls of lime for son George at 9d Bus'l.
        Acknowledged two Deeds, one for Richard the other for Giles
        Reed.

26   Surveyed for Henry Hofman 150 Acres forth of Mt Carmel Tract.

27   Resurveyed Phil: Colvens Plantation.

29   Paid to Adrian Hegeman 4:18:5 for Smiths work in manner
        following vizt: £1:2:6 by Jos: Hegeman 17s. By himself for a
        Deed and 2:18:5 in Cash.

May 1751

1   Robt Calcot had one Bus'l of Wheat

4   Uria or George Trimmer paid for a Deed. Sent by Jos: to the
        Landing. The last Mo sent to buy nails by Daniel 12s. Returned
        2s:7d.

6   Barnet Achenbach paid for a Deed.

7   John Hoff sent by Cath: Ryerson[100] for Deed etc. Set out for Trenton.

8   Being at Trenton met the Freeholders and Justices. Cancelled the 330[?]. Went over to Mahlon Kirkbrides.

9   Went to Burlington tended the Council of Proprietors.

10   Set out homewards where I arrived that night. Expenses.

13   Payed Mich'l Henry for support of the Ministry.

14   My wife went home intending for New York. Took with her in cash about 28:10:0. Son George also went with her to whome I gave for his use 9:0:0. Payed Ditto on Account. Payed for Bricks Boards etc. to build with. Sent by son Daniel to pay Mr Broughtons Account.
Sent the Return of the Calf Pasture to the Surveyor General.

15   James and Jere: Thatcher paid for 2 Deeds 28s and for one days Surveying 10.

17   Adam Tates Payed for Recording of a Deed. Tho: Martin finished his work at Georges House.

19   Robert Calcot had one Bus'l of Indian Corn (So far is Robert Account taken oft).

23   Martin Shipley had 2 Bus'ls of Wheat.

24   Gave son George 10s to buy Boards. Andrew Trimmer paid for a Deed.
Philip Beven had 6 sheep being ewes upon hire of one pound of [wool?] per year for three Years. Returning as many and as good at the End of the Term.
John Payed back money that I lent him this Spring NYC [New York Currency?].

25   Sam'l Kitchin paid 25s:8d being one third for the Charges of Resurveying of the land at Pohohatcong the whole being 35s and 14s for a Deed. Payed him at the said time for a Plow in said Reconing a third is 11:8. Accompted with F: Passion Charged for the Deed 14s, 2 Bonds 2s Surv: 3 Several times 15s.

---

[100] CATHERINE (COXE) RYERSON (b. 1713). Wife of Martin Ryerson. Ryerson, *The Ryerse-Ryerson Family*, 18.

Tho: Martin had 24 yds of Ozenbridge.[101]

27th John the Shoemaker had one b'l of Wheat. Godfrey Peters paid for a Bond.

Jacob Zutphen paid for 2 Acknowledgments. Sent to Philadelphia by Bro: Luke to buy Parchment.

Signed an Instrument to pay to Mr Biram[Bryam][102] 5£ per Annum to be paid quarterly or by the half year for his support in the Ministry.

30   Some time this Month debited to Wm Curry a Taylor had upon Will: Coelback's account 2 Bushells of Wheat.

June 1751

3   Set out upon a Journey to the uper part of the County.

4   Received at Sam'l Greens for the Acknowledgment of 2 Deeds.

7   Payed to Sam'l Brewer for his Assistance.

8   Payed to Jno and Wm Wright for their assistance 7/6 each. On the same day returned home. In my absence Wilhl'm Coelbach had 2 bb of Wheat.

11   Eliz: Harney paid for 6 Barrels of Cider at 10s per bar.

13   Francis Williams Earned by work at son Georges with myself 1:12:3 after a deduction for credit by George. Remained 1:4:3 from which I Deducted the making of 2 pair of Trowsers there remained to Balance which was paid the sum of 2:13:5.

18   Gave Mr Coxe for advice concerning the Bog meadow.

19   Lawrence Haff paid the Remainder of the Surveying. When at Trenton paid Benj: Yard for a spade; shoeing my horse.

21   Yerie Eike paid the Balance of Wm Hanns Account for Acknowledging and Recording.

26   John Youngblood paid for a Deed. Delivered Mr Jos: Stout an order granted to Sam'l Emley for 197 Acres to him afterwards 172 ½ acres being Surveyed forth of the same.

---

[101] Or Ozenburg, linen; originally made in Oznabrück, Hanover, Germany. Alice Morse Earle. *Costume of Colonial Times* (New York, 1894), 174.

[102] ELIAB BYRAM (1720?-1754?). He was the first pastor of the Amwell Presbyterian Church, graduated from Harvard in 1740. Rev. George S. Mott, D.D. *History of the Presbyterian Church in Flemington New Jersey, for a Century* (New York, 1894), 28-30.

29   George Beatty paid towards the Consideration for land the sum
      of 41:14:6.

July 1751

1   Bro: Luke Ryerson had one Bus'l of Buckwheat. Began the Corn
      Harvist.
8   Sent Thomas Atkinson by Son Daniel towards Bolting etc.
11th Payed Morgan Leonard for 3 ½ Reaping at 2/6 per day. Payed
      Jno McGrau for 12 days Mowing of grass at 3s per Diem 3s:8.
      Ditto Cradling of Winter Grain at 4/8 per Diem 36s and one
      Ditto at Burning of Brush 2/6.
      Son Daniel Returned the money sent Tho: Atkinson, not wanted.
12   Joh's Yory Binder worked 7 days at Harvist at 5s per Diem came
      to 35s out of which is to be deducted 7s for 1 1/4 lb of Wheat
      remains 28s for which he is to be Credited.
15   Joh's Yory Binder had almost one Bus'l of Buckwheat. Gave
      Benj: Howell for Service in the Harvist 1:02:6.
23   Son John 2 Pieces of Eight.[103]
24   Payed Peter for 6 days Mowing of Grass 12/ which with 6
      borrowed is 0:18:0.

August 1751

1   John the Shoemaker had one Bus'l of Wheat.
2   Paid John McGrau for something more than 5 ½ day mowing
      grass.
5   Payed John Van Est towards the Support of the Dutch Ministry
      and towards purchasing of more land by the Parsonage.
6   Set out upon a Journey to Burlington. Called at Trenton. Arrived
      there the night. Lodged at Mahlon Kirkbrides.
7   Arived at Burlington made a Council of Proprietors.
8   The Council of Proprietors continued their sitting until the 9th
      and Adjourned about noon. Went to Trenton that night.

---

[103] A Spanish silver coin equal to £0.23 sterling in 1766. McCusker, *Money & Exchange in Europe & America, 1600-1775*, 10.

9   Payed to the Surveyors Office for Jno Youngbloods Return. To a Writ of Resurvey 5:9. An order thereon 1/ for my own order 1/. To the Executors of Isaac DeCow for services don in his lifetime 9:3:0. To the Deputy Secretary for an abstract of a Deed.

17th   Received from Daniel Howell for Survey of Tho: Wests Plantation Paid for carting the Desk from Trenton to Christ'r Search. Paid to Daniel Howell his and his Bros Jno and Jos: their shares being their share of £9:0:8 3/4. Henry Hurlocker's Interest money having paid to D'k Zutphen and Benj: Howell 30:00:3 on the 14th of said Month their shares the whole being 7:10:7 ½. Robt Braiden left for Wm Force for axletreeing a wagon.

16   Went to John Burcham to Resurvey his and the Ruckmans Plantation.

17   Returned home. Paid Wm Force the money left by Robt Braiden.

21   Gave Mr. Byram as part of his Sallary Subscription.

22   Martin Layman Payed for half a Deed and half of some charges. Lent black Peter 40s.

12   Peter Yager Payed money for the use of the Mess'rs Coxes.

24   Payed Molly Stevenson for Quilting. Payed Cathrine Marshall for Spining.

26   Reconed with Robert Calcott and Balanced Accounts. Robts account came to [amount].
Gave leave to Azariah Read to live at the Great Meadows at Horton's Cabin. Terms not agreed on.

31   Lent to Jno the Shoemaker in cash a pieces of Eight. Payed Henry Landice the Sadler by cash sent him by D'k Hogeland. About the last week in this Month since the Reconing Robt had half a bushell of Indian Corn.

September 1751

7   Bought of the Widdow of George Hatton 143 lb of Beef. Sent by Thomas 17/6. Remains still to pay 7/4.

12   Payed Mr. Wm Montgomerie the Balance of Accounts being [amount].
Payed John McGrau for Mowing here to fore and at present.

Payed to Mr. Wm Coxe left in my hand by P'r Yager for 51
Acres.

13 Received from John Burcham for an Order 1s/. For Surveying
10s.

14 Wm Genoe paid for a Deed.

16 Payed Peter for the Widdow Hatton the remainder for the Beef.
Set out for Burlington arrived there that night.

21 Went to Mr Beattys.

23 Returned to Burlington.

27 Set out homewards. Arrived there that night. Payed to the
Surveyor Generals Office for Recording Morris Creature Return.
To said office for Recording G. Reading Return of 303 Acres. To
said office for a Certified Copy of 230 Acres its Return. To an
order for Jno Garrish.

To Dr Jon: Smith for Castile Soap, Alloes and Liquorish. To
Horse Pasture and Expenses at Bristol. To Expenses and
Ferriages upon the Road.

In my absence my wife reconed with Molly Mathews her work
coming to 2:10:8 which was paid her in part in cash and part in
goods.

30 Set out for Burlington. Lodged at Mahlon Kirkbrides. Son
Thomas[104] went with his sister Betty home. Ferriages.

October 1751

1 Arrived at Burlington where I stayed till the 5th. Then returned
home found family in good health.

---

[104] THOMAS READING (1734-1814). Married Rebecca Ellis of Gloucester, New
Jersey. He was involved with unsuccessful mining and iron works in the Muskenetcong
valley prior to the the Revolutionary war. During the war he was a Captain in New
Jersey 3rd Reg. and campaigned in the Mohawk valley in 1776. He later assisted the
Continental Army's Quartermaster in procuring supplies. Thomas was one of two
original elders of the Flemington Presbyterian Church. Leach, *Memorials,* 52; Peter O.
Wacker. *The Musconetcong Valley of New Jersey, A Historical Geography* (New Brunswick, New
Jersey: Rutgers University Press, 1968) 103-104, 115; Mark E. Lender and James Kirby
Martin, editors, *Citizen Soldier: The Revolutionary War Journal of Joseph Bloomfield,* (Newark:
New Jersey Historical Society, 1982), 60; and Mott, *History of the Presbyterian Church in
Flemington,* 43.

Payed to John Trapneel at a Club. For my Horse Pasturage Ferriage and Expenses upon the Road.

In my absence Wm Montgomery sent up two pieces of Linnen. Paid Willm Cherry the Shoemaker.

8   My wife and Daughter Eliz set out for New York. Ordered her to take money with her from Henry Lanes. Gave son Daniel for to buy some things at the Landing and Expenses and my wife.

Set out for Burlington. Returned from thence on the 12th. Expenses for Pasturage and some other Expenses.

Sent by Son John to buy Parchment (and lent him 10:6).

Gave leave to Richd Metcher to setle below the Forks of Muskonetung. Terms to be agreed upon when I go up thither (he is to have the Land on the lower side of the said River. Gave leave to Yerie Rush to suply Fletchers). Had Oct the 14th 1752.

15   Set out for Burlington Where I arrived that Day. Where I remained 'till the 23d and arrived at home the 24th. Payed for my Boarding. It being going on in the 6th week. Expenses at Fretwell Wrights and Jno Trapnells. Other costs and Charges for Washing Shaving etc. To my Horse pasturage etc. at Bristol. To Expenses upon the Road and Ferriages.

Payed Jos: Holinshead for Fashioning 2 pair of Buckles.

18th   In my absence my wife Returned from New York and had expended and layed out the sum of 25:00:0 which she Received from Henry Lane due for Wheat and Flower, and she brought from said Lane in Cash for the use of the above said 25:00:0. Son Dan'l sold at the Landing 15 bl of flax seed at 7s Bu'l.

26   William Force made a Cider press Beam. Sold 2 stiers to Sam'l Stevenson 3:13 per piece. Peter Dirdorf paid for 2 years Interest of 20£.

28   Morris Creature paid towards the Consideration of 88 Acres and Surveyor Generals fees; Remains to pay for said Land Charges £4:3.

29   Payed to Ishmael Shippy for 25 days work at Georges house

31   Henry Forst[?] paid towards a Bond Received in part of pay for a black woemans pair of shoes.

29   Payed Tho: Atkinson for Bolting, Grinding and Packing 100 bls.

John Reading's Diary

November 1751

1   In part of pay for a pair of Woemans shoes as above.
Sent a Return for 100 Acres and a Deed to John Mullat. Reconed with John Hely and rests to Balance to me 1/9 besides a kamer[?].

5   Set out for Burlington. Lodged at Trenton.

6   Arrived at Burlington. Stay'd there till the 9th. Returned home.
Received from Wm Branson at Burlington. Expenses out and in and when at Burlington.
Accompted with Jno Ladd for 1000 ft of Boards and 1000 of Shingles paid him by Bond Bill of Cash.
In my absence Henry Lane sent up the Remainder of the money for Wheat and Flower being the sum of 33:08:10 which with what my wife had, and had formerly sent up made the sum of £108:8:10 York Currency.

12   Lawrence Haffe paid for Benj: Jones's Deed.

13   Fredrick Hubert Foxe paid for a Mortgage to Her: Kline and Wm Alback.

15th   Payed the Fuller for some Kersey Cloath.

20   Reconed with Joh's Binder and rested due from him to Balance. Leather for a pair of shoes Sept the 18th 1750.

22   Payed Wm Coolbogh towards his Account.

25   Christopher Falkenberg by Christ: Sharpenstine paid the sum of and Delivered a Bond Cancelled for the sum of 20£ dated Apl 24, 1750 payable in 1751. Questioned whether he has not paid too much and whether at the Taking of the Bond I did not allow for the want of measure 24:18:0. Reconed with Wm Force and remained due to me besides the Bond and the Land there was almost one Bus'l of Buckwheat had Sep'r the 15 last not reconed for in the above Setlement besides the leather for the shoes.

December 1751

2d   Dennis and Joel Wollverton paid for 2 Deeds of Exchange.[105]

3   Signed a Reconveyance of a Deed of Trust[106] (made over from
        Coll Daniel Coxe[107] to Myself and others) to Daniel Coxe[108], Jno
        Coxe and Wm Coxe[109] to be applyed to such uses as Coll Coxe
        derected in his Will.

7   Gave to a Charitable Use.

9   Lent to Jos Yerry Binder the sum of 0:07:4.

10   Received from Jno Youngblood for 44 A. of Land a Deed and
        Surveyor Generals fees.

13   Martin Shefly had a bl ½ of Indian Corn.

10   Lent Mr Charles Beaty to be paid upon Demand. Paid John Jones
        Jur for Halling 2000 of Shingles.

17   Joseph Hegeman paid for a Deed.

20   Gave son George 25s which Henry Forst paid towards a Bond.
        Jacob Burdsall paid by son George for services don and
        Recording; his account is 17s:7d paid five pence too much.

23   To six Bushells of Wheat to Martin Shifley. Bought fish to the
        Value of [amount].

25   Son Daniel with his Bro: George went to Brunswick.

26   Payed Mich'l Henry on Annual Lottery account for Wm Force.
        Received from Derrick Murlat for a Deed and Surveying.

28   Received pay for 38 bls of Barley at 3 1/4 per Bl Light Money.
        Son Daniel gave an account of Money Expended.

30   Two hams of Venison from Jas Hanna weighed 40 ½ lb.

---

[105] When two persons mutually transfer the ownership of land for the ownership of another, neither thing nor both things being money only, the transaction is called an exchange. http://www.lectlaw.com/def/d020.htm (July 23, 2010).

[106] Transfers title to land to a "trustee", usually a trust or title company, which holds the title as security ("in escrow") for a loan. When the loan is paid off, title is transferred to the borrower by recording a release of the obligation.
http://en.wikipedia.org/wiki/Deed. (July 23, 2010).

[107] COL. DANIEL COXE (1673-1739). Son of Dr. Daniel Coxe (1640-1730). Dr. Coxe became the largest West New Jersey proprietor in 1687 with the purchase of shares from Edward Byllynge's heirs. Cox, *The Cox Family in America*, 211.

[108] DANIEL COXE (d. 1758). Son of Col. Daniel Coxe. Cox, *The Cox Family in America*, 212.

[109] WILLIAM COXE (1723-1801). Son of Col. Daniel Coxe. Cox, *The Cox Family in America*, 213.

1752

January 1752

2d   Bought Barelled Codfish ½ a Barrell at 14/6 and three shillings worth more for Son John paid to son George Light Money.

5   Payed for leather bought by Jno Smith at Trenton.

9   Agreed with Thomas Hunt for the place whereon George Hatton formerly lived being 49 Acres Consideration 100£; 50£ part thereof to be paid the beginning of May next; the Remainder is to go upon Interest from thence and to be paid the next fall. The Widdow Hatton is to live thereon till next Spring to have firewood for her use out of the drie trees. A Title to be made if said Hunt thinks fitt at the payment of the first 50£ he giving Bond to pay the [remainder] as above.
      Gave to a Charitable Use. Michl Van Boskirk paid his and his fathers Account.

14   Son Joseph went down to Phila by whome I sent to buy sundries.

15   Will: Force had six bus'ls of Wheat. Received from Tunis Kase for a Deed from Jno Hawkins.

16   Payed the fuller at Charles Huffs his Account. Payed Son George a Balance of the said fullers account paid in 1750. Payed a Balance of Ch: Huffs Account.

18   Received from Dr Cadwallader on account of the Estate of Mr Lamb.

20   Payed Christ: Search for his care and Trouble about the Boards and the Shingles.
      To Expenses at John Woods on the affair of the Lotterie.
      Received from Joh's Bossenberg the Balance of a former Account. James Martin by Thomas Martin paid for a Deed.

24th Son Daniel went in search after some young horsekind found 3 and brought them home. Charges for Keeping and posting.

25   Abraham Zutphen bought 2 __ of Hay.

29   Peter Hofman paid for a Recording of a Deed. Henry Winter paid for the Recording his Deed.

30   Sent son Daniel to Sam'l Swazey at Roxiticus for salve and looks after young mare missing to whom I gave [money].

31   Derrick Zutphen paid for his Will and a debt.

26   Force had two bu's of Indian Corn and had some time before this month 2 b'ls more at 2/6 part of pay for a slead.

February 1752

3   George Reading borrowed the sum of £2. Returned it again.

5   James Stout paid for Tanned leather.

6   Wm Force had four B'ls of Indian Corn.

7   Tho: Hunt paid towards the Consideration of the above 49 Acres of Land (Return dated the 8th).

12   Martin Shifley had four bus'ls of Wheat.

17   Wm Force had One bus'l of Rye. Payed to Philip Kase for 2 Gallons of Train Oil.
      Son Joseph Returned of the money he took to Phila.

19   Thos: Hunt paid towards the Consideration of the above land. Receipt dated the 19.

27   Martin Ryerson took the Acknowledgment of three Deeds paid him by Discompted upon Hemp and Tow and 1/6 in Cash.

29   Paid Matte Corsen by son John for a Weeks Spining. Wm Force and Myself Accompted and every affair was setled upon the Consideration for the Land and the discharge of a Debt due to Tobias Tenyke. I passed a Deed for the Land and he gave a Bond and Assurance by Deed to Reconvey the said Land back again to My Self and Son George for Security my Debt being 13£: 15s and George 20£. The said Wm Force Indebted for writings upon said Account.

March 1752

2d   William Force assisted at the shaping of a Canoe.

5   Payed to Alex: Miller for the making of a Wigg.

9   Received from Christ: Harshel, And: Redrick and Peter Yager.

10   Sent by Jos: Hollinsghead a D'b D'b Loon for Robt Smith.
     Sent by Tho: Marshall to Phila to buy some silk and Daffy's
     Elixir.[110] Payed Knitting of 3 pair of stockings at 3/. Wm Force
     this week had 1 ½ b'l of Rye.

13   Received for use of the Family of the Coxes £130. Paid it to
     them. Morris Creature paid the remainder of his Consideration
     money and Surveyors fees.

16   Tho: Marshall Returned part of the money sent to Phila.

29   George Reading paid for his Unkle Mart: for spectacles. Wm
     Britain had 5 bl and 30 wt of Hay.

23rd Coonradt Hemerigh paid for 2 Drafts of his Land. Gave son
     George to buy Triming etc.

25   Bought a Deer Skin from Tho: Scott. Jno Smith bought 2 -0- of
     Hay. Son George bought triming as above which came to L[ight]
     M[one]y [amount]. Returned the Rem't.

28   Wm Force had two b'ls of Oats. John Cock had one b'll of Oats.

30   Son Daniel left with David Connor for __ Duckworth.

April 1752

2   Lent Mr Byram [an amount]. William Force had 2 bls of Oats.
     Morris Creture paid for a Deed.

2   Payed to Wm Coxe Jos: Thatchers money. Thomas Coat paid for
     the Acknowledgment of a Deed.

4   Payed Willson Hunt for Halling of 7055 ft of Boards and 2900
     shingles.

6   Mich'l Henery jur paid for a Deed.

7   Set out for Burlington Lodged at Trenton.

8   Arrived at Burlington. Opened Meeting of the Council of
     Proprietors.

9   The Council Proceeded to Business. Payed to the Surveyor

---

[110] One of the most popular and frequently advertised patent medicines in Britain
during the 18th century. It is reputed to have been invented by clergyman Thomas
Daffy rector of Redmile, Leicester, in 1647 http://en.wikipedia.org/
wiki/Daffy%27s_Elixir (July 23, 2010).

Generals Office. Ditto to the Clerk of the Council in Jno Burchams affair. To Dr Smith for Physick.

8   To Jos: DeCow for 2 Calf Skins had the last year. Expenses in and out.

In my Absence Eliz: Harney had 5bls of Oats. Wm Force had 2 B'ls of Wheat. John Gock had 1 ½ bls of Oats.

Payed to the Currier Tho: Flood.

11   Sam'l Fleming had 5 __ of Hay. Wm Kinny paid for a Deed. Henry Deldine bought 1 ½ of Oats.

13   Jno Edmonds had 2 bu'ls of Wheat.

15   Bought a Cowshide from Mr Sheply weighed 43 lb and another of his which was at Henry Graves weight unknown. Wm Force had two B'ls of Oats

John Reading jur lay'd out for use at the Landing. Payed Molly Matthews for spining. Martin Baker made 8 pair of Shoes to be Accompted for with son G[eorge]. Paid Paul Bottner for 3 Collers at 3/2.

17th   Harm: Dildine and Court Hemerigh paid for 3 Acknowledgments.

18   John Jewell paid for an Acknowledgment of a Deed.

21   Payed Wm Coelbagh the remainder of his Account.

22   Peter Romine paid part of two years Rent.

24   Went to Trenton and Penna.

29   Payed to Adrian Hegeman for smithwork. To cash expended in Phila for sundry things. To 2 ½ of Oats at 2/2 per B'l.

May 1752

2   Received from Tho: Hunt £16:6:3 which with 2 other payments is £50. The first payment for the Land which was to be by May 1st.

Thomas West paid for a Deed. Sam'l Fleming paid for Hay. Bought a Kip Skin of John Edmonds weight 20 lbs.

4   John Berner and Christ: Koel paid for a Deed and Surveying. Mich'l Henry paid for his sons Daniels and Deeds the whole being [amount].

6   Set out on a Journey to Burlington. Arrived there that night.

7   At Burlington.

8   Returned home Expenses in and out. Received for acknowledgment of a Deed. Martin Shifly had better than ½ a b'l of Planting Corn. Wm Force had ½ a b'l of Rye and ½ a b'l of Oats.

9   Received from Jacob Runk and Job Warford for 2 Deeds.

11   Mart: Shifley had 2 Bus'ls of Wheat and 2 Bus'ls of Rye. Jacob Erwine paid for the Recording of a Deed.

12   Set out for Trenton. Arrived there that night.

13   Prepared for the Freeholders by Bundling up the Principal of the Paper Money in order to be Cancelled but for the want of one Freeholder it was not proceeded on.

14   Stayed at Trenton till near night. Set out homewards. Lodged at Nath'l Moor's.

15   Came home. Expenses out and in.
In my absence my wife paid for my Tax to Amwell Collector 2:16:10. To the Collector of the Township of Reading 0:6:0. Jos Francis had in cash 0:13:6.

18   Accompted with Benj: Howell for weaving of 256 Ells at 6s per Ell Comes to £6:8 the half whereof we are indebted to him 3:04:0.
Matthias Houselt and Jacob Housilt paid for 2 Deeds. Philip Kels paid for one Deed. Jacob Quick and Wm Wertgen paid for 2 Deeds of Exchange @7/6 and Surveying.

19   Towards night set out for Trenton lodged at Jno Rouses next day.

20   Arrived at Trenton stayed there 'till near night on the ___.

21   Then set out homewards where I arrived on the ___ in the Morning.

22   Expenses out and in being [amount].

25   Henry Hofman paid for Surveying and Bonds in his Land Affair. Sent by Eliz: Harney to buy sundries at New York.

27   Sent by Son George to Brunswick for 3 Deer Skins. Returned it again.

30   Payed Philip Chapman for Combing 25 lb of worsted.
Philip Calvin having bought from me a Proprietary right to 41 Acres of Land at the rate of 20£ per 100 Acres which with the

Charges of Resurvey etc. came to the sum of £10:02. He paid the sum of ___ Remains to pay 14:6.

June 1752

1   Payed off son Georges account which was Light Money. Sent by him to New York to buy Sundries. Sent by Ditto to buy Parchment. Received from George Biggs for a Deed.

2   Payed son George upon Mr Beker's account 16, Benj: Howells Account ___.

5th   Thomas Lambert paid for a Deed.

3   Received from the Deremus's the remainder of a Bond and 4 Years Interest. Martin Shiply had 2 bls of Wheat and 4 Bul's of Rye.

8   Went to Trenton. Expenses 2/8 by the Way; 1/8 Seal to a Writ.

9   Returned home. Paid Dr Lewis for ointment and a Viol.

4   Bought and fetched 800 ft of Cedar Boards.

11   Set out upon a Journey to Whipany and Else where. Lodged at Roxiticus that night.

12   Went across the Country to Jos: McMurterie's. Lodged there.

13   Set out from Abra: Howes homewards. Signed his Lease. Expenses whilst abroad not much; agreed for a young horse with James Wills for 15£ Light Money. Hester Coat in my absence paid 7/6 the supposed Balance between her late husband and My Self. Gave a Receipt for it.

16   Mr Byram paid back the money borrowed excepting the Remainder of his half Years Sallary.

18   Received for the family of the Coxes from Henry Cock one Year Interest for 135:9:09.

19   Payed Jos Francis the full for 1 month Service and other work. Peter Romine for two Years Rent in all paid the sum of 9:04:6 which with 4£:12s formerly paid made £13:16:6 which was short 3/6, But I gave him a Receipt for the whole.

22d   Sent son Daniel to James Will's for a Young horse which I bought for 15£ light money paid him by his own and his bro Johns Bond and Interest due thereon. Brought him home.

27   Bought three Deer Skins from Isaac Light.

30   Lent David Bartron 384 foot of Boards. Paid them back in
      August.

July 1752

7   Began Harvist in the Winter grain our own hands and Wm Force
      cuting and Jos Binder binding.

15   Finished cuting the Winter graine and geting it up. Payed Wm
      Smith for Binding 3 ½ days. Wm Force Cradled 7 Days. Jos
      Binder Raked and bound 8 days. John Mc Gray Cradled.

22   Jonathan Quimby proposes to take out of the Falls below
      Canbys[111] Ferry two Rocks. The one called Pena Gulf Rock the
      other Known by the name of Pursly's Rock. Engages to Clear out
      and take away and make a safe Passage down the said Falls
      Provided a sufficient sum of money can be raised to defray the
      Expense. The Subscribers to the said Proposalls do promise to
      pay the several Sums by them Subscribed to Jon: Quinby or his
      Order as soon as the said work is completed. The said Proposalls
      or Engagement dated the 21 of July 1752. Subscribed toward the
      said work the sum of 2:0:0 (in 1753 Payed said Quimby 4d).

23d   Bought a Cutlash from David Fetters.

24   Set out on a Journey to Mr Beattys with my wife. Returned the
      —.

27   Expenses about [amount].

28   Lent son John and took his note for (to buy a Servent) £16:0:6.
      Gave son George to buy a Servent £16:15.

30   Payed John McGray for Mowing Grass and Corn. Son John
      bought a pint of Linseed Oil (cold drawn) with a Bottle.

31   Received from Jon: Stout and Isaac Leet for 2 Acknowledgments.

---

[111] BENJAMIN CANBY (1704-48). On 29 Oct. 1745 Benjamin bought a portion of the
ferry tract, including the ferry, from John WELLS. After Benjamin's death his wife Sarah
married in 1751 David KINSEY, who continued to operate the ferry. It was sold in
1764 to John CORYELL, and the ferry became known as Coryell's Ferry (now New
Hope, Pa.).
http://freepages.genealogy.rootsweb.ancestry.com/~paxson/balderston/canby.html
(July 23, 2010).

August 1752

1   Son George Returned of the above £16:15:0 (less) 1:15:0.

4   Set out on a Journey to Burlington. Lodged at Trenton. Arrived there the next Day. Payed for Expenses out and in. Payed to the Secretarys office for Recording of Ph'p Calvins Deed. Ditto to the Surveyor Generals Office for an order for Martin Ryerson. Ditto to Jos: Holinshead for the Remainder of the stay. Payed the Interest Money to the Treasury £15:10. In my absence Daniel carried to the Landing 13 3/4 B'ls of Wheat. Sold it for 5s Light Money per Bus'l. Paid for Shingles the Remainder thereof brought back. Bought Melassas paid for it at 5 ½ Bus'ls of the above Wheat being the B[alance]. Payed for Freight of Flower to New York [entire line obliterated by water stain]. Burlington cost [amount]. Christian Harshall paid for a former account for Writing and Surveying.

8   Jno Behtelsimer and Justus Raniel paid for writing and Surveying.

10 John Job by P'r Young paid for Writings and his share of the Resurvey. Payed John Ford Sherrif of Morris for the return of a Writ Non Est.[112]

12 Jos Binder had in Cash [amount].

13 Martin Shifly brought a Calf Skin weighed 15 lb.
    When Daniel was down last at the Landing he brought me up for 32£:0:4 of flower being 17 Casks Accompted weight at 15s [New York] Money per 100 comes to 25:6:0 for 3 Casks of Cornell weight 5 lbs.

15 Joseph Kitchin and his Bro: Sam'l Henry[?] paid for Resurveying and Returning the Tract of Land at Pohohatcong. Sam'l Kitchin [blotted].

18 Received from Ch: Hoff and Abraham Bonnil [Bonnell] for Surveying

20 Wm Force Borrowed __ paid it in Jan'y 1753. Philip Beven brought home the 6 sheep which he took to hire but no wool nor money for hire. Has since paid it in Indian Corn.

---

[112] The returning of a sheriff's writ when the person to be arrested or served with it cannot be found in the sheriff's jurisdiction. *Dictionary.com Unabridged.* http://dictionary.reference.com/ browse/non est (March 13, 2010).

24   To Cash Expended for 440 feet of Oak boards.

25   To cash Received for the Acknowledgments of two Deeds. To cash lay'd out for lime.

28   To cash paid to a Cooper for 2 cedar pails and a Well Bucket. To cash paid M: Ryerson for taking two acknowledgments and Deeds.

September 1752

Day of the month Altered. N[ew] stile introduced.

This month from the Second Day was left out 11 days to Introduce the N[ew] Stile.

15NS   Set out for Trenton.

17th   Returned home Expenses out and in about [amount].

18   Isaac Laning paid for a Deed; for a Bond. Payed Benj: Stout for 3 Days work.

23   Thomas Atkinson paid for 250 lbs of Wheat.

22   Benj: Stout worked at the door frames.

23   Payed Thos: Atkinson for grinding etc. 100 bls of wheat. Payed said Atkinson for 20 flower casks. The said Atkinson paid for 2 lb of Wool. Payed for 200 of Oysters to Abm Delamater.

25   Gave to a Charitable Use.

27   Bought 250 Bricks more which with 500 more on the 19th.

30   Nich's Weykoff and Jacob Vanderbilt paid for 3 Acknowledgments. Payed the Tax for the Land in Reading 0:2:0. Martin Shifly brought home a German Servant from Phila first cost 12:14:8. Debt due to the ship £1:10 Money in hand 7/6 Expenses 5/4 being 20s more than what I sent gave him credit upon his bill.

This Month Martin Shiffiy had soal Leather.

October 1752

2d   Set out on a Journey to Muskonetcong. Arrived there that night.

7   Returned Home Received for Service in Surveying to Christ: Falkenbergen (besides13:2 credit in a former account). Tho:

Martin Debtor to one days work.

In my absence my wife Received from Bern's Van Brike for 200£ of Wheat heretofore sold at 5s Light Money per Bushel.

Gershom Lee had ___ of Lime at 9d per Bus'l. My wife paid Joh's Francis the sum of 1:2:0.

10   Payed Matte Corsen for Spining etc. Put by for Sarah Moor for spinning Worsted.

Gave to a Charitable Use

[Wm] Force had two Bus'ls of Wheat. Received from Peter Dirdorf for Interest.

13   Sent to the Landing by son John to buy Melossus.

14   Paid to Jos Francis in Cash.

18   Paid to son George for Sundries bought at Brunswick.

21   Received from Sam'l Kitchin the Balance of his account.

Received from Phil: Calvin the Balance of his account for Surveying and Surveyor Generals fees.

Payed John Cock for the waggon and axletreeing; one per sides son George's account [rest of page torn].

23   Payed Joh's Francis the Remainder for his 2 Months Service and 2 days.

24   Payed to the Collector for the Provincial Tax 0:18:11. Paid to Ditto for the Poor Tax 0:13:3. Payed for Oysters __ 300.

23   Received from And's Redricks for writing his Will.

November 1752

3d   Payed John Smith for 2 Month service at £4:5 the sum of [amount] which with 18s kept in my hands to pay the Doctor makes 4:05:0. Bought from Edw'd Harrington 76 lb of Beef at 2 ½ per lb.

4   Peter Woolever paid for the hire of 6 sheep for one year John Wood paid for a Deed and Balance of an Account.

7   Payed to Mary Chapman for weaving 45 yds of Worsted.

8   Set out near noon on a journey to Burlington. Lodged at Trenton that night.

9   Went over to M and J Kirkbrides had two Deeds signed arrived at Burlington after one of the Clock Sat in the Council of Prop's.

10   Sat in Council.

11   In the Afternoon returned homeward. Lodged at Trenton.

12   Rainy weather. Came home about 4 of the Clock.
     Paid for a copy of Jno Mullens Will and Inventory. Expenses at Bristol. Trenton and by the way. Bought 1 pint of sweet oil and [B]ottle 3s, a pair of stockins, 2 sheepskins 10 oz of Nutmegs. Received by my wife in my absence for the hire of 6 sheep, 9s for Acknowledging of Jos: Johnson's Deed.

14   Joh's Binder reconed with me and I fell in his debt upon a Balance for sundrys the sum of £1:6:4 ½ which was given credit for on the back of his Bond.

15   Set out on a Journey to the heads of Rariton. Arrived there.

16   Run severall lines of my Land there.
     Went on to Muskonetcong 18th. Returned home. In my absence Eliz: Harney returned from New York and Expended on our account the sum of [amount].

18   [obliterated] from Wm Housell.

20   Samuel Kitchin for his brother paid in full for surveying at Pohohatcong. Bought at Union Furnace Tallow and soaps.

22d Bought Brass Buttons ½ a gross of small ones at ½ per doz: and one Doz. of Large ones at 1/8 per Doz.

23   Then accompted with Martin Beker on all accounts and herein am indebted the sum of suposing Cesars pay taken home not Accompted for and also 1s for the blacking the side of Uper Leather.

24   Expended with Const'n O Neil for Linnens and Worsted stockins.

25   Set out with Mr John Coxe in a Journey to his land and Moravians. Lodged at Pat'k Nixsons.
     Dined at Easton in the Forks and arrived at Bethlehem near night.

27   Spent the fore part of the Day at Bethlehem. Lodged at Easton.

28   Spent the fore part of the day in viewing of Mr Coxes Land as to its situation on the River. Lodged at Patk Nixsons.

29   Arrived at home in the Evening Expenses paid by Mr Coxe

In my absence was paid and Answered by son George to the Currier who used 5 gall of oil which cost 5s per gall and bought lamp blk.

Bought one Hide from Jacb Woolever. One Ditto from Ja'b Gray. Arch'd Stienson paid for Taning and Currying a Kip Skin.

1753

January 1753

1	To Jacob Gray for a Yearling Skin	0:03:1
6	To Ditto for a Cow Hide	0:10:5
	Lent Mr Beatty by his Negro John	0:05:0
	Jos Binder had a Quarter of Beef Wt 100 lb at 6d per lb	
		0:16:8
7	Son Richd brought home a horse called Punch from the Horners	
	Cost	1:05:0
	Bought Cowhide from Thomas Marshall Wt 60 lb	0:12:6
8	Paid towards the Supt of the Ministry ½ year for 4 seats in	
	Gally	5/60:11:0
11	Paid for a Cowhide to And Hegeman	0:08:6
	to the Everitts to Survey Stayed there 'till the _____	
18	Received from Dk Hogeland a Balanceupon all accounts0:05:9	

_____ from Jo Opdyke for 2 Deeds One for himself1:10:0

Went to Cornell Stevenson's in Amwell to Re[survey] and continued There the 19. 20. and 21.

Received at that time for services don and to be don   1:02:6

Received from Jno Boyce for Service and a Writ of Resurvey 0:13:3.

Seeking _____ suring the lines of Benjs Stouts land in the ___ 0:15:0

Payed _____ Wood light money   1:01:1

Went to Survey _____ Island_____ paid him the
Balance being   0:05:0
Son John brought home the Landing 500 Shingles a ____ pr 100
1:17:0

30   Payed _____ for a Deer Skin   1:00:0
      Payed Son George in full of Accounts being_:19:4
      Cash Received from Peter _____ from _____ and a Balance of
      3/10 Sent By him to Phila being 16/6 _____ paid [an
      amount].

February 1753

1st   Received from John Cowan for the Writing of a Deed   0:09:0
2   Signed a Return _____ 66 acres for George
3   Son Jos: Returned back 12s.   0:12:0
6   Set out upon a Journey to Burlington. Lodged at Bristol
7   Went over to Burlington. Stayed there 'till the 10.
9   Lodged at Trenton.
10   Came home. Expenses out and in about 20s.
      Payed to the Secretarys office for Recording a Deed for Paul
      Buyer. I had to upon of his rent which Buyer brought along with
      for the Said Buyer to pay the next May for the per Year if no
      more
      _____ to Come one acre of Swamp to be cleared yearly and
      be put in good fence.
13   Benj: Johnson paid for his and his brothers Deed and Surveying
      1:06:0
      Received for 2 Acknowledgments of Deeds.   0:06:0
      Spent on Account of the Lottery at John Woods.   0:01:9
17th Received from Morris Kreture for a Deed.   0:10:0
      Received from Corns Low jur for the Acknowledge of a Deed.
      0:03:0
20   Payed for 6 Ga of melasses at 3s per Gall at the Landing.
      0:18:0.
      Bought a Barrel of Codfish Cost at Brunswick __ light money.
      1:08:0

Martin Beker had 4_3/4 of' uper Leather at 20d per lb and 1s
blacking.   0:8:0
Ditto had 5 lb of Soal ditto at 1s per lb.   0:5:0
Lawrence Mare Sometime ago had a Calf Skin.

27   Wm Force had 2 Bls of Wheat.
Tenyke paid for Surveying and other work done in 1749. Charged
2:3:9 paid.   2:02

March 1753

1   Tho: and Benj: Curtis paid for a Deed of Bargain and Sale and
Defeasance   0:12:0
Aaron Schyock Payed for the Acknowledgment
of a Deed   0:3:0
Philip Kline paid for a Deed.   0:12:0

7   Son Joseph Returned from Middletown Expences.   1:03:3
8th   Cristian Coil paid for a Deed.   0:15:0
9th   Martin Shifly had two Bushls of Wheat.
19   Christian Harshall paid the Balance of his Account for Surveying
and Writing.   1:07:6
Wm Force had 1 Buslls ½ of Wheat.
24   Gave Wm Rightinghousens Daughter Hannah 15s.   0:15:0
27th   _____ Wood had in Cash.   0:2:3
31   Bought 6 lb of Flax of Pompe at 6d per lb.   0:03:0
Reconed with Adrian Hegeman the Smith and paid him
Lt Money.   1:18:11
Paul Flagg paid me for a Deed wrote in 1745.   0:15:0
Ditto paid for Surveying of 2 Acres.   0:03:4
Bought for Said Money 1 lb of Gun Powder.   0:03:4

April 1753

3d   Set out in the afternoon on a Journey to Whipany lodged at Ab:
Van Horns.
4   Went to Coll Fords Returned back as far as _____.
5   Bought a _____ bay Horse from _____ at Roxbury. Lodged at

P[ete]r Woolevers.

6 Surveyed 100 Acres for Saml Bruglar in Greenwitch. Went to Jos: McMurteries.

Bought a bald face Bay horse from James Hannah 1 Cost 20£ lodged at Corns Anderson's.

7th Returned home. Expences about 4s. Payed to Ob: Seward for the horse 21:00.

8 After meeting Set out for Burlington. Lodged at Mahlon Kirkbrides.

9 Payed to Mahlon Kirkbride for 200 acres of Land. Arrived at Burlington   17:00:00

10 Went from Burlington to Trenton.

11 Arrived at home Expenses at Burlington 5s (Ferrys 1/9 at Bristol).

/2 for Sundry Fees to the Clerk of the Council 10:8 to the Surveyors Office.

Expences at Trenton 4/10. At Mr Ringoes 2s.

Paid for To Moor Furman for the Gazett.

14 Agreed with Wm Templar for diging of a Celar 26 by 22.

Gershom Lee paid for the Acknowledgment of a Deed.

19th Gave John Allison in part for Services don   0:07:0

23 Went up on a Journey with the Coxes to _____etc   0:02:

25 George Schamp paid for writing of his Will.   0:15

26 Philip Kline paid for Surveying 56 ½.   0:10

Payed a third part of my Subscriptions and my Sons towards buying a parsonage   5:03:4

Wm Davison paid for a Deed etc.   1:01:6

28 Payed Molly Matthews for Spining.   2:03:9

Payed Byram towards his Sallary.   1:10:0

30 Payed Wm Templar in part for the diging of the Celar. 1:00

May 1753

2d Went to Burlington Returned on the _____.

4 Expences out and in 12s. Payed for 2 Deeds in the Secys Office 18s.   1:12:0

Peter _____ for Recording came to 9:8 he paid me 15s being
5s.4d over which I am to keep and Account for when his Deeds
are Acknowledged and Recorded   0:15: 00

7   Joel Woollverton paid for a Deed.   0:10:00
       Aaron Davis by his father Coenradt Davie paid the Sum of 3:00:7
       being ____ Short of his Account.
       Gave my wife for to buy goods and necessaries at Brunswick 8: N
       [New York money]

9th   Set out upon a Journey to Greenwitch. Lodged at Godfry
       Melock's this day and the 10th. Run round the 1ines of his and
       his brother Johns Plantation.

10   _____ Tho: Martins Plant: upon Muskonetcong.

11   Went to Jos Warfords. Purched 181 Acres of unlocated land @ 7
       lbs per 100.   12:13:1
       Received from Jos McMurtery, Rob Mc Murtery and their
       Charges for Writings being 12.6 per piece.
       Robt Houe having paid before and Tho: to Receive from
       _____ Ryerson his Share _____ with.

12th   Run a back

17   Payed_____for Joseph other ___Expence Journeys about
       0:5:0

19th   Paid wm Templar more Cash towards the Celar.   1:0:0

21   Received from _____ Deed   0:9:0

June 1753

1   Set off from Burlington homewards. Lodged at Trenton.

2   Arived at home about 11 of the Clock.
       Expences while abroad besides Boarding.   0:08:8
       In my absence Peter Romine paid his yearly Rent being 7:0:0
       And as he Supposed paid 3/6 what was behind in the last Year.
       But having Accd two Pistoles at 28s Each it wanted 2s
       Payed Sarah Moor 10s l.my[light money] the remainder 0:10:0
       John Burcham in my absence paid for Surveying   0:12:6

4th   Set out for Burlington. Arrived there between 1 and 2 of the
       Clock where Stayed till the 8th day.

	Then came to Trenton	0:19:5
9th	Came home about noon For Sunday Expences.	
	to my board and lodging	1:00:00
	In my absence was paid to__McLane the Taylor	4:10:0
11	Tunis Trimmer paid for a Deed and Recording	1:06:8
	David Connor paid in Cash for Some Occasion	
	Robert Calcot had 2 Busls of Wheat	
12	Philip Wise paid for the writing of one Deed and	1:17:6
18	Payed a Tinker of Work don	0:6:10
	Son Daniel Came home from John Fords.	
20	Payed Isaac Neams for Grubing 12 acres of Land	3:12:0
	Joseph Thatcher paid for a Deed Surveying and	1:12:0

Daniel Returned from the Landing who had taken down 20 bls of wheat.

	Sold the Same at 5/3 per Busl. Came to	5:05:0
	Brought up 500 of Shingles at 3/18 pr 100. Came to	1:09:0
	Bought a Scyth at 6/ and dressing an _____	0:8:4
21	Returned in Cash	2:17:8
	Went up into the Country on Account of a Writing.	
	Expences on the Journey	0:4:2
	For Cedar Boards 1000 feet	3:10

July through December 1753

[Unavailable]

1754

January 1754

3rd To [illegible]

4 James Woods the fuller brought home _____ To 37s said Light money Payed him.

22   Daniel returned a piece of 8 from the money he went 7: being
      about 2:3s _____.
26   Jeremus Horn paid for surveying in 1748.
      John Opdyke paid for a _____ from Jno Jewell.
      Bought of Negro Tab 2 lbs of flax.
29   Bought a Gal: of Rum at Sam L_____.
30   Gave son Joseph _____ went away about ____.
      Sent by Bro: Ryerson to pay into the Surveyor General Office

February 1754

2   Negro Tab bought 36 lb of Flax to have 6 per lb.
      I paid for a Title Bond.
      Received by son George [an amount].
4th   Reconed with son George he fell in my debt to Jan'y the 4 ____.
      Wm Force per account with son George paid in part for a Steir.
      Payed to son George for Jno Edmonds by a store Hog[?].
6   Wm Stevenson of New York g_____ (by his son Wm). Payed a bill
      I sent him of charges for surveying some unlocated and Surveyor
      Generals fees.
      Son George _____ Account Payed the £6:0 formerly
      borrowed.
8   Yarus Barracalow Returned 10 sheep of 12 which he had taken to
      hire having had them 5 years. One Year Rent paid 4 years due.
      Remainder of the 19:6 and for 2 sheep of 6/ each is _____.
7   Will: Force had uper'd sole leather came to _____.
15   Bought of Saml Fleming 300 foot (wanting 5) of Cedar Boards.
17   Had from Martin Shifly a quarter of Veal weighed 10 ½ lb.
18   Son George had a side of Soal leather weighed 9 lb
      Received from Pr: Praul for a Deed.
20   Payed Jacob Coursen for ½ Dozen of chairs by 3 Bus'ls of
      Wheat.
      Rob't Calcot had his shoes soaled.
21   John Edmonds worked 3 ½ days at the Barn.
      Wm Force worked 4 ½ days at Ditto.
      Dittto had Harness leather at _____ Returned _____.

John Edmonds had Leather came to ____

26   Garret Van Campen paid for surveying his Deed and other services.

27   Payed for 2 oz of Salve 2/6 left unpaid.

Payed to a Turner for mending 2 spining wheels.

28   John Anderson paid for a Deed and Surveying.

Patrick Travers Payed for _____.

March 1754

1   John Edmonds bought a black Mare. He is to give me £5:0 in the Fall. _____ Accounts I fell £0:17:2 ½ in his debt which ___ pay for said mare.

4   Reconed with B Jewell for weaving and was ___.

5   Payed Benj: Howell _____.

Gave to a Charitable use.

6   Son Daniel bought 4 Spring and B_____.

Ichabod Leigh by Henry Peter paid for a D[eed].

8   Son George had 13 pairs of mens shoes @ 7/4.

Son Daniel expenses when abroad being about _____.

Shoemaker the last time earned _____ had a pair of shoes made.

Robert Calcott had a pair of shoes soaled.

13   Left with Son Joseph for his Carpenters the sum of 22:04:8.

12   Paid Tho: Atkinson for a quarter of Sugar light [money].

11   Will Force axeltreed the hinder Wheels of the wagon.

18   Will Force had 2 b'lls of Wheat.

20   Will Force had 1 tt of hay at _____.

Payed to Morris Woolverston for haling of Plank etc.

Payed to Peter Coons wife [an amount].

27   John Dilts spoke for a Deed and paid for it. The week before Martin Shifly had 2 bls of wheat.

Paulus Botner made 6 towe collars @ 2 per piece.

Sold him 3 tt of Hay at 2/6.

April 1754

5th   Philip Bevin finished Pruning the trees for the doing of which he had earned 47s which Sum together with 2/8 of Mart: Ryerson money made the sum of 2:9:0.
      Payed him the sum of _____.
7   Martin Shifly brought a quarter of Veal wt 10 lb.
8   Set out for Burlington from Mah Kirkbrides. Arrived there about 11.
9   Stay'd there till the 10th. Arrived at home on the 11th.
10   Out and in 15/1 and for Sundries bought at Burlington.
11   being cash.
8   Martin Shifly has 2 bus'lls of wheat.
      Son Daniel lay'd out for latches and a lock.
      Detained in his hands supposed to be for Expenses on the Journey.
15   Payed Hugh Hunter 45s (left unpaid 5 / to give him a fortnight notice).
18   Cornelius Low Payed the Remainder of the money _____ upon the due upon the Land and Returning.
19   Isaiah Quinby paid towards a Deed and charges of Surveying and Returning.
      Robert Calcot had two bls of Wheat.
      Robert Calcot had helped on Grubing 20 days @ 2/6 per day.
22   Paid Nanny Woods in cash for _____ earned in Spinning.
      Set out on a journey to Pompten.
      Absent from home to the _____.
26   Expenses 5s beside 7/6 given towards the obtaining of the Bill in Chancery.
29   Then accompted with Bro: Luke Ryerson and Remains due from him to Balance besides his Sisters Legacie the sum of Proc money _____.
      Peter Folper paid for a Deed.
      Paid for 30 Busls of Lime for Daniel.
30   Jno Durland paid for a Deed.
      Payed towards the expenses of Mr Byram's funeral etc.
      John Edmonds had leather for Bell Collars.

John Reading's Diary

May 1754

1 Set out on a Journey to the Mine above the mountain at
   Pahuckqualong.[113] Arrived there about 3 in the afternoon on
2 the 2d day where we went and viewed the mine and Mount. On
   the 3rd day settled the affairs of the Mine.
   On the 4th day and some of the Company. Set off homewards.
   Cost to this time of £7:00:6 which I Payed and 1/6 over.
6 Arrived at home. Expenses on the journey about _____.
   In my absence Mart: Shifly paid me for Wheat.
   M: Shifly had 3 bls of Wheat.
   I _____ Sallary to the late Mr Bryon.
9 Sent _____ to pay for Daniels Hatt.
   Paid for 2 salt at 3 per __.
   Received from _____b Swallow for Surveying _____ for
   fulling cloaths (12/8 behind).
   Rec_____Bas____ Dl of Sund[ries]. Accompted with Israel
   Shippen for Building Daniels house who Is _____ the _____
   of which I paid 13:06:0 W ____6:14__ formerly paid makes
   ____.

   Wm Force had leather for a Bell Collar of Hopples.
13 Wm Force had two bls of wheat on Son George Account.
   Received Mart: Ryerson from the Treasurer on the Gov'rs
14 w___.
   Received from ___tys R____ sil for himself and on behalf of Jas
   Behtelheimer. On Bonds the sum of 49:5.
15 Payed Tho Atkinson for sundries then and before bought.
   Ands Gardenier paid for a Paper Deed and one
   Acknowledgment.
17th Tobias Tenyke paid as Executor to _____.
20 Paid to Wm: Peirson part for in smiths _____.
   To Martin Shifley 3 bls of wheat.

---

[113] The mine referred to here is undoubtly the Pahaquarry Copper Mines originally
believed to be excavated by the Dutch. Herbert C. Kraft provides a compelling narrative
that dispels that myth and describes John Reading's involvement with mine in The
Dutch, the Indians, and the Quest for Copper: Pahaquarry and the Old Mine Road (South Orange,
New Jersey: Seton Hall University Museum, 1996), 97-108.

22nd To Cash to buy Nails etc at the Landing.

23rd Johs Bossenberg paid for a Deed.

Bought some melassas at Tho Atkinson's on the [Kline] affair.

Robt Calcot worked last time 3 ½ days.

In the time of Roberts last working he had 2 per of soals for his and his wives shoes.

To a piece of 8 to Coenradt Tarr when he went up.

25 Reconed with Tho Martin for Mason's work at the House due to him for work done at Georges House 4:/4s, for Dls House per Agreement and further for 33 days work at 4s per day 6:12 in all. 34:16:0.

To Ballance which I have credited aganist him for Loan Office money upon Hy Stewarts account 2:14:9 for _____ surveying. Suveyor Generals Office and My own Trouble.

I am to pay son George (and Interest till paid) the sum of Which when paid in full of all accounts _____.

Daniel upon his Journey into the Country with the Miner's _____ Mr ____'s furnace.

For a streak upon the Wagen Wheel.

Expenses upon the journey _____.

27 Payed negro Tab for flax had in the Winter.

Payed Woods for said Tab.

Payed son George in part of the above sum for Tho: Martin.

Received from Yacus Barracaloss by one of his sons the Remainder of the money for sheep.

Payed Thomas Atkinson for 2 Galls of Melasses.

28 To Robt Calcot 2 bls of wheat.

29 Fred Jno: Meleck paid for surveying.

Abm Gray paid for a Deed.

30 Ab: Howe paid towards a Years Rent.

31 To expenses in a Journey to Mr Kirkbrides in Pensylv.

To Parchement bought 13 skins @ ___.

To the Publick Paper paid for to Mr Reeds.

June 1754

John Reading's Diary

1 Gave son Danl in cash to buy Cloaths 20 pieces of 8.
   Money for Expenses on a Journey to Freehold.
   Payed Stephen Chandler for Weaving and Shearing Sheep Lt money.
   Gave Robt Gould to Retain Mr Ogden[114] a Solicitor in the Bill of Chancery.
2 Gave to a Charitable Use.
3 Received for 2 acknowledgments from Jers: Lambert and Johs: Housil
4 Payed Philip Beven by Cash and Wool.
   Received from Tunis Case for Surveying and a Deed.
   Danl expended for latches for his House and returned the above.
6 Set out on a Journey for son Joseph to Mr Beatty's.
   Arrived there on the 3d day.
7 Remained there to the day _____.
8 Returned home. Expense for ferriages and etc.
   Payed Jos: Howell for the Laying of an Axe.
12 Went to Paquanoch River to Bro G: Ryersons in order to find out the Bounds of the Newarkers Exdr[?]:
13 I employed Mr. Jons Sarjeant for that purpose. Were almost 2 days about it that is in _____.
14 In Reruning the courses of the Mount.
15 I set off homewards. Gave Mr. Gould 15/3 for entering my appearance in the Chancery suit and the Rest for other Services.
   Bought a Belr[?] 1/8. Expenses 3/ in all.
   Bought a Bay horse from Bro: Luke Ryerson.
   Tab's paid for by Cash due to me per account in April.
17 In my absence my wife lent Robt Calcot 5/9 worked at the dung[?] 2 days.
   Bought 1/4 of -0- of Rice at 5/6 Light Money.
18 Cornelius Weycoff Jun Payed the supposed Balance of _____.
   Sent to son Jos: to pay Wm Rightinghousen and _____.
   Sent to New York by Son George t[w]o pieces of 8.

---

[114] Probably ROBERT OGDEN (1716-1787). Governor Belcher appointed him a Surrogate Jan. 27, 1753 and Aug. 14th of the same year, "one of our Clerks in Chancery." William Ogden Wheeler, compiler, *The Ogden family in America, Elizabethtown branch, and their English ancestry* (Philadelphia, Pennsylvania: Lippincott, 1907), 78-84.

20   Lent Wm Force upon son George his allowing thereof a ___.
21   Martin Shifly had 2 bls of Wheat.
22   Saml Holcomb[115] paid for a Deed.
21   Robt Calcot had 2 bls of wheat.
26   Bought from Saml Johnson 175 net of iron ___.
27   Hunter had 6 ½ lb of Uper leather.
29th   A man for Thatching of the Barrack[116] charges 9s light money.

July 1754

1   Bought one bus of Buckwheat from Tunis Cole.
2   Mart: Shifly had 3 Busls of Wheat. Payed in Cash.
3   Payed Mrs Byram for Kniting 2 pairs of Linnen Stockins.
6   Received from Obediah Pi_____ for Acknowledging a Deed.
     Robt Calcot worked this week 2 ½ days.
8   Lay'd out with two Indians for Trap and Baskets.
10   Payed John Vang for 12 ½ days Mowing of Grass @ 3s per day.
     Robt Calcot had wheat 1 ½ busl.
     Robt Calcot worked this week 3 days working from breakfast
     time.
22d   Finished Wheat Harvist. Wm Force Cradled 4 days @ 5s.
     Stephen Chandler Cradled Wheat etc.
     Hugh Hunter Raked and bound wheat 5 ½ days.
     Jos Binder Raked and Bound wheat.
     Nanny Wood Raked and Bound wheat.
23d   Bought Linseed oil 2 1/4 galls.
24   Bought an Axe and Matlock for son Daniel.
25th   Bought 2 oz of Indigo.
26   Payed Stephen Chandler for 12 days mowing of grass.

August 1754

---

[115] SAMUEL HOLCOMBE (1711-69). Son of John Holcomb Jr.
http://freepages.genealogy.rootsweb.ancestry.com/~jonkh/RegJohnHolcombe.htm
(July 23, 2010).
[116] A structure used to store hay. It consisted of four posts and movable roof. Wacker,
The Musconetcong Valley of New Jersey, 99.

John Reading's Diary

1   Dr Van Wagener had in cash a piece of 8 in Light Money.
2   Paid to John Cockin part for a Wagon.
4   Hugh Hunter bound and Raked _____ in the _____.
     Robt Calcot worked this week ___ day and from Breakfast Time
     Thursday.
     Matthw Breimer the Like Time.
10   Payed John Francis for 2 days cuting of grass.
     Received from Hendrick Snider for a Deed.
12   Daniel came home _____ Expenses - buying some things at the
     Landing.
     Received from Saml Smith[117] for attending the Council 1753.
16   Payed Nanny Woods for House work, Spining etc.
     Payed Hugh Hunter the Balance of our accounts by Leather and
     a Beaver Hat and cash in 6:11 (his Harvest and Shoemaking
     Account came to £3:15:9).
     In which at time he had made 22 pairs of new shoes out of which
     son George had 9 pair; 9 pair for the family. Nanny Calcut one
     pair and mending of one pair for her; Matte Caursen one pair.
     Molly Matthews one pair and John Vang one pair (which is
     Accompted for).
     To the mending of Stephen Chandlers shoes.
21   Payed son George £10:19: being the Remainder and in full of
     Tho Martin's Bond and three Pounds before paid towards it so
     that ther remains due to _____ Mart: on all accounts between us
     the sum specified in May the 25th being 11:8:9.
22   Matte: Coursen paid for a pair of shoes.
     Payed to Tho: Ridge Joseph's Carpenter (vizt left it with Jos: for
     him).
     Bought 4 lb of shott at 6d per lb.
     Payed to the Thatcher for the Barrack.
27   Payed to Benjamin Howell the Balance of our account (and 3d
     over) being ___.

---

[117] SAMUEL SMITH (1721-1776). Son of Richard, a historian and Quaker. Recomended by Gov. Belcher for the council but rejected by the Lords of Trade. Treasurer of the Western Division of New Jersey Assembly from 1751-75. Whitehead, *Colonial History of New Jersey*, Vol. VIII, 416.

30th Set out on a Journey to Walpack arrived there on the 31 about 11 o Clock.

September 1754

1-4 At Walpack. Spent in viewing the Mines. Examining into the _____ and Payed off the miners and other Expenses therein. A 6th part whereof the House besides ___ Dr Maxwells[118] share amounted to the sum of ____ which I paid besides advanceing more than my share the sum of £17.0.3.

5 Set out homewards in Company with Mr Nevil[119], Mr Kearney[120] and Mr Ryererson.

6 where I arrived the next day in Safety. Expenses out and in _____.

9 Payed to John Cock for the wagon etc.
In my absence at Walpack Hugh Hunter had leather to the value of _____.

17th Payed [hole in page]rt his aprentice for what was _____ some of Dls House.
Payed Jacob Lare the Remainder and in full for Mason work don for son Ab:
Payed William Force for 33 lb of Beef

21 Send down to Phila by son Dl to buy Servents and ____ £39:18:6.

27th Son Dl returned from Phila. Bought two Servents. The Boy for my self the man for son Dl.

---

[118] ANTHONY MAXWELL (b. 1711?). Trained Doctor who lived in Sussex Co. Partner with Martin Ryerson and John Reading in the Pahaquarry mine venture. Kraft, *The Dutch, the Indians, and the Quest for Copper:*, 98.

[119] SAMUEL NEVILL (d. 1764). He inherited large tracts of land in New Jersey from his sister, the second wife of Peter Sonman's, one of the Proprietors, and came to New Jersey in May, 1736, and settled at Perth Amboy. He was a judge of the Court of Common Pleas, Mayor of Perth Amboy, second judge of the Supreme Court of the Province, beginning with the March term, 1749, and filled several other important offices. Edward Quinton Keasbey, A.M. LL.B, *The Courts and Lawyers of New Jersey 1661-1912* (New York, 1912) 301-303.

[120] PHILIP KEARNEY (d. 1775). Lawyer, member of the Legislature of New Jersey, 1746-47. Resided in Perth Amboy. *Proceedings New Jersey Historical Society* 3rd ser. (1906-07) Vol. V No. 1 (Paterson, New Jersey: 1908) 4-8.

John Reading's Diary

October 1754

2d Payed Thomas Atkinson the full of his Shop Account per receipt.

4 Valentine Shultus Payed for two year Hire of six sheep.

Payed for some Shirt Buttons to a Pedlar.

7 Mr Beatty paid for two Steirs sold about 2 years ago to him.

Payed some money indebted to Ditto for Preaching (per Account for the steirs).

John Wood bought 6 lb of Soal Leather 4 3/4 lb of upper Ditto.

14 Payed Mr Beatty the money left by G: Beatty being 25:17:6.

Payed for half-years Supply's of the ministry by Preaching.

Set out on a Journey to the Mines. Expenses out and in.

20 Returned Home.

21 Nanny Calcot paid for a pair of Shoes.

23 Payed for 3 lbs of salt by son Jon.

Received from Hend: Lane the Balance of our Account for flower and Wheat 100 lbs.

Cash Received before by son Dl for 8 bl Con:emd[?] flower and Kernel 10 lbs.

And at another time for 33 bls of fine flower.

Deducted Georges for __ measuring and weighing.

Deducted the cost for Grinding, Bolting, Packing and Casks.

26 Payed Tho. Atkinson for Grinding 250 bl of Wheat, Casks, Bolting and Packing.

29 Payed the Tax for support of government and the Sinking Fund.

31 Payed by John Casper Lup for a Deed.

Payed by Anthony Waldrof for a Deed.

Sometime before the 20th of this month gave son Joseph for Lime bought of William Rightinghousen 22s and his Tax about 8 __ in all about 1:15:0.

November 1754

1 Payed to John Cock the remainder for Jos's Wagon and mending of the other.

Ab: Howe paid towards the Years Rent.

2 Payed Jno Francis for 8 days mowing at 2/9 per day.

Payed to the German Doctor for help in Daniel's sickness.

4   Robt Calcot had one bl and ½ bll of wheat.

5   Set out for Burlington. There till the 9th day. Expenses out and in.

In my absence I Payed for a Beaver Hat to Jno Yard £ __.

For some medicines bought at Burlington.

Robt Calcot had 2 buls of wheat to Sow.

Reconed with Stephen Chandler for weaving and Harvist work which paid for a horse @ £3:10 and £1:11 ½ over which is Daniels.

16   Payed Paul Flag for Sundry's had.

30   Reconed with Johs Binder and paid the Balance due to him.

Payed Mr William Montgomerie for a pair of Linnen Cloath and for the Dying of some blew Cloath.

Richd returned from Phila. Payed Mr Montgomerie for Linnen and for dying 10 yds of Worsted and a Balance for some parchment.

Payed for Sundries bought at Phila by son Richd.

Robt Calcot worked a[t] Stubing this week 4 days.

December 1754

2   Robt Calcot had two Busls of Wheat

3   Tho Martin having worked about 2 days in Jobs charged 8s. Payed him in 2 busls of Wheat @ 5s per bus. Payed me 2s in cash.

4   Cohoon paid his act being 2:12 and other Charges in deer leather. Bought some fish.

James Ashton paid for Surveying etc.

21   Reconed with Herm: Simonse. Paid him the Balance (besides son Georges Account which is £1:11:4).

Reconed with Robt Calcut and remained from him to Balance

____.

25   Bought a Gall of Rum.

27   Received from Jos. Golden 55d for Writing and other Services on a Commission granted out of the High Court of Chancery.

30   Bought fish to the Value of [an amount].
      Calcot had 2 bls of Wheat.
31   Gave son Daniel 25 to pay for a Drum.
      Payed son George the money due upon Hermanus Simon's
      account

1755

January 1755

3d   Received for Surveying for Lawrence Haff.
      For Tho: Expenses with his sister Eliz to Mr Beatty.
7   Robt Calcot had a pair of shoes for his wife and a pair of shoes
      ___.
10   Gave to a Charitable Use.
      Johs: Binder had one Bushell of wheat.
11   Payed for a Wheat Ridle and a Cockle Sieve.
13   Johannes Binder had a pair of shoes for his wife.
      Francis Passion paid by son George for Surveying and Writings.
19   Will: Wiggins paid toward his Account (for 2 Deeds and charges).
20   Joh. Binder had 2 busls of wheat at son Georges.
23   Received from Jere: Thatcher for the acknowledgments of three
      Deeds.
24   Reconed with Hugh Hunter for the making of 27 pairs of shoes
      Payed to said Hunter a pieces of Eight.
      Gave towards the obtaining of Charter for the Presbyterian
      Congregation in Hunterdon.
28   Herbert Hommer paid for a Deed.
      Jacob Geerhart paid for a Deed and Surveying.
      Some time this month Joseph Worford answered Tho: Martin by
      Di_t[?] which paid sum is in full all Accounts between us vizt:
      Tho: Martin and myself.

Jacob Woolever had 5 lbs of uper Leather and 7 3/4 lb of soal paid per son Danl.

February 1755

4   Set forth on a Journey to Burlington (by Trenton).
        Where I stayed and by the way to the 8th. Expenses on said
        Journey _____.
        Payed to Surveyor Office for Recording 2 Deeds for Henry Lane.
        Received for acknowledging of a Deed for P: Praall.
        Payed to Mr Cottenham by Bill Given to Wm Pierson.
8   Johannes Binder had 2 buslls of wheat.
        Received on my Journey from Wm Godly for attendance at
        Trenton Court.
10   Henry Graff paid for a Deed.
13   Received upon account of surveying and other trouble from Wm
        Voreheis.
        Payed to Ch: Carriers 3 ½ Liquar 8[?].
27   Robt: Calcot had 2 Busls of Wheat.

March 1755

11   Peter Dirdorf paid for Interest.
        Lent son George 2:05:0.
14   Payed Hermanus the Currier 33s. Indebted to him 5d.
17   Robt Calcot had 2 blls of Wheat.
27   Received from ____ Poland for Tanning and Currying about 29__.
29   Expenses in a Journey to Mr Beatty's.
31   Johannes Van Este paid for a Deed.
RP   Rich'd Porter paid part of a Bond £25.

April 1755

5   Robt Calcot had 2 busls of Wheat.
8   Payed to son John upon Adrian Hegeman's account
        Set out on a Journey to Burlington. Arrived there on ___.

9   Returned home on the 10th. Payed in the Surveyor Generals Office.

10   To the Secretarys Office 1/3 for Wafers. 1/6 Expenses and fees to the Gazet. 10s for 50 Limes 2/6.

To a W[ri]t of resurvey for William Case 5/9 order thereon.

Payed to Nanny Woods pieces of 8.

Payed to Adrian Hegeman.

11   Setled Accounts with Dr Van Wagenen and paid him the Balance.

12   Payed to Charles Baird 3:5:19 which with 1:5:0 paid to Jno Yard is being the full of his Account for Mason work done at son Joseph's.

15   Payed Paul Flagg his account for Sundrys had.

Payed to the Fan maker cash 1:17:6 and a pair of shoes.

16   Set out on a Journey to the upper parts of the Country absent to the 22nd.

Payed J__es __on for weaving 83 Ells @ 6d and per Ell.

Robt Calcot finished grubing being 8 days.

26   Payed Ishmael Shippen in _____ (ought to have been three Pounds)

John Cock had 6 Bls of Oats.

Danl Grigs bought ½ bl of oats.

Liz: Harney had 4 buls of oats.

Joost Habbagh for a Deed.

28   Wm Force had 6 bls of oats.

29   Jno Anderson had 19 1/4 of Harness leather.

30   Paid to Tho: Ridge by son Joseph.

Payed to Michael Henry towards the Supplys by Mr Hait[121] and Subscribed for the support of the Ministry the next year 2:0.

Philip Bevin the last week had leather to the value of ___ to answer to Saml Fleming.

---

[121] BENJAMIN HAIT (1734?-79). The Rev. Benjamin Hait graduated at the College of New Jersey in 1754 and was licensed to preach the gospel by the Presbytery of New Brunswick October 25, 1754. He was ordained December 4, 1755 and installed pastor of the Presbyterian Church at Amwell, New Jersey until 1765. Mott, *History of the Presbyterian Church in Flemington*, 30.

John Reading's Diary

May 1755

2d   Payed to a Charitable Use.
      Received from Teunis Middagh and Cornelius Lore for Writing.
      Payed by John Anderson the remainder for the Harnes Leather
      and ___.
3   Michl Henery Payed for Leather.
5   Abr: Zutphen had 3 -0- of Hay at 2/6.
7   Saml Fleming had 6 -0- of Hay.
6   Wm Henery paid towards an Account relating to Land Affairs.
      Alexr White by Wm Henry paid for a Deed.
7   Saml Fleming had another 6 -0- of Hay.
8   Corn: Weycoff had Soal Leather and paid for currying a Side in all
      ____.
9   Payed further towards Mr Haits Supply.
12   Hugh Hunter had 4 3/4 lb of Uper leather and 6 lb of Soal Ditto.
      Christ: Coul paid for a Writing of a Bond and other Services.
13   Set out for Burlington. Absent the 14th. Returned home the ___.
16   Expenses on the Journey and to the Secretary's Office.
      Received from Mr John Stevens[122] on a former Account and for
      my attendance at Court.
      My wife paid in my absence to Nanny Woods by Mrs Hoff.
      To Ditto to a Pedlar.
      To Hugh Hunter in Cash.
      Bought 3 pairs of Linen Stockins.
      Gave to a Charitable Use.
      Richd bought Sundrys at Brunswick on the Landing.
19   Received from Jos: Boss and Tho: Martin for Writing and
      Surveying.
      Received from Johs Housil for Examining the lines of a Lott Sold
      ____.
20   Received from James Williamson for a Deed.
22   Received from Buyer in full for 2 Year Rent about ___.
      Received from Abraham Howe for Indian Corn Sold.

---

[122] JOHN STEVENS (1715-1792). Properous merchant and member of the General
Assembly in Perth Amboy. http://en.wikipedia.org/wiki/John_Stevens_(New_Jersey)
(July 23, 2010).

23 Payed Ishmael Shippy by Cash Sent by Robt Calcot.
    Payed James Wood the Fuller in full on Accounts.
    Payed more towards Supplys in the Ministry - in all for 2/3 of ½ year.
24 Gave to a Charitable Use as also on the 20th day.
    Martin Shiply had 3 bl of Wheat.
26 Reconed with Hugh Hunter for the making of 22 pairs of Shoes.
    For 27 pair made heretofore in January.
    For mending of shoes and boots.
    For making of boots 4 pairs.
    By Credit to cash and sundrys had.
    By Cash paid him excepting 4d.
    In the above Account there has been shoes made for Sundry Persons.
    For Patrick Traverse one pair.
    For Robt Calcots and daughter soaling his wive's shoes.
    For Johs Boltenhammer 1 pair paid for by the F__.
    For Wm Force one pair.
    For Dl Terrat the cooper one pair charged to George.
    For Hermans the currier one pair.
    For the Miners 3 pairs.
    For John Beam 1 pair.
    For Gershom Lee soaling and heel taps.
    For Adrian Hegeman Soaling one pair.
27 Payed towards the Fencing in the Graveyard at the Meeting House.
29 Received from Abm Zutphen for 3 -0- of Hay.
    Reconed with Saml Fleming who fell in my Debt to Balance about __.
31 Gave son Richd to buy 2 Jackets and trimming there to and per other ___.
    Received from Wm Young for acknowledging a Deed.
27 Payed Willm Young the Smith the Balance of our accounts.

June 1755

-    Payed Philip Kase for 8 ½ Galls of oil.
3   John Anderson paid on full for Surveying and Writing.
     Richd returned from Freehold. Expenses on the Journey.
     Layed out at Brunswick for 2 Jackets and Trimming.
     Ashforby Cock paid for a Deed 12s which was accounted for by weaving of Coverlids.
6   Wm Vorehise gave a Bill for the payment of 4 lb the 1st of Oct. next.
7   Saml Kitchin paid for a Deed and towards payment of 2s for other Writings.
     Payed John Opdyke for a Barral of Pork.
8   Hugh Hunter borrowed 2 pieces of Eight.
9   Corns Bowman paid for a Deed from the Coxes heretofor paid the Charges.
     John Edmonds Creditor to 14 lb of Veal.
10   Tunis Corsen had one Bl of Rye and one Bl of Wheat.
9   Edwd Berry had 2 Bls of Rye paid per Mowing.
11   Jacob Gray Payed for Surveying the first 80 Acres 7/6. A title Bond 2s one other Ditto. 2/ for last 50 Acres.
     Surveying the same 7/6. Deed by Bargain and Sale from Wm Wood 7/6. Divided the first 104 Acres and Bond for Wm Wood for the consideration of the last 50 Acres not in the Account.
     Jacob Gray paid by son Daniel for Leather of Sundry Soal.
     Payed John Rake for 6 lbs of white lead a gal per lb 14-6 of __.
12   John Edmonds worked at the Frame for the Arbor and a New Gate 3 days.
17   Payed John Cock towards Daniels wagon.
23   Gave to a Charitable Use.
     Robt Insworth Payed the Balance of his account which for 15 sheep @ 4:5:5 and for 5 lbs of Soal leather.
     Credit for 2 hides 19:2 and 3 -0- 1/4. 2 lb of Iron @ 27/6. Comes to _____.
     Son Richd gave his Receipt for the Sum paid as above.
     Pr Yager paid for the Acknowledgment of a Deed.
25   Sent by Daughter Ann to New York [an amount].
26   John Gever paid for a Deed.
30   John Edmonds borrowed [an amount].

Theods: VanWyke at New York. Flower and Kernel sold at New York vizt: 14 casks of flower at 15:6. 7 Of Casks of Kernel @ 13:6. Sum total with the Casks of £29:8:9. Comission for charges of etc. Deducted 14:9 nett Proceeds £28:14:0 (Boating to be paid for).

Edwd Berry about the Last of this month or the beginning of Next had 2 bls of Rye.

July 1755

14th   Ab. Laushee paid for a Deed

19th   Payed Tune Coursen for mowing of grass, Raking and Binding 6 wt and Rye deducted.

Andw Haun after his Servitude worked with me 12 days.

2/4 d per day came to £1:8. Harvist work 5 ½ days @ 5s per Day came to 27:6 to NY in Proc ___/13:0 cash gave him 7/6. All is 3:3:8 paid it.

Will Force worked at harvist 5 ½ days @ 5s per Day.

Hugh Hunter Raked and Bound 6 days @ 5s light money per Day.

Wm Force had 1 ½ bl of rye @ 3/3 per busl.

Payed Hugh Hunter in Cash.

August 1755

Set out upon a Journey to Trenton and Burlington. Absent till the__.

Expenses on the Same besides Council Fees about _____.

Received at Burlington more than Expenses ___.

George Barton paid for a Deed.

Gave to a Charitable Use.

Reconed with And: Haun. Remains due to him for work. Payed him [an amount].

23d   Expenses on a Journey to Dl Lorecs and Trenton on the Mining Affair.

Ferriges 1s and Expenses at the last Court paid of this time.

25   Payed Negro Pompy for Harvist work.

29   Josiah Clawson paid one Bond and Interest and part of another. In all being L[ight]. M[oney]. 50:0:0.

30   John Johnson paid towards a Bond and Interest. Sum due for Interest to Sept. On same day paid the further Sum of £1:3:1 ½ being his share of a Bond for 6£ interest due thereon.
Paid Mr. Beatty for Baxter Xtian Directory.[123]

12   Payed to Tho: Atkinson part of his Account per son Richard.

September 1755

1   William Housel paid for a Deed from the Coxes.
Jno Edmonds part of a day at the Gate in the old Field charged ____.

Payed to John Cock the Balance of Accounts for a new Wagon and mending Wheels.
Payed Martin Ryerson for the use of the Mine being ____ need for purposes agreed on by The Company for one twelfth part.

12   Payed for weaving a piece of Checked Linnen.

13   Reconed with Eliz: Harney and Payed her for Harvist Rum 11 Galls.

18   Payed Boid for weaving 83 Ells of Linnen Cloath.

19   Accompted with Henry Landis and paid him the Balance being [an amount].
Received from Henry Landis for a Deed of Bargain and Sale
    For a Defeazance thereon
    For a lease
    For a Bond
Which was accounted for with other Charges of Recording and Writing and settled at the same time.

22d   Payed or left in the House for Wm Force for 82 lb of Beef.
Johannes Null[Hull?] paid for a Deed for the Coxes.
Payed John Rake the Painter in pieces of 8 for painting Jos: House.

---

[123] Richard Baxter. *The Practical Works of Richard Baxter, Vol. I, A Christian Directory*, (London, 1707).

24th   Lay'd out in Expenses at Philipsburg and Journey.
29th   Gave to a Charitable Use.
        Gave to daughter Mary when she went up to the Moravians
        about 9-6. Lay'd out in expenses About 6s.

October 1755

1   Bought two Hogsheads from Paul Flagg.
3   Thomas McMurtealy paid for writings etc. Formerly don.
        Payed to Wm Piersons wife for Smiths work (being Part of his
        account).
        Payed to son Joseph for the hire of a man for one Month.
        Gave also to son Joseph a pieces of 8.
6   Payed to the Widow Smith for Cureing a Rupture in a Negro
        Boy.
        Left with Mr Beaty for to buy a Map and Mr Hardy's
        Meditations.
8   Philip Grandin paid for a Deed.
14   Payed my Land Tax for the Township of Reading 0:03:7.
15   Payed to Adrian Hegbeman towards my own Smiths work and
        part for Daniels wagon.
17   Received from Fredk Maurison for writing his Will.
19   Received from Dl Grigs for Writings.
        Son Richard Expended when went for the Cattle.
20   Received from the Grandins and the Roger's for Surveying.
21   Payed Wm _____ for a Beaver and Felt Hat.
23   Lay'd out at the Potters.
28   Payed to the Collectar for the Provincial Taxe In Amwell 1:10:0.
        Peter Woolever paid for leather being the Balance of his Account.
        Sent by son George to New York which was Layed out in Cloth
        for self and Daughter Sarah.[124]

November 1755

---

[124] SARAH READING (1738-1809). John Reading's youngest daughter. She married
Augustine Reid and lived in Roxbury, Morris County. Leach, *Memorials*, 53.

1   Adam Snuke paid in full for Writings etc.
4   Set out upon a Journey to Burlington. Expenses and fees to Offices paid.
6   Returned Home. Son Richard sold 20 lbs of flax seed.
     Carryed out to John Rake 4 busls Ditto.
7   My wife with son Richd went to Brunswick with
     30 bls of Barley. Sold the same for 3/6 per busl.
8   Returned home and Expended the money for the Barley and in Cash.
10   Payed for Supplys (this last half year) in the Ministry.
15   Hugh Hunter had 30s towards his pay for shoe making.
26   Lend son Daniel 15s when he went to Easton.
28th Lawrence Low paid (supposing it to be the whole) for Land and Surveying.
29   Sent by son Thomas to the Furnice to buy Tallow and Scraps.
     John Edmonds worked 2 1/4 days.

December 1755

1   Expended with a Pedlar
9   Bought an Hog from John Stiers wt 163 lb.
11   Gave son Daniel one 6s Bill at the Training.
13   Richard Porter paid part of a Bond.
23d Payed for a Gall of Rum at Paul Flags.
14   Let son Daniel have (when he went to the Uper Parts of the Prov) [an amount].
23   Richd Porter paid Some more of a Bond.
     Payed Benj: Stout for 2 days work formerly don (one is said yet to pay for).
25   Nichs: Williamson had a side of Uper Leather.
     Bought 2 lb of Powder 2 lb of Lead and 6 Flints.
27   Gershom Lee Debtor to soaling a pair of Shoes.
     Debtor to Hugh Hunter to the making of 22 pairs of shoes.
     Account with Hugh Hunter _____ and charged him for for Cash and Sundries had and there. Remained Due to him 9/9 which I paid.

Received from Nichs Williamson for leather had as above.

29th Adrian Hegeman had a side of Uper Leather.

John and Corns Wyckof Payed for Releases etc.

30 Acknowledged a Deed for Simon Simonse. 3s not paid for.

1756

January 1756

3d John Edmonds shod the wood slead.

5 John Edmonds had a pair of soals.

6 Debtor to John Edmonds for 17 Squares of glass.

Bought from David McKinny hardward to the value of _____.

Payed to Boyd the weaver for Nanny Woods.

8 Bought from David McKinny per son Daniel 9 lb of powder and 2 lb of lead.

7 William Henry paid towards his account 15s.

9 Payed Benj: Stout for 2 Chests making @ 15s per chest and one days work.

John Edmonds whet and set a Saw and made a Stove.

17 Wm Voreheis paid a note underhand.

23 Received from Willhelmus Wertegen for a Deed.

24 Received from Wm Henery the Balance of Account to this day.

26 Received from Saml Moors for Acknowledging some Deeds.

29 Payed to the German Doctor for Thos legg and Richds finger and medicines.

30 Setled with Lawrence Low full in his debt which I paid him.

February 1756

3d Payed John Rake 3/6 which with 3/12 and 14s in flaxe seed makes 6s 2.

5 Gave to a Charitable Use.

13th   Reconed with Ashfordby Cock and paid him the Balance.

21   Sold 600 -0- of hay.

25th   Received for acknowledging three Deeds.

26   Received for Acknowledging One Deed.

27   Received of Mordecai McKinny for a Deed.

Bought 2 ozs of Indigo.

Jno Binder some time this month weaved 13 Ells of Linsy Woolsy

The same No. of Ells to Jno Ecbird.

March 1756

Met at the Meeting House about the Parsonage.

Concluded to Keep the Remainder of the Land and Build for the minister, accordingly; a subscription was drawn and I subscribed 50s, the one half to be paid at the raising, the other half within 6 months after.

Payed Wm Norcross for a felt Hatt.

11   Josiah Clawson paid part of a Bond.

John Edmonds had 2 -0- of Hay.

16   Tunis Coursen had 2 -0- of Hay.

20   Lent son George when he went to Phila.

Sent by him for the use of the girls.

22   Lent Will: Force in Cash. Paid it per Son George.

23   Bought Cotton at the Landing.

24   The Weaver Mrs Brand had 2 -0- of Hay

Some time this month John Binder weaved 18 Ells of Linen and Ditto @ 6/ per Ell. The same no. of Ells to John Ecbird.

April 1756

2d   Payed the German Docter for medicines etc.

Received from Jacob Anthony for a Deed of Gift in Paper.

3   Received from Corns: Bodine by his Bro: Jno on Account of the [Arbitration].

4 Received from Wm Snuke in full of a Bill for 16s and acknowledgment of a Deed.

  Lent Philip Bevin in Cash [an amount].

6 Sold to Garret Van Campen 500 -0- of Hay.

7 Sold and paid for to Tho: Marshal 500 -0- of Hay.

12 Payed Bro: Ryerson for Peter Middays Return in the Surveyors Office

  Nanny Woods had cash to buy Flax.

14 Christian Coul paid for a Deed.

16 Payed for 6 shads.

19 Johs Binder weaved and brought home 41 Ells of Linen and wool, the half to Jno Ecbird @ 6d per Ell. The half comes to

  _____.

  Son Joseph had in Cash and Flax.

20 Paulus Botner had 3 busls of Oats.

21 Jno Aller and Abm Zutphen had 1 ½ -0- of hay. Paid for it afterwards.

  Jacob _____ had one Bl of Wheat and one Bl of Rye.

22 Matthias Brand the weaver had 2 bls of Rye

26 Payed to Joseph Reed for a Barrel of Pork.

  James Baird paid the Balance of an Account.

  David Eveland paid for running the lines round his Plantation.

30 Aaron Starke paid for one Years Rent for the Calf Pasture. Gave a Receipt.

May 1756

3d Layed out for Lime for the Parsonage (and fetched it home).

4 Set out on a Journey to Burlington. Absent till the 7th day then returned home; my expenses in and out.

  Payed to Jon: Thomas Wm Henery's Fees for getting a Warrant from the Council.

  Payed to Moore Furman for the last years Gazett.

  Sent to the Landing to buy Melasses, Cotton, Salt etc.

11 Edward Berry had 2 Bls of Rye.

12th   Received for an acknowledgment of a Bill of Sale from John Thomas to Col[?] Wm Dilts and Powel Sharp.

15th   Dr Vieselius, debtor for Surveying 3s and Writing a Deed.

17   Matthias Brand Debtor to two Busls of Rye.
       To cash lent to John Edmonds as he said by Request from David Eveland.

20   To one gall of Rum at Paul Flags. Payed for it in Light Money.

22   Edward Berry had 3 Bls of Rye.
       Philip Bevin paid back the cash borrowed April the 4th.
       Payed to the support of the ministry £2:0 (the whole) to the parsonage 1/0.

24   Payed Jos: Howell in full for Smith's work.
       Matts Brand had two Busls of Rye.

27   Payed Ishmael Shippy towards the Balance of his account (remained due £8:16).
       Lay'd out with a Pedlar for Fustian[125] etc.

29   John Foxe paid for a Deed.

31   Payed Wm Norcross for dressing of two Hatts.

June 1756

1   The Everitts paid for the acknowledgment of two Deeds.

4   Expended with David Kinny for Buttons.
       Johs: Binder wove and brought home 48 Ells of Linnen Cloath.

7   Bought 26 busl of Lime.

8   Richard had Cash to pay for making a Plough.

10   Peter Rivenberg paid for 2 pair of shoes had in last Feb.
       Gave to Daughter Molly when went to Freehold.

14   Payed to Wm McKarty for making son Thomas a Fustian coat.

12   Gave son Richard to buy Fustian for a coat 30s and money to bear his expenses in a Journey to Freehold 8s and to daughter Molly for Expenses upon said journey.

---

[125] A stout fabric of cotton and flax; a fabric of stout twilled cotton or of cotton and low-quality wool, with a short nap or pile. http://www.websters-online-dictionary.org/definitions/fustian

Setled Accounts with Martin Shipley and remains due from him to Balance upon all Accounts the sum of £10:3:10 1/4.

16   Received to defray the Charges of an arbitration between Jons Hampton[126] and Dd Allen.

Expenses upon Said arbitration paid for accommodations in said Journey.

17   Payed to James Cowley's wife for Pasturing and taking Care of one 2 year old brindled Heffer the last year.

21   Ran in debt to Pedlar Thomas Lowry.

Martin Shifly 2 Bls of wheat at son Georges Mill.

23   Payed John Cock for mending the Wagons.

30   Received from Abrm Drake in past for 22 Acres of land @ 20s per Acre. Rems due to pay (for which he gave Bond) the sum of £8:00.

Sold to John Cock some grass.

Sold to Matts: Brand some grass for 5s if he could not give 1:10:0.

Sold to Martin Shifly some grass.

This month Jos Binder wove 35 Ells of Linen.

July 1756

1st   Then accompted with Adrian Hegeman and fell in his Debt to Balance 4:11:2 which was accordingly paid.

Johs Binder had 1 ½ bl of wheat from mine in store @ Georges Mill. Paid for by Balance.

3d   Edwd Berry had 2 Bll of wheat from the above place.

12   Received from Mr Wm Coxe 6 skins of Parchment sent up to Moor Furmans by Douglass.

17th   Paid Jno Rous for near three days Mowing.

21   Payed Aaron Hankinson for 2 ½ days mowing of wheat.

---

[126] JONATHON HAMPTON (1717-1777). Prominent citizen of Elizabethtown, New Jersey. Appointed in 1755, one of the commissioners to purchase supplies for the soldiers during the French and Indian war. Whitehead, *Colonial History of New Jersey*, Vol. VIII, 393.

Payed Tunis Coursen for Mowing of grass and Raking and Binding.

Payed 2 Reapers for 2 ½ days.

Payed Tunis Coursen on Nero's account for fetching a load of Lime.

Jos Binder earned for 5 days work.

Robt Calcot had 2 ½ load of hay.

August 1756

2d   Jos Binder wove 59 Ells of Linnen @6d per Ell
     Jos Binder had in cash _____.
     Payed Hugh Hunter 1/16 for Harvest work.
     Payed Nanny Woods for Spining etc. being in full 1:16:0.

3d   Set out on a Journey to Burlington. Expenses at Trenton.

4th Arrived at Burlington. Continued there till the 5th in the afternoon.

5   Lodged at Newtown in Pensylvania. Thence to Mr Beattys and thence to son Joseph's; Lodged there and thence home on the 7th. Expenses at Burlington etc.

7   Mary Eveland paid upon Jno Edmonds account.
     Payed Thomas Lowry the Pedlar the former account.

10   John Case paid an Old Account for Surveying 10s and Writing 2 Releases.

19   Son George paid towards the Payment for 60 bls of Wheat.
     Lent to Ishmael Shippen by my Wife when she Went to N.Y.; the Balance 8:18:0.
     Received from Peter Meddagh in part of an Account between us.

21   Payed John Rake the remainder for Painting Jos's House.

20   Joh Binder brought home 60 Ells of Linen.
     My wife when she went to York to buy Sundrys for daughter Sarah had for the Flower £60:15. Ishmeal Shippen's money 8:16 from son George returned out of money the sum of ___.

23   Payed Mr Beatty for Whiston's Theory[127] and Maundrel's
      Travels[128]
30   Received for the acknowledgment of four Deeds.
31   John Edmonds had two blls of wheat which Jacob Yockle paid
      back.
      Son Daniel bought and paid for 4 bl of Shot.
      Tho: Atkinson returned for the sum of £12:5 to buy feathers the
      sum of _____.

September 1756

4   Then accompted with Jno Egbert and Jos Binder for weaving and
      paid John Egbert in cash and per Johs account. The Balance
      being _____.
6   Peter Meddogh paid the Balance of account between us.
11   Payed Eliz: Harney in part for Harvist Rum etc.
      Payed Ruth Potts for a part of Stays for Eliz:
25   Accompted with Jno Edmonds and due from me to Balance_.
      Payed son Daniel for a quarter of Beef weighed 91 lb.
      Received from John Gulick for a Deed by Jocam Grigs.

October 1756

6th   Daughter Elizabeth Returned from N York Expenses in the
      Journey _____.
7th   Lent Jno Johnson by Johs Binder _____.
9   To 8 ½ lb of fish @ 2d/per lb.

---

[127] William Whiston. *A New Theory of the Earth, From its Original, to the Consummation of All Things, Where the Creation of the World in Six Days, the Universal Deluge, And the General Conflagration, As laid down in the Holy Scriptures, Are Shewn to be perfectly agreeable to Reason and Philosophy* (London: Benjamin Tooke, 1696).
[128] Henry Maundrell (1665–1701) was an academic at Oxford University and later a Church of England clergyman. His *Journey from Aleppo to Jerusalem at Easter A.D. 1697* (Oxford, 1703), which had its origins in the diary he carried with him on his Easter pilgrimage to Jerusalem in 1697, has become an often reprinted "minor travel classic." It was included in compilations of travel accounts from the mid-18th century. http://en.wikipedia.org/wiki/ Henry_Maundrell (July 23, 2010).

To expenses in fetching some Cattle from Black River viz: Wm Douglas.

15 Received from Jno Sharpenstien for the fees of Recording his deed by Wm Kase.

19 To Expenses in fetching the Cattle from Edwd Hunts.
Received from Abm Howe by son Richard being the Balance between us.

21 Payed Mr Hacket[129] for four Hogsheads.

23 Payed Jno Edmond in part for some work done and the above Balance.

25 Payed my Land Tax for the Township of Reading 0:3:6.

26 Payed my Provincial Tax in the Township of Amwell 1:6:10.
Payed for a quarter of Beef to Nichs Egbert.

27 Payed Jos Binder 9s light money in full to this day for weaving.

29 Tho: spent in Looking the Cattle [an amount].

November 1756

1 Paul Leonard by son George paid an Old Debt.

2 Payed for an Hog[shea]d to Mr Jno Hacket.
Payed to a Charitable Use.

3 Payed for 21 lb of fish.

5 Sold 12 ½ bl of Flax Seed and 9 bl of wheat.
Bought some necessaries for the house use.

8 Son George borrowed 6 lb wanting a gr[?] of Uper Leather.
Received from Josiah Clawson in part of a Bond.

11 Payed to Jacob Mattison for the Parsonage – for the Ministers Salary.

12 John Coxe had ½ a beef weighed 192 lb.

13 Nathl Pettit by his son Amos paid part of a Bond.

---

[129] JOHN HACKETT (1728-1766). Hackett was employed by William Allen and Joseph Turner. Hackett operated the Union Iron Works in what is now High Bridge for them from about 1749 until 1760, when he took over the management of the Andover Furnace near Waterloo. He married John Reading's daughter Elizabeth in 1755. Hackett was appointed a Justice of the Peace in Hunterdon County on May 18, 1751, a post which he held until he moved to Waterloo. He was appointed a judge of the Court of Common Pleas of Sussex County in 1760. Leach, Memorials, 51 and http://www.hackettstown.net / history.html (August 1, 2010).

15   Richd Porter paid part of a Bond.
16   Payed off Tho: Atkinsons Account for Shop Goods.
     Payed him also for a Coat Cloath and Trimming.
26   Payed Blk Tom for dressing 3 sheep skins.
     Expended in Oysters and Clams.
     My wife layed out at Freehold for Cheese.

                    December 1756

1   Accompted with Edwd Berry; paid him the Balance.
     Accompted with Nanny Woods paid her the Balance.
2   Gave son Richard to pay the Stubber.
3   Payed John Edmonds the Balance of Accounts.
     Philip Binder stubed and worked seven days.
     Robt Calcot stubbed 10 ½ days.
9   Accompted with Hugh Hunter. Was in his debt £2:9:20 whereof
     was discompted upon account of his board and the remainder 9s.
     I paid him.
15   Received from Pr Cook for acknowledgment of a deed.
24   Son Tho: when he went to Freehold with Augn Reid.[130]
     Expended __.
26   Gave son Jos: to pay a Stuber in a swamp [f]or Isaac
     Rightenghouse.
24   Robt M'Kracke had a Barrel of Cider.
30   George the Tinker had a Barrel of Cider and Mart: Shifley had a
     Barrel of Cider.
28   Mats: Brandt had 2 Bls of Wheat

1757

                    January 1757

---

[130] AUGUSTINE REID (1731-1807). Son of Col. John Reid and Mary Sands. Married
Sarah Reading. Leach, *Memorials*, 53.

1   Payed Mr Beatty the Balance of our Account for books etc.
       Payed Casar for some Raked wheat and to pay for a Hat.
       Gave to daughters Eliz and Molly for Jocky Caps etc. in cash.
       Received for Writing from Michl Shurt.
       Tho: expended when at Freehold.
3d   John Wood had a Barrel of Cider.
4   Gave to a Charitable Use.
8   Payed Mr Hacket for Tallow and Scraps.
15   Philip Binder debtor to 2 Blls of Wheat.
17   Received from Justs Martin money Recovered from Jo Willson
19   Received from Tunis Cole in part of 15s for a Deed.
20   Payed Martin Tegan for 7 days Work.
       Expended with a Pedlar.
24   Edwd Hunt paid part of One years Rent.
       George Shank paid for a barrel of Cider (the Tinker)
       Jno Washer paid for a Bond and a Bill of Sale.
       Tunes Coursen is Debtor to 2 bls of Wheat the price when I sell
       –.
25   Antho Dirdort paid for a Deed.
28   Lambert Brink had a Barrel of Cider.
30   Son Richd bought an Horse from one of the Drakes.
       Cost £12 paid £8:6:3 part thereof by a Bond from Abm Drake.
       Expenses on said account Being [an amount].
       Son Tho: fetched an Heifer that strayed away last Spring near
       Union Furnance. Cost to Wm Silverthorn on account thereof –
       Expenses on said account and on Heifer.
26   Payed Isml Shippen £9:8. The supposed Balance of our Accounts
       but wants 2s.
27   Wm Force borrowed Cash; paid it since –

February 1757

4   Bought a wove Cotton Cap.
5   Sold to Peter Fox a Barrel of Cider.
       Gave to my wife out of the money paid by Gershom Lee last
       Aug. to me the sum of £8:6:6 it being upon Bro: L: Ryerson

Account. I having wrote to him Concerning the Receipt thereof and Requesting that I might have the Same upon Account of his Sisters Legacy the whole sum Received from said Lee being £20:0:0. Remains to my own use the Sum of 11:13:6.

15   Agreed to sell Adam Snuke a Tract of land for 250 lbs Proc and sent him a Memorandum of our Agreement in these words vizt, Be it Remainder That I John Reading have agreed to sell to Adam Snuke a tract of land Lying on both sides of the Muskonetcong River in Morris and Sussex county containing 219 Acres for the Sum of 250 lb Proc. Money to be paid in manner following Vizt. The sum of 100 lb on the first day of May next Ensuing. 75 lb the Remander on the first day of May 1759. Upon payment of the first 100 lb I am to signe a Deed of my own cost and the said Snuke is to give Bond with Issac Demot for the payment of the remainder in manner aforesaid. Bonds and Bear Interest from the first of May 1758 upon thise Terms. The said Snuke may Enter upon the Land and prepare timber for a building of he sees meet.

               Feb the 15, 1757 Witness Jno Reading

A copy of the above is sent to Adam Snuke [along side of page].

Agreement with Adam Skuke May the 14th 1757.

Payed towards the agreement £100. June the 4th 1757.

Payed the further Sum May the 8th.

Payed the full Consideration – 16 Augt 1757. Granted a Deed for said Tract and half the mines General Warranty.

Agreed with Francis Tominlson for the Carpenters and Joyners work of Richds House containing from outside to outside in length 37 feet in breadth 30 to be well sufficie[?] and workmanlike don in all respects for the sum of 30 lb Proc. Money to be paid as soon as conveniently I can. The Building to be but one stay above the Celar, the Beams to go thoughout the house if to be had if not then to Frame with a A Summer and Small joysts for the Particularies of the work as discovered of I refer to another memorandum.

14   Payed by Son Richd for the last years Gazette.

18   Bought from David McKinny 4 ½ lb of Gunpowder.

21   Setled all accounts by Bill Book or Accompts in reference to Cash with Bro: Martin Ryerson and he fell in my Debt the Sum of

£40:10 for which he gave me his note under hand dated the 21 of Feb 1757 to be paid upon Demand.

22   Received from Wm Force paid of 33s formerly Borrowed. Hugh Hunter since past Settlement has made 3 pair of men's shoes, a pair for Patte and mended mine.

25   Gave to a Charitable Use.

March 1757

2d   Payed Richard Cook for following a piece of Blanketing.
Received from the German Taylor for 1 bl of Indian Corn.

5   Payed Jacob Drake for the use of Abm Drake Jur (Per Bill Due)

8   Received from Wm Force the remainder of the 33s borrowed.
Jno Edmonds had a lb of Indian Corn (1 or 2).

4   Robt Calcot had one lb of Indian Corn.

12   Payed for the weaving of a Coverlid.

15   Matt: Brandt wove 23 yards of Cloths.
Gave to the repairations of the fences of the Parsonage. Towards the putting in of a Garden 2/6, for firewood 5:

19   Received from Bro: Luke Ryerson part of his Sisters Mary's Parcon.

21   Gave son Richard in Cash.

23   Wm Force had a Busl of Indian Corn, paid for it.
Nanny Woods had in cash.

25   Wm Force had a Bushl of Indian Corn in Ears.

29th   Paid Richard's Well digger for 1 month Service.

April 1757

1   Received from Joseph Titus for Writings and other Services.

2   The German Taylor had a bl of Indian Corn.

4   Received from Jacob Gray for a Deed.

7   Sent by Daughter Eliz: to Phila to be Expended in Cloath etc.
Payed Nanny Woods in Cash.

9   To a Journey to Burlington in which with Fees to the Surveyor Generals Office. Sundrys bought and Expenses.

11	Received from Jno Anderson for a Deed.
12	Philip Binder had 2 bls of Wheat.
14	Payed peter Edelman for Hedging.
18	Recd from William Kinney for Changing Pennsylvania Bills into Jersey Ditto.

18   Recd from William Kinney for Changing Pennsylvania Bills into Jersey Ditto.

Daughter Eliz: Returned from Phila bought for myself a Coat Cloath 4 cte[?].

Besides Expending the above money for Cloaths.

(Gave Mr. Beatty 10s which with 11:2 ½ left of Money of the Coat to buy Parchment makes ___.)

22   Received for Service don Gart Van Fleet and the Widow Rosa.

23   Payed Philip Bevin for trimming aple trees.

29   Received for further Service for Garret Van Fleet's.

30   Received from Nichs Off for a Deed.

Received from Jacobus Kinny for a Deed and Surveying for himself etc.

Lent to Hugh Hunter in Cash 3 pieces of 8.

Edwd Berry had 3 bls of Rye.

May 1757

Sent to Richard's stuber.

3d   Sent to Ishmael Shippy to pay the Balance of Accounts by son Tho:

Sent to the Widdow Hegeman to pay for 2 Coverlids.

Sent to buy Boards etc. money Returned.

Received from Francis Quick for a right to Land etc.

4th   Payed to Mr Andrew Reed for a Barrel of Beef.

Payed for a pair of Sheep sheers.

Payed to Expenses on a journey to Trenton.

Maths Brandt had ___ of Rye.

5   Edwd Berry had 3 Bls of Rye.

10   Sent to Richds Well Digger in Cash. Rd paid for it.

For Lime.

11   On a Journey to Trenton and returned home the 12th.

12   Payed for 600 feet of Boards.

Payed for carting Boards and Beef and Pork.

11   Cancelled the Deficiency in the Loan Office before the Inst and Freeholders being the sum of ___.

Payed to Mahlon Kirkbride part of a Retaining Fee.

16   Payed John Coxe for a Wagon and for mending of an old one several time besides an account against him being £3:8 and in Cash also the Sum of ___.

14   Payed to Richard's Well Diger.

Received from Adam Snuke the first payment of the Land.

Received form Chris: Coul for a Deed.

June 1757

3d   Payed to Henry Grapp for Hops.

4th   John Egbert wove 45 Ells of Linnen Cloath.

Payed Nanny Woods in Cash.

Received from Adam Snuke on Account of the Second Payment for the Land which ought to have been 75 but Interest Being ____ 70:4:4.

5   Received for the use of Luke Ryerson from Gern Lee by a Bond of £40 taken up in cash £8.

9   John Egbert by Js Binder wove 41 Ells of Linnen Cloth.

10   Expended with a Pedlar for goods.

11   Christian Sharpenstein paid for a Deed.

13   Will: Bardack paid for 2 Releases and a Deed.

Bought 2 galls of Rum for Richard.

Received back from Jacob Mattison money lent to Support the Ministry.

14   Matths Brandt by an order to son George for 2 bls of Wheat.

Frances Waldron is credit to the weaving of ____.

20   Sent by Richard to pay the Housekeeper as part of her wages.

Payed Anghe[?] Carter for 11 days Service.

21   Payed towards making up and deficiancy for the Building Parsonage House. Each of the managers paying the said sum of ____.

22d   Sent to New York by Sarah Marshcollock to buy sundries.

Sent by son Thos: to buy Sundrys and bear Expenses on the Journey.

Aaron Starke paid one years Rent for the Calf Pasture.

To a scythe 6; 1 Bl of Salt 6; To one Board.

27 To Expenses for a Journey of son Richard to Freehold.

28 To Dr Vieselius the Balance of Accounts upon a Reconing.

Received from Henry Cogh for a Deed.

30 Payed for a pair of Horses bought from Ab: Van Campen and Benj: Dupue 20:0:0.

Received from Jacobus Kinny for a Deed.

Payed towards the Parsonage House to Tho: Martin The further sum of 0:01:6.

To a Busl of Indian Corn to Robt Calcot.

July 1757

1 Sent to Tho: Atkinson to buy feathers.

2 Payed to Henry Schamp for money borrowed by Son Rich'd and Interest.

Payed for a Sheep at the raising of Richard house.

4 Payed for the weaving of thread Stockings.

7 Philip Binder mowed a Little more than Eleven days.

Paid him per account ten shillings in cash.

Lend said Binder in Cash.

11th Payed Joseph Reed for a Barrel of Pork for Richard.

Payed the Widow Harney the Balance of Account.

15 Payed Gershom Lee for some work done to the Barn floor.

18 Son George Returned money from Sarah Marshcollock. She expended [an amount].

21 Finished Harvist. Payed to the several persons following Harvist wages vizt:

   To Jno Corwine and his apprentice

   To Josp Corwine and his Ditto

   To Moses Reed

   To Richd Giles

   To Saml Oliver

To John Pidcock

To Johs Binder

To Robert Calcot for 6 days reaping.

Payed Patrick Traverse for work about the new ground.

22   Nanny Woods had in Cash.

Payed Michl Yerianse his father for 10 ½ days work.

23   Payed Nanny Woods the Balance of Accounts.

Payed Lettice Newbank for 13 weeks Spinning.

26   Robt Calcot had about a half a busl of Buck Wheat.

August 1757

1   Gave son Richard to pay his Tender and some Harvist men.

6   Received from Edwd Hunt on part of Rent.

Sent to Wm Norcross by son Tho: subscriptions for Mr [Gilbert] Ten[n]ants sermon.

18   Payed Daniel for Tanning 6 calfskins and currying the same and 2 side of harness leather – the Whole is 8d paid him.

19   To son George for Peg; and to Nany _____.

23   Payed Mr Hacket for som Linnen and Binding Bought at Phila.

26   Payed to Dr Watson for Morony and Jalap.

29   Gave son Richard to pay for two Bells.

September 1757

12th   Set out for Trenton in Order to get rellief for My Sore leg.

Boarded at Doctor Norton who was to administer by Physick or other ways what should be thought needfull there to and Arrived there that night.

Edward Berry mowed grass 4 ½ days.

13   Mathias Brandt mowed grass 4 days wanting 4 hours.

21   Edward Berry Debtor to Rye 2 Busls.

24   Martin Ryerson Borrowed 2 bls of seed Wheat.

25   John Reading jur Debtor to 2 busls of seed Wheat.

NB[131] The above articles were set down by son Tho: while I was away.

---

[131] Nota Bene (Latin). Note well.

John Reading's Diary

October 1757

5   Debtor to Patrick Travers for one Day work. Son Tho: paid.

7   Johannes Binder Debtor to two Busls of Rye.

10   Joseph Reading Debtor to one pair Mens shoes.

21   Paid to Christ: Man the Weaver for Weaving.

      Paid Tho: Atkinson the account for shop goods in full as per his Rect bearing each date appears.

      Received from son George for Flower sold at New York.

27   Payed half years support of the Ministry to Mr Hart [Hait]

      To ____ the weaver

      To Oysters.

      To Nanny Woods.

NB   These articles were Received and paid at home in my Absense.

      Expended this month at Trenton for Cloathing and Sundries.

November 1757

1   Payed my Provincial Tax to Lewis Chamberlain.

      Ditto to Saml Tucker for Cloath for a Jacket and Trimming.

3   Payed to the Barber at Trenton.

      Payed to the Taylor for making a Jacket.

      Payed the Doctor for Boarding of Self 7 ½ weeks and Molly 7 weeks.

      Gave to the Doctor's Servent.

      Payed to Lettice Newbank a spinster.

11   Payed to Richards Well diger in full.

14   Payed Richards labourer Saml.

      Received from Richd Porter in full for his two first bonds.

      Lay'd out in Wine and Rum.

      Bought from Gasham Lee 128 lb of Beef.

15   Payed Mr Beatty for two books vizt Clark's Lives and Lex Parla.

      Payed Joseph Smith for weaving a piece of Dieper.

18   Payed to the Widdow Harney for 5 qts of rum in full.

21   Payed to Wilson Hunt for a cheese weighed 17 lb.

      Payed to Richd money borrowed from Obed Howell.

Received from Jacob Mattison part of the money disbursed on account of the Parsonage.

15 Subscribed by Mr Beatty for Mr Bradford's America Maga[zine][132]

24 To one Hog wt 114 lb sold to Jos Binder.

28 Payed to Saml Tucker for Cloath and Trimming for a Jacket.
Payed Wm Clayton for 5329 foot of Boards.

26 To 2 lb of Razens.

29 To a Quart of Wine.

December 1757

10 Payed to Christean Man for mowing.

15 Johs Binder had 4 bls of wheat.

12 Payed John Wright for Riding Express to Mr Saltar.[133]

22 To Barber at Trenton for Wigg. To shavings.

12 Received for 3 Military Commissions for the Rangers.

16 Received for Seal to a Writ of Replevin.[134]

23 Payed to the Doctor Norton for Board, Medicines etc.
Payed to said doctor for a visit in the Fall.
Payed to the Servants.
Gave to son John when he came to fetch me home for Sundrys and Expenses home from Trenton.

30 Martin Shifly had 2 bl wheat.
To cash when Richard and Tho: went to Phila to buy cloathes.
To cash when went to Freehold with Sarah.
To Ditto to Richard and Thos at Richards wedding.
To Hannah Brewer Richards Housekeeper in full.

---

[132] The American journalist William Bradford (1722-1791) published two of the best colonial periodicals, the Pennsylvania Journal (begun in 1742), a weekly, and the American Magazine (1757), a monthly. http://en.wikipedia.org/wiki/ William_Bradford_ (American_Revolutionary_printer (July 25, 2010).

[133] RICHARD SALTAR (1699-1763). Member of the Council in 1745, Commissioned as associate judge of the Supreme Court 1754. Whitehead, *Colonial History of New Jersey*, Vol. VIII, 412.

[134] A Writ of Replevin is a court order to regain personal property held or retained by another. http://www.co.rock.wi.us/index.php/ civilprocess-writofreplevin (August 2, 2010).

To cash Payed for Richards Cloaths, a gown for Molly.

To a pair of Breeches for Thos and gloves.

To Glass's white Lead.

To Patrick Ryely for a Hatt for Richard

1758

January 1758

2   Gave Richard to pay for Hair to Plaster with.

3   Gave to Richard to buy Bolts for Shutters.

5   Jacob Demot by his Bro: Isaac paid for a Deed.

    Isaac Demott paid part for his own Deed.

    Received from the Treasurer by virtue of account paid to Mr Read.

6   Lend son Daniel _____ paid it back again on the 9th.

9   Martin Shifly paid for 2 bls of wheat.

18   Payed Nanny Woods in Full.

19   Johs Binder had two busl of Wheat.

    Payed Francis Waldron for weaving 240 Ells.

    Payed Paul Botner for making three Towe Collars.

    Payed Pompey for 23 lb of Flax.

23   Gave to Sister Blandina Hall[135] the money left for her by her brother George being the sum of 29:11:9.

24   Also paid her cash left with my wife formerly Payed to William McCartee for taylor work.

    Payed to Fran: Tomlinson part for the building lent by Richard.

29   Received for sealing a Writ of Replevin Jere: Stillwell vs Jer: Stillwell.

30   Cash to Son John at Trenton.

---

[135] BLANDINA (RYERSON) HALL (1706-1747+). Sister of Mary, Luke, George, Elizabeth and Martin Ryerson and sister-in-law to John Reading. She married George Hall in 1735. Ryerson, *The Ryerse-Ryerson Family*, 22.

John Reading's Diary

February 1758

1   To cash Payed to John Yard for a Hatt.

2   To son Richard to pay his Account at John Opdykes.

4   To Cash paid to Wm Peirson for Smiths work.
    To cash with son Thos: to Brunswick to buy Fish.

7   Payed Dr Norton for a Lotion and some ointment and 3 doses of Physick.

8   To expenses when my wife went to Mr Beattys sent per Richard.

7   Frances Tomlinson gave a Receipt for the money.

14 Payed Joseph Higby for sending Lord Loudon's[136] letter per Express.

18 Payed Jos Binder for his wife's Kniting of Mittins.
    Received from Peter Dirdorf in part of a Bond.
    Received from Peter Wert for acknowledgment of a Deed.

17 Payed Benj: Stout for work don at the old Roof.

28 Gave son Thomas to buy Calf Skins one for self and Two for Daniel. Danl had one of the calf Skins @ ___.

27 Debtor to Charles Hoff for 3 -0- of Iron.

March 1758

1   Payed to Moor Furman for the Gazette.
    Payed to Nathl Parker for carrying me to Bristol and Diner etc.
    Signed a Certificate for a Vessels Property Record.

11 Lent James Hanah 15d and 10d for grinding of two Raisors.

18 Payed Mrs DeCow[137] for a Weeks Board.

23 To Lycencing Two Attorneys at Law vizt: Ebn Bryant and Pr Selvester.

---

[136] LOUDOUN, JOHN CAMPBELL, 4TH EARL OF (1705-1782). A British nobleman and Major-General. In 1756 Loudoun was sent to North America as Commander-in-Chief and Governor General of Virginia. As Commander-in-Chief, he planned an expedition to seize Louisbourg from the French in 1757. While Loudoun was thus engaged in Canada, French forces captured Fort William Henry from the British, and Loudoun was replaced by James Abercrombie and returned to London. Fowler, *Empires at War*, xiv, 97.

[137] HANNAH DECOW (d. 1780). Widow of Isaac Decow Jr. DeCou, *Decow Family*, Chart J, 173.

28   To the Great Seal of Proof of 2 _____ Bonds.

14   In my absence Wm Pierson to a Barrel of Cyder.

      To Cash to Richard when he went to Freehold.

18   To Dr George Viselius 5 ct of Hay.

26   To John Wright Clark for Schooling.

      To cash lent Son Richard.

18   Lent James Hannah when at Burlington as above.

April 1758

11   To the Proof of a Power of Attorney under the Great Seal.

17   To Doctor Dehart for Purging Rlls[?] to be sent by The Rec
      _____officers.

19   Payed to Mrs Hannah DeCow for Dyet, Washing and Lodging.

      Payed Mr John Shaw for several Dinners and Clubs.

      Payed to the Barber Jno Hancock.

      Received from the Treasurer a quarter's Salary to the 21 of Feb.

      Payed Wm Yard for accomodations at Sundry times.

20   Payed Mr Abm Hulings for Lignum Vita and sitck liquorish.

      To Expenses at Pennytown.

21   In my absence To daughter Molley for New York expended.

24   Payed Nanny Woods in full for Spinning.

      Payed Obadiah Howell in part of Pay for Building Richds House.

      Received from Adam Snoke in part of the consid: For a Tract of
      Land.

14   To Dr. Viscelius 4 -0- 1:2 3 lb of hay.

24   Edwd Berry had 2 bls of Wheat.

      Payed James Stout the Remainder of the Subscription For the
      Parsonage for self; son John; for Son Richd.

25   To son Daniel in cash.

      To son Richard in cash.

27   To Coenradt Cotts for a horse and chair per agreement.

      To Nathl Parker for a Chair and Expenses to Bristol.

      Payed to Henry Landes for Sadlars Ware.

May 1758

6   To cash to Son Thomas on expences on a Journey to Bergen County and to New York.

10   To Expenses to and from Trenton.

To cash for a Writ of Error Received.

16   To a Great Seal to a Will and Proof thereof being George Douglass's.

20   To Mrs DeCow in full for accommodations.

To the Two Daughters 5d each.

To the Negro Woman.

To the Barber.

21   To Mr Tho: Marriot for a Chair and Horse.

22   To Expences at Will: Yards in full.

To Moor Furman for Postage of Letters.

To Saml Pearl for Assistance.

In my absence Richard has had Cash of Two Sundry Times vizt to part of pay for a wagon and to Fran: Tomlinson.

24   Received from John Wood for a Barrel of Cider had last year.

Payed to Jacob Mattison for part of the Minister Sallary and for my part of fencing the Meeting House and Grave Yard.

Set off with 26 Cattle for the upper part of the Country. Went as far as Mr Hackets that night.

26   Returned this day in the afternoon from the Upper Part of the Country.

Lay'd out expenses about _____.

30   Sent Dennis Woolverton per Richard for carting of Boards.

Payed Obodiah Howell £9:0 in full for Richards Mason work about his house.

31   Payed Thomas Lowrey in full of his account.

Account of some affairs transacted in my absence from home.

4   To cash paid by Maths Brandt for 2 bls of wheat

5   To Joseph Hankinson Credit by cash supposed to a Deed Matthias Brandt [?] Debtor to one bus of Wheat.

12   Martin Shifley Debtor to three busl of Wheat.

20   To Cash paid to John Helts in part for ditching.

Payed to Wm Norcross for the one half of Subscription For Mr Tenant's Sermons.

John Reading's Diary

June 1758

3   Johs Binder weaved 30 Ells of Linen.
    Accompted with Johs Binder Credit on his side for weaving
    comes to £5:8 and debit for grains had at Sundry times, comes to
    4:1:6 the Balance due to the said Binder is £1:6:6 on Allowance to
    the price of Wheat is to be made according to the Price I shall
    make with son Geo: for the wheat sold him.
    Payed him in cash 23/4 /3 lb of butter formerly had 2/3.
6   Gave to Daughter Sarah in cash to buy Sundrys wan___
13 Pr Prall Paid back money heretofore advanced.
17 Received from Jasper Carman for a Deed part of surveying and
    other trouble.
19 Sent down to the Landing to buy Sundries.
22 Coll Van Campen paid for 7 Military Comissions.
    Martin Shifly paid towards the above Wheat.
27 Payed to Philip Painter in Cash.
28 Martin Shifly paid in Cash for Wheat.
30 Gave to a Charitable Use.

July 1758

4   Son Joseph borrowed Cash.
10 Son Richard had to pay for a Bever Hatt at the Landing.
    Payed to Philip Binder in cash 32s in all for Mowing Grass.
13 Payed Willm Fleming to a former Account in Law.
21 Payed Joseph Corwine for 5 days Harvist work a piece for Self
    and ____.
    Payed John Corwine for 5 days harvist work.
22 Payed to Wm Force in Cash.
24 Gave to Daughter Molly when went to Mr Beatty's in cash.
28 Payed for a Boxe of Pills from Eliz: Town by Mr Hampton.
29 To Expences on a Journey to Burlington and home again.
31 To 2 busll of Wheat to Mr Sheply.
21 Hugh Hunter's wages in Harvest Came to [an amount].
    Hugh Hunter when he had the Small Pox debtor 5 ½ of Butter
    @ 2d per lb. 11 ½ of Gammon Bacon @ __d per lb.

135

Payed to Mr. Hampton for the use of Dr Barnets for a Box of Pills.

28   Received from the Treasurer a Quarters Salary to the 21st of May.
Received form Nathl Pettit by his son Nathl being part of a Bond.

Debtor to Mart: Shipley for Harvist Work by himself and Boy.

August 1758

4   Hugh Hunter Received part of his Harvist wages.

6   Daughter Molly returned of the money I gave her.

8   Received form Richd Porter part of a Bond and due upon another.

9   Gave to Mr John Hacket part of his _____ set out for __
        1 doz of Chairs
        To a Dressing Table and a Chest of Drawers
        To 2 Looking Glasses; a bigger and a lessr
        To a piece of diaper [cloth]
    Payed to John Helt the Ditcher the Balance of Accounts for ditching.

10   To son Thomas in Cash when he went to Mr Montgomeries.

17   Lent to Philip Binder in Cash by Bill.

18   Payed Charles Hoff for 3 -0- and 1/4 almost of iron for Richard.
Payed Mr Jno Hacket for one Sugar Loof.
Philip Binder paid part of the above Bill.

22   Son Thomas returned back of the money I gave him when abroad.

23   Payed Henry Bemmer in cash 6:6: and part by some grass.
Settled with son Geo: to the 9th of this month and then paid him and remains a balance due to me.

September 1758

1   Gave to a Charitable Use.

2   Gave to a Charitable Use.

4   Paid to George Shank for the use of Ml _____ m grass in Cash.

5   Paid for another Box of Pills from Eliz: town per Bro: Ryerson.
7   Reconed with Nany Woods and paid her the Balance
     Paid Son Danl for Taning and Currying 5 Hides of neals [?]
     Lether and one Calfskin.
     Paid Son Daniel also on Stephen Chandlers account.
     Received also from son Danl on Robt Calcots Account.
     Son Daniel also paid for Money borrowed to pay Daughter
     Elizabeth on Sarah Mack Hullens[Mullens] Account.
9   Will: Force worked almost a day at the Cider Press and Mill.
11   Payed to Hugh Hunter in Cash.
15   Paid to Dl Bray (by son Georges Carter) for 2200 of Shingles.
16   Payed to Lewis Chamberlain's son for Haling 1600 shingles.
18   Payed to Henry Landis the Balance of our Account.
     Payed to Joseph Reed for a gall of wine called Port.
19   Sent to Trenton by Jno Wood to buy Boards 200 foot and
     Haling.
20   Received from John Hawkins 6 Barrels.
22   Bought a big basket.
25   Benj: Johnson paid for a Deed.
26   Bought a gall of Wine.
12   Philip Binder paid more of the Before mentioned Bill.
     Lent to son Richd by his Mother.

October 1758

1   Payed Adrian Hagerman for Smiths work.
     Paid to James Willson for Medicines against the Flux.
4   Henry Stole paid for a Deed from his Bro: John for 87 Acres.
9   Gave D[octe]r Kennedy for a visit.
     Aaron Starke paid the last years rent for the Calf pasture.
12   Payed the widow Smith on Mr Haits Account (being his money).
13   Bought ½ Gall Lisbon Wine.
     Johs Binder wove 34 yards of Woolen Cloath.
18   Daniel Reading per Hugh Hunter borrowed 30 s.
10   Debtor to Hugh Hunter for going to Mr Beattys.
19   Payed Gershom Lee the Balance of Accounts being [an amount].

20   Benj: Stout with Daniel, V: Boskirk and Gershom Lee 20 Days work @ __ per day. Came to £4 being for Work at the Roof. Paid him.

Bought ½ Gall Lisbon Wine. Let Dr Viscilius have a quart thereof. Sometime this forepart of this Month had Beef of Son Daniel.

23   Payed Tho: Williams for 12 days work 10 of them in the Swamp.

26   Payed John Rous Jr for Combing Worsted.

Bought from Wm Norcross 104 lb of Beef.

27   Payed Dr Viselius for Several Drugs bought at Phila.

28   Payed half on Years support to the ministry for Mr. Hait.

30   Bought half a Gall of Wine.

31   Gave to Amos Swazy for fetching the widow Vansicklen.

November 1758

2   Bought half a Gall of Wine for Patty's[138] funeral who departed this life near day the night before.

7   Expenses when I went home with Daughter Beatty.

8   Payed to Nanny Woods for Nursing the Sick.

Payed Blk Tom for dressing Skins and for a Small Sheepskin.

Payed the Provincial Taxe on the 7th day per son Tho.

9   Payed to Jos Binder for weaving and Balance upon all Accounts.

13   Hugh Hunter had in cash.

Payed to Jacob Verity for altering a Chimney.

15   Received from John Stiers, a Fatt Hog wt 154 lb in part of a Bill.

16   Son Daniel had 74 lb of Pork.

18   Payed Mr Charles Hoff upon the fullers account due this day.

Payed to Son Daniel to pay for beef to Wm Norcross.

25   Payed John Jewel for Speying of Sows.

28   Received from John Meleck and Frederick Meleck for two Deeds.

30   Received from Harmon Kline for a Deed and Acknowledgment.

---

[138] MARTHA BEATTY, age 4, daughter of Ann Reading and Charles Beatty. Patty was commonly used as a nickname for Martha. Greenwood, *The Researcher's Guide to American Genealogy*, 42 and Beatty, *Family of Charles Beatty*, 67.

John Reading's Diary

December 1758

1   Payed for a Gallon of Wine.

2   Payed Dr Viselius his account in Cash and Credit per my Account.

6   Received from Nathl Pettit by Cash and on Horse in full of a Bond.

11 Settled with Hugh Hunter to shoemaking etc. Two years board; due to us. Received from Mr John Lawrence on an old Debt of his Fathers.

12 Tho: returned from a Journey to Freehold. Expended on the same.

15 Received for a Warrant to make distress for Rent from Peter Hoff.
    Received from Tunis Cole upon Edwd Harrington's account part for a Deed. Gave to a Charitable Use.

16 Payed Francis Tomlinson the remainder for Building Richards house and some alterations and additions therto being the full and 2d over. He promising to finish what is left undon when called upon.

21 Received from Aaron Van Campen for a Deed of Mortgage.

23 Payed Tho: Atkinson the full of Accounts to this day.

29 Payed settlement for some days work after Harvist and in the Fall.

1759

January 1759

2   Received from son George for the Recording of a Deed.

8th Received from the Widow Cock by her son Ashford by for Recording an Agreement.

12   Paid Will: McCartee in full for Taylor work.

17   Sent to Adam Keiner for diging Patty's grave by son George.

Sent at the same time for the relief of the said Keiner and Jno Edmonds.

20   Payed Aaron Hankinson for dressing of a Deerskin.

26   Payed Mart: Ryerson the half of sw_____ Acknowledgment.
      Payed him also for his son Geo: Journey to Morris County and expenses.
      Payed to Mr Beatty for the Pena Magazines.

30   Joseph Smith wove 23 ½ yards of Linen Woolens.
      Money when son Tho: went to Crosswix about ___.

27   Lent Wm Force per Bill – paid.

February 1759

3   Payed Benj: Stout the remainder for his work last Fall.
      Payed Sam Stout for the making of a Wood Slead.

5   Dr G. Viselius Debtor to 500 -0- of Hay and haling.

16   Received from Will: Kase for Writings.

21   Subscribed towards building a Bridge over the S Branch at John Grandines 2d half to be paid at the raising the other half at the finishing.

22   Received from Mr Charles Read by the hand of Will: Brown sent from _____ £100.

23   Payed Wm McCartee for making a pair of Breaches for son Thos.

26   Son Tho: had for to pay for a pair of Bend Leather Soals.

28   Gave son Richard to buy a Barrel of Mackral, 1/4 for Joseph.

27   Received from Jonathan Hull for a Deed.
      Will: Kase paid the Remainder of the Account per binding of a Bible.

28   Payed Joseph Howell for a Falling axe.

March 1759

3d   Payed to Negro Pompey for 3 days Swingling of Flax.
      Lent Bro: Martin Ryerson (sent by his son George) in Cash.

9th   Paid Philip Dilts on Mr Beattys account for an horse.

10   Martin Shifly had a bl of Indian Corn.

Gave my wife for Daughter Molly a fifteen shilling Bill.

14   Gave son Richard to pay Joel Woolverton for 15 lb of Flax.

13   Son Thomas returned. Expences in his journey about _____.

15   Payed the Widdow Kase for 12 lb of Tow and 6 at 3/6.

Payed to Jacob Mattison the full for the Parsonage 20s and towards sinking a well.

17   Paul Coul paid for writings as one of the Devisees of Pp Kases Will.

19   Wm Force paid the sum borrowed Jany the 7 th.

22   Gave to Daughter Sarah Reid for to buy a dressing table etc.

23   Received from Aaron Starke for Rent for the Calf Pasture.

Received from Mr Read per Mn Ryerson upon a Warrant per order of Assembly.

31   Gave to a Charitable Use.

Some time this month Payed Peter Rivenberg for a day's work.

April 1759

2d   Lent John Helts per Note.

3   Dr Viscelius had 3 -0- of Hay.

5   Joh: Binder had 1 ½ bu of Wheat.

9   Received from Philip Dilts for writings some of the Devisees of Pp Kases Will.

11   Payed Will Shelby for half of the weaving 23 ½ yds of Linen and woolen.

12   Received from John Anderson in full of Accounts

13   Johs Binder wove 70 Ells of Linen Cloath.

Payed to Johs Binder for weaving.

Payed Wm Peirson the Balance of Accounts for Smith work.

14   Payed Wm Norcross a Subscription for the East Meeting House.

17   Payed for Flax to son Richard being 10 lb.

Henry Farnsworth paid for the acknowledgment of a Deed.

18   Bought 13 Shad.

21   Gave Son Thomas to Expend for Cloathes at Phila.

To Pocket Money for expenses on his Journey.

To a Charitable Use.

24   Edward Hunt paid 3 lb part of Rent. Gave bond for £20: the Balance between –
       Received from Mr Beatty the money paid for an horse.

25   Lent son Daniel in Cash.

26   Lent Joseph Smith in Cash per note Lt Money.
       Payed to Amos Swazey for 3 pails.

27   Son Tho: Returned home and returned of the Money given him.

T.R.   Supposed to be the time of his preparat for marriage.
       Supposed son Tho: was marryed about this time.

May 1759

1   William Force had four Buslls of Wheat from Son Georges Mill.

2   Lent son Joseph 40s besides £6 I gave him for part of pay for a Horse which together with 30s formerly lent him.
       Gave son Richard for Smithwork for the wagon £4:6 and for tools for the Wall.
       To pay son George on Saml Kirkbrides Account for making the wagon.

4   Payed to Mrs Beatty for weaving of a Coverlid.

5   Payed Nany Woods in full for Spinning.
       Payed Pompy for 5 days work.

8   Reconed with Saml Fleming he paid me the Balance of Account being 3:18:9.
       Recompted with Tho: Lowry and Payed him towards the Balance there being 31s behind which was left towards pay for _____.
       Bro: Ryerson repaid the money borrowed in March last.

11   Payed Thomas Marshall for a quarter of Veal.

12   Received from Michl Demot for a Deed and ½ of two Acknowledgments.

14   Martin Shifly had 4 Busls of Rye.
       Isaac Demot upon Adam Shukes account paid off a bill for which with £17:2:6 formerly paid and cash paid last week £39:15.
       Compleats Adam Shukes consedt[consideration?] for the land bought at Muskonetcong.
       Lent Mr Beatty towards pay for a Cow bought from Abm Smith.

15   Martin Ryerson paid to the Surveyor Generals office for a Return.
16   Upon an Examination at Trenton.
17   Continued at Trenton 'till near night. Cost at the Widdow Yards.
      Bought 1/4 of a hundred lemons.
      Job Robins paid for Acknowledgement of a Deed.
      Son Thomas in Carrying out the flower Expenses and for goods
      bought.
16   Sent Young Cattle into the woods at Ed: Hunts. Nt 23.
18   Expenses and Som Lemons bought at Trenton.
21   Son Thomas went to AllenTown. Sent money by him for
      Expenses in his intended marriage.
      My self went into the Upper Parts of the Country on Surveying.
      Expenses.
22   Johs Binder had 1 ½ bls of Rye (supposed to be son Thos
      Wedding Day).
24   Payed the Ministers half year Sallary to Jacob Mattison.
25   Martin Shiply paid towards the Rye formerly had.
      Son Jos: paid money borrowed to pay for the Horse.
26   Son Thomas Returned of the money gave as above.
      Gave son Richd to buy Oil and Paint.
31   Payed Gershom Lee for 3 quarters of Veal.
      Some time this month son George Payed for the Gazet to Moor
      Furman.
22d   Johs Binder wove 70 Ells of Linen.

June 1759

1   Martin Shifly paid for the Rye formerly had.
4   Adam Poke gave me for Services on Account of the Title to his
      Land.
      Received from Wm Force due upon Bond and Interest.
      Received in part of Perquisites from Mr Read by John Arrison.
6   Gave to son John in Cash.
      And set out on a Journey to the Upper parts of the Country.
      Expenses.
11   Payed for 3 quarters of Mutton.

12   Son Daniel paid back some Cash borrowed.
      Payed for repairations of the Parsonage.
13   Payed for 1600 of Shingles.
      For Expenses and fish.
14   Joseph Smith had 2 Buslls of Rye. Paid for on[e] Busll.
      George Biggs paid for a Deed and Will.
18   Jos Binder wove 53 Ells of towe Cloath.
      Jos Binder had 1 ½ Bls of Rye. 1 Bus Indian Corn.
21   Bought a Cheese from Jon: Hills wife.
27   Payed Mr Beatty for a pair of black stockings/two small books.
      Mr Beatty paid 5s / borrowed and 1 sh for finding of Cloaths
      lost.
      Payed Gershom Lee on son Tho:s account in part for a horse.
      Payed G. Lee for ½ days work by his Bro: in making an Harrow.

July 1759

3   Johs Binder wove 33 Ells of Cloath.
      Johs Binder had 1 ½ of Rye at 3s/ per Busl.
11   Johs Binder wove 36 Ells of Cloath.
      Payed in Cash to Johs Binder.
13   Payed Tho: Lowry for 1/4 of lb of Indigo.
14   Received from Christ: Smith [?] for near two Pecks of Buck
      Wheat.
17   Payed for 1/4 lb of Rice.
21   Payed to James Cherry for Cradling wheat for almost 4 days.
      Payed Robt Shaw for said work and said number of Days.
      Payed to Jacob Bartholomew for Harvist work.
24   Payed to the Bennits for 1 days mowing Rakeing and binding.
      Received from son George in Cash from Mr Read the remainder
      his money.
29th Payed to George the Tinker for work.
      Payed to Henry Yager for 1 ½ days Cradling Wheat.
      Payed to Jos Binder for Harvist work and an abatement of 1s for
      rainy weather.

25   Then Settled Accounts with William Force from July 1755 to this present time and paid him the Balance upon all accounts. Accompted with Jos Binder and there remained a Balance (which was paid).

26   John Post Debtor to 1 bl of Indian Corn.

August 1759

3   Reconed with Son George to Augt the 9th of Last Year who Payed the Balance to me.

4   Payed Henry Beammer for 11 days mowing by grass.

6   Payed Nanny Woods for 4 days Rakeing in Wheat Harvist. Johs Binder had two Busls of Rye which was paid for in the above settlement.

7   Set out on a journey to Burlington. Absent from home four days. Expenses being paid by the Proprietors Clerk whilst at Burlington by myself on said journey.

10   Received from Mr James Kinsey[139] part of Mr Byerly's account.

16   Payed to Coenrdt Philipse and Wm Hunter for mowing of Grass.

17   Received from Abraham Emmans for writing his fathers Will.

22   Johs Binder had 1 ½ bl of Rye.

30   Gave Son Richard 3£ to pay Interest Money for his Negro.

23   Hugh Hunter Pitched Hay and Wheat.

September 1759

1   Lent son Thomas to pay the remainder for his Horse

11th   Payed Mr Jos: Stout the half of the above £25 Received from Mr Kinsey. Returned me for some services in the affairs over and above his part.

---

[139] JAMES KINSEY (1731-1803). Son of John K. Kinsey. James was born in Philadelphia and like his father, a lawyer. Resided in Burlington. Elected to the New Jersey assembly in 1772. Kinsey was elected in to the Continental Congress 1774, resigning in 1775. He continued his legal practice, and was appointed Chief Justice of the Supreme Court of New Jersey in 1789, serving until his death in 1803. http://08016.com/kinsey.html and http: //en.wikipedia.org/wiki/James_Kinsey (July 28, 2010).

15th   Paid to Wm Force for work done at son Daniels Kitchin.

21   Payed Pompy for work don.

22d   Received from son George on the Wheat Account for the year 1758.

       Debtor to Nanny Woods for 9 weeks Spinning.

29   To Expences on a Journey to Morris County etc.

       Sent by my wife to New York to make a doz of Silver Spoons.

14   Gave to son Richard to pay in part for a Negro for which he gave bond.

October 1759

1   Received from son George on the Wheat Account as above.
       Gave to son Geo: £4:5:6 to make up the above. Sum £14 New York currency and c[arrie]d over to pay for an Horse bought by V Campen.

2   Andrew Bray paid for Surveying and for a Deed.

5   Payed Pompy for 5 days work.

9   Son Thomas Returned from Trenton. Sold some wheat. Returned in Cash.

11   Payed son Danl for some Beef bought from one ___ Young.
       My wife came home from N York. Returned of the money sent.

9   John Post had 2 bls of Rye wanting 3 Quarts.

13   Payed to the Parsonage towards a Study and mending the ___.
       Gave to ___ a Captivated and Retaken Manner.
       Received from Henry Winter for Writing and other Trouble.
       Div of Pp Case.
       Payed to the Collector for the Township of Reading Prov Tax.

19   Daniel Lake paid an old Account for Surveying; for Acknowledgment.

22   Reconed with George the Tinker time being 4 ½ days which came to £2:15:6 deducting 20s for grass paid him the Balance.

24th   Son John paid 30s in part of £3/10 for a fat Cow.

25   Son Danl paid for 76 lb of Beef.

26   Received from John Anderson for 3 Sevl Dls[?] of his Land.
       Payed Michl Lamb for 6 ½ days work.

27   Received from Yacom Griggs for surveying Service.

       Sent to Mr Beatty by son Tho: Pay for a Riding Chair.

30th Cost in Ferriage for Horses and Chair.

       Payed the Town Collector for the Provincial Tax.

November 1759

1s   Received from the Shurts for writings don.

2   Payed John Miller the Mason in full for his work.

6   Wm Welch paid for a Deed and Acknowledging.

       Lawrence Hager paid for a Deed and Acknowledging.

       David Van Doren paid for a Deed and Acknowleding.

10   Payed for half of the acknowledgments of three Deeds.

11   Gave to a Charitable Use.

14   Payed one half years Support of the Ministry to Wm Norcross.

19   Sold to Jos: Reed 721 lb of Pork deducting 12d per head.

       Bought a stock Lock. Out of the above money gave son Tho: [an amount].

24   Payed Mr Hackett the Balance of our Account.

27   Received from Jos: Reed on a Mistake of 100 lb in the Hogs. [missing line].

December 1759

3d   Had from son George 8 skins of Parchment bought at New York.

4   Son Thomas paid the Sums borrowed at Sundry time.

7th   John and Joakim Griggs paid for two Releases.

       Peter Hoffman paid for a Deed Acknowledgment.

6   Paid to Wm Barnes for laying of two axes.

14   Payed to Henry Bemmer in full of Accounts for mowing.

       Received from Michl Moore for writing a Deed and Assignment.

15   Jos: Habbogh paid for a Deed and Acknowledgment.

       Adam Poke paid for a Deed and Acknowledgment.

20   Henry Bemmer Debtor to one Busl of Indian Corn.

22   John Kase paid for an agreement between him and John Foxe.
      Ordered Wm Hacket to give Credit to Robt Shaw's wife.
26   Payed Mr Beatty for some books bought at Phila.

1760

January 1760

14th   Martin Shifly Debtor to one Busl of Indian Corn.
17   Daughter Molly returned from Freehold. Expenses.
21   Payed Mr Hackett for goods ordered to Robt Shaws wife.
22   Son Thos returned from the Great Meadows. Expenses for the
       Company.
25   Gave to a Charitable Use.
30th   Payed Benj: Stout the remainer for work don last Fall.
       Payed Wm Case for Book binding.

February 1760

1   Payed to son Richard an account of his _____.
4   Reconed with Doctor Viselius. Payed him the Balance.
8   Gave to Daughter Molly in cash.
       Nanny Woods Debtor per Hugh Hunter account for mending
       shoes.
       Hugh Hunter brought in his account amounted to ___.
       For Balance at last settlement 2:5:5 to two years Board. The Diet
       Account for to May 1760.
9   Accompted with Tho: Atkinson and paid him in full.
11   Received from Matths Kase for writing an Agreement.
12   Payed John Grandine by Jno Imlay a subscription for a Bridge.
14   Payed George Shank the Tinker for mending etc.
23   Received from Jno Updike and Abm Laroe for a Deed and
       Surveying.

John Reading's Diary

March 1760

4th   Payed son Thomas for a pair of Breechs bought at Phila and for a Turkey.

7   Payed to Adam Aray[Bray?] the Post Rider by Tho: Lowry.

11   Payed Pompy for dressing of Flax and 4 days work.

12   Martin Shifly Debtor to 2 busls of Indian Corn.
Martin Shifly had 2 -0- of Hay.
Martin Shifly paid in cash towards the Corn and Hay.

13   Sold a Negro wench Dinah to Benj: Low for 55 lb L. Money.
Gave his bond for 55:0:0.

15   Payed Tho. Atkinson for 4 lb of Resins.

18   Sold to Wm Disher 4 hundred of Hay.

20   Payed to George the Tinker for mending Pewter.

24   Payed by Hugh Hunter to Wm McCartee for makeing a suit of Cloaths.

28   Payed the Physician Mr McKane for Innoculating of Daughter Molly.

29   Payed or sent to Mr Huff for Expenses at the Innoculation.

April 1760

1   Received from Aaron Starke for the Rent of the Calf Pasture for 1759. Had a quarter of Veal from M. Shifly.

2   Payed Molly Emley for nursing at the Innoculation 9/. To a boy 1/3.
Received from Executors of Corns Weycoff Jun and from Corns Weycoff Senior for Surveying and Writings etc. the sum of _____.

5   Abraham Bonnell paid for 7 lb of sugar bought at son G[eorge]s
Bought a quarter of Veal from Mr Shifley.
Payed to son John for 100 feet of Boards bought at Kings Sawmill.

8   Wm Douglass paid upon exchange of Cattle formerly made.

14   Martin Shifly had 200 of Hay.
Received from George Morden for one years Rent for the Uper place at Menusigay.

15   Gave Son Daniel towards pay for the building of his Barn.

16   Gave Daughter Polly to pay for the Instruction in Singing by Mr
      Milly.
17   Sons Joseph and Richard had a load of Hay apiece. Richard a
      barrel. Gave to son Richard to pay the Painter and more Cash.
21   Gave to a charitable use to a German.
      Martin Shifly had 2 bl of Oats sometime last week.
22   Sold to Antho: Louzier 10 bll of Barley.
      Martin Shifly had 2 bl of oats.
21   Jos. Binder had one Busll of Indian Corn.
23   John Lake by Ab: Zutphen paid for a Deed and Mortgage.
25   Wm Rea paid for a Deed.
23   Adam Poke paid for 6 bls of Oats
26   Jerome Emmans paid for 5 bls of oats
      Payed to Lottis Newbank for Spining
28   Gave to son John Reading to pay in part for a Negro for which
      he gave Bond.
      Antho who I sent over to Delaware came home and brought 6
      shad.
29   John Post Debtor to one bll of Indian Corn.
30   Received from Francis Woolveton for a Deed and Bond.
      Received from Edward Hunt the remainder of 20 £ Bond.
      This month Jos Binder wove 3 Ells of Linnen and Woolen.

                              May 1760

1   Received from Frederick Bodine for a Deed.
      Gave to Daughter Molly to buy her a gown.
      Gave her to bear her expenses on a Journey to her sisters and
      Phila.
3   Peter Dirdorf paid for a Deed.
      Christ: Coul paid for a Deed.
6   Tho: W_____ paid for a Deed.
7   Thomas _____ for an Heifer and a Calf.
      Peter Bellows paid for a Deed and Surveying in 1738 in Am[well].
8   Tho: Lowry Debtor to 19 bls of Rye.
9   Sold to a butcher 6 Sheep.

Sold to Tho: Jones 2 bls Rye.

10   Payed to Moor Furman for the Gazette.

Payed to Dr Norton for Physick and a visit.

12   Ephraim Oliphant paid for a Deed to Peter Nevius.

Gershom Lee paid for 3 -0- ½ of Hay.

13   Joakim Griggs paid for a Deed from Christian Bergh.

Daughter Molly paid off the money given her when she went into Pennsylvania.

14   Sold a Lamb to the Butcher.

15   Received from Josiah Clauson the Balance of a Bond __.

Returned him 18s out of £7 Bill overpaid him.

17   Payed Benj: Stout for Carpentary work about the Barn.

19   Martin Shifly had 6 Blls of Rye.

20   Bought a quarter of Veal from Saml Harman.

21   Received from Benj: Smith for a Deed and D[raf]t of the Land

22   Johs Binder wove 61 Ells of Linnen and Woollen.

23   Payed to Js Binder in part for weaving

26   Sold to Casper Shavers son a Barrel of Cider.

22   Jos Binder had 1 ½ bul of Rye.

26   Jos Binder Debtor to 2 bls of Rye

28   Payed Augn Reid for a Bottle of Balsam Mirablis Sent from Freehold.

30   Gave to Daughter Sarah Reid for Sundry uses.

31   Paid unto son George upon Nanny Woods account for Oil.

June 1760

3   Johanus Binder Debtor to a Busl of Corn 6 lb of Wool.

4   The Widdow Sarah Van Sicklen had a 7/6 piece which when she receives the money from David Cock she is to repay.

Payed to Wm Norcross the half of the Minister yearly Salary.

9   Jno Hawkins paid the Balance of his Account on Account of 2 Deeds and Share of Surveying.

11   Reconed with Benj: Stout for the Barrack; for the Chair house and on adition of 6s which was not Received in the former account ___.

Paid Benj: Stout of the above Account.

12 Paid George the Tinker for mending the Tea Ketle etc.

Paid Rachel _____ for helping to clean the house.

23 Gave to son Richard towards the Pay for his Barn.

Joseph Smith wove 22 yards of towe Linen.

Payed Justice Ryerson for 5 Acknowledgments being one half.

25th Payed son George for 8 Skins of Parchment; 2 pairs of Corse thread Stockins and ½ an ounce of Wafers.

26 Payed to James Wills upon Benj: Stouts Account.

Jos Binder some time this month had from Georges Mill 1½ of Rye.

July 1760

2 Bought and Payed for 25 lb of Cheese.

4 Benj: Stout paid the above. 1/9 over paid.

8 Jos Binder wove 93 Ells of Linen.

Bought a pair of Linnen Stockins.

17 Received from Christ: Koul for a Deed to Richd Roberts.

22 Jos Binder had one Busl of Indian Corn.

Jos Binder had one pound of Corse Wool.

26 Accompted with Nanny Woods for Harvist work Spinning etc.

29 John Ringo[140] paid for a Deed from his Brother Cornelius.

Cornelius Ringo paid for a Deed from James Baird.

August 1760

2d Daughter Molly Returned from Princetown. Expenses. Having lost her Horse out of the Pasture sent H. Hunter after him. Returned on the third day with him. Expenses and time Lent by him to be board (18 vos of the Univ: History).

4 Payed Wm Pierson for Smiths work for my share.

Payed Mart: Ryerson for 2 Acknowledgments.

---

[140] JOHN RINGO (1736-79). Son of Philip. Married Martha Henson in 1757. Lived in Ringoes, New Jersey. Ringo, "What Ever Happened to the Ringoes?"

5   Went from home upon a Journey to Burlington and Retured the
      __.
8   Expenses out and in etc.
      Payed for the Recording Benj: Stouts Deed.
5   Payed to Henry Landis for mending and New Seating my Sadle
      etc.
12   Payed Tho: Atkinson for a quarter of Veal.
16   Payed Johans Binder in part for Weaving.
23   Expended for 2 pair of Worst stockings. The on[e] thread the
      other Cotton.
27   Edward Hunt paid off a £15 Bond and almost 4 month Interest
      thereon wanting near _____.
29th Payed Joseph Reeder for a New Wagon.
30   Derrick Atten paid by John Pellinger for a Deed.

September 1760

1   Jos: Hegeman paid for a Deed and Acknowledgement.
2   John Barber paid for a Deed and Acknowledgement.
4   Received from Mr Theo: Van Weyk for sale of 11 Casks of
      Flower
10   Received from Peter Shultus for a Deed.
16   Returned from a Journey from Mr Beatys. Expenses on Said
      Journey.
      Payed to Joseph Howell for an axe and mending the riding Chair.
      Left money with Daughter Beatty to buy an Handkerchief for her
      Mother.
20   Payed Katy Wood for Spining of Flax etc.
25   John Barber paid for a Paper Deed from his sister Mary.
      Payed to Richd Crock the fuller for Dying and Dressing Cloath.

October 1760

4   Having been on a Journey to Freehold this day returned home.
      Expenses.

23   Returned from the Jury on view on the lines of the Society's Purchase. Exps about ____.

26   Gave to a Charitable Use. Vizt: for Provision made by Mr. Bernard[141] for the Civilized Ind[ian]s.[142]

29   Payed to the Collector the Provincial and Poor Tax.
Received for 3 Cattle sold to a Butcher of Phila.
Gave to Dl Howell for the use of his son Reading Howell.[143]
Sold to Son Tho: a young heifer.

November 1760

3   Payed to Nanny Woods the Balance of All Accounts to this day.
Received from Wm Kase and Christ: Stranzfell for three Bonds.
Received from Peter Aller for Writings and other Service on the Estate of J.P. Kase.[144]

4   Sett off in a Journey to Burlington Supream Court
Expenses there at ____.

8   Returned home in Safety.
Johs Binder Received in my absence per my wife for weaving.
Antho: in fetching home some Cattle spent ____.

10   Let to Johnstone Imlay upon hire for 2 or 3 years 6 sheep vizt: one White Whether 3 ditto ewes 2 blk Ewes for one pound of

---

[141] FRANCIS BERNARD (1712-79). A British colonial administrator who served as Governor in New Jersey and Massachusetts. He was first educated at St. Peter's College and then spent seven years at Oxford, where Christ Church granted him a master of arts in 1736. He was appointed governor of New Jersey January 27, 1758, and arrived at Perth Amboy on 14 June. His service as Royal Governor of New Jersey ended on July 4, 1760. Whitehead, *Colonial History of New Jersey*, Vol. VIII, 381.

[142] Refers to Brotherton near present day Indian Mills, the first and only Indian reservation established in New Jersey. George D. Flemming, *Brotherton, New Jersey's First and Only Indian Reservation* (Medford, New Jersey: Plexus Publishing, Inc., 2005), 43.

[143] READING HOWELL (1743-1827). Son of Daniel Howell. Leach, *Memorials*, 165.

[144] JOHANN PHILIP (J.P.) KASE (ca.1680-1756). Born in Anhausen, Germany. He married Anna Elizabeth Jung on 29 November 1703 in Anhausen. He was naturalized in New Jersey on 8 July 1730. A 1738 deed transferred land in Flemington, New Jersey, from William Penn's sons Thomas, John and Richard to John Philip Kase (soon Anglicized to Case). Buried near Chief Tuccamirgan in Flemington. Elias Vossetter, "Reminiscences of the Kase Family", 1907, (rpt *Case-ette* No. 2 Summer, 1965), 7.

good wooll for Each sheep per annum when Returned to be as good in quality Age and Kind.

15   Paid for 3 Seats in the Meeting House, half years salary, and one shilling per seat for firewood.

18   Received from John Kase for a Deed and Acknowledgment.
      Sold to son Daniel a fatt Cow and Stier.
      Sold to son Joseph a fatt Cow to be paid in the Spring.

20   John Opdyke paid for a Deed to himself and Benj: Severns.

22   Let Danl have thirty pounds part of 50£ towards pay for a Negro.

27th Lent to John Wood in Cash (to be paid in a fortnight).

18   Sold to several of my sons some Cattle amounting to in the whole 40:0:0 for which Bonds or Bills are to be given and I am to be paid the yearly Interest till Paid.

December 1760

13th John Williamson and Peter Rockefeller each paid for a Deed.
      John Wood Payed back the money borrowed.

23rd Received from Wm Bergh for agreement and Bond of Performance.

1761

January 1761

6   Abraham Emmans paid for some Writings.

9   Payed Widdow Hegeman for the weaving of a Coverled.

13   Bought a pair of Stockings from son Richard.

22   Received for Writings, Vizt: a Deed and 2 Bonds in the Doctor Vescelius affair.
      Payed to Doctor Viscelius his Account for last Year.

29   Payed to a Book Binder at Nassau Colledge for binding the Universal Histy 20 vol.[145]

February 1761

_____ Johs Binder on all Account Balance in his favour.

_____ Shills Ten pence which I paid.

_____ by Exam the Accounts I find one article in Aug to cash paid by my wife £1:10 Proc charged in my Account with him but 17:16 light money so that I have over paid him 17:6d.

17   Payed Wm Van Fleet for mending the Chair Wheels new spokes and felows.

Payed to the Smith for putting on the Tier and making some new Nails.

March 1761

3d   Son George paid for a Deed from Alexr Rogers to himself.

6th   Richard Porter paid off his Bond as supposed Principal and Interest being Rec[eived].

9   Payed the Balance of Tho: Lowrys Account (his whole Account better than ____).

6   Received from son George for a Deed from Alexr Rogers to Mr Ryerson etc.

11   Sold a Bull to a man from Derliy in Pennsylvania.

9   Left with Thos Lowry for Joseph Redman the Post Rider.

19   Reconed with Tunis Hendrickse and Accounts were Balanced.

23   Paul Hardung and Michl Cole paid for a Deed and Surveying.

Received from Christ: Harshal and Pr Yager for 2 Deeds and Surveying.

Payed to Mr Mills[146] for a Supply (to the Elders).

---

[145] *An Universal History, From The Earliest Account Of Time*, 65 volumes published in London between 1747 and 1768.

[146] WILLIAM MILLS (1739-1774). Reverend William Mills was graduated at Princeton, 1756, studied theology, was licensed to preach by the Presbytery of New Brunswick, March 1760, and in 1762 became pastor of the Presbyterian Church at Jamaica, Long

John Reading's Diary

Received from Jacob Zutphen for a Deed.
Subscribed to the discharge of a Deficiency on the payment for
the Study at Mr Haits being disbarsd by Jacob Zutphen.

28   Payed for a ferril to my Cane.
     Received from Henry Peckel for 2 Deeds.

April 1761

11   Cornelius Weycoff paid for a Deed from him to Thos Atkinson.
17   Payed for 6 skins of Parchment.
18   Payed a Subscription to a Bridge over MiddleBrook.
25th Gave to a Charitable Use a french Pistole who had his house and
     goods burned.
     Gave to son Jos: towards building of his Barn.
     Received from Bartholomow Thatcher for a Deed.
29   Received from Jere: King and Saml McPherson for 2 Deeds.
30   Received from Barthw Thatcher for his 2nd Deed.
     Lent to son George per Bill.
     Lent to Martin Ryerson the sum of per Bill.

May 1761

5   Set out on a Journey to Burlington. Cost and Expenses besides
     those at the [council].
9   Attendance at Council. Returned the ninth.
     To Dr Norton for Physick.
     To the Council Board for a Treat at the Elections of their
     Members.
18   Received form Edward Hunt for one Years Rent.
     Received from George Moeden by the hands of Edward Hunt
     one Years Rent.
21   Received from Francis Stewart by Wm Colluel for a Deed.
25   Received from Henry Mershon for a Deed and Mortgage.
26   Sold to Mrs Beatty 14 Sheep and a Lamb.

Island. He received an honorary degree of Master of Arts from Yale in 1771. He married
John Reading's daughter Mary *ca.* 1760. Leach, *Memorials,* 52.

28   Received from Wm Bergh for a Deed.

          Received for an agreement inter Pr Foxe and Michl Moyer.

30   Received from Wm Coats for a Deed, Mortgage and 3 Bonds.

          Received from Benj: Force for a Deed and Bond.

          Payed to Richd Crook the Fuller for Blanketing.

          Sometime this month Benj: Stout paid for the Recording of a Deed.

June 1761

2d   Martin Ryerson paid for Js: Van Estes Deed; for Wm Camback Ditto. To Ditto from Ditto to Derk Zutphen Deed.

          To charge on a Reference.

          Payed said Ryerson for 2 acknowledgments.

5th   Received from Adrian Hegeman for a Deed.

17   Received from Tho: Ruckman the Balance of an Account.

23   Received from Aaron Starke for the last Years Rent.

19   Received from John Lodor by his son Benj: for a Deed.

27   Had a quarter of Veal from Martin Shifly.

July 1761

1   John Anderson paid for a Deed.

          Lent son Daniel by son Thomas in Cash.

4   Payed son Richard for a Horse lately from him bought.

6   Payed for 2 Boxes of Lockyer Pills.

          Received from Gershom Lee for ½ of a Deed; a Mortgage one Bond.

10   Gave to a Charitable Use.

20   Johannis Binder paid back what I overpaid him per Account in February last.

21   Hugh Hunter brought in his account for work done since last summer; Settlement amounting to £11:10 which deduct from his former Balance there remains due from him the sum of __.

August 1761

8th   Expenses to Burlington on the Journey out and in the sum of
      ___.
      Received from Mr John Lawrence on Mr Jas Kinseys Account.
      Payed Mr Joseph Stout the half thereof.
      Mr Stout paid me for 6 acres of unlocated Land and Deed and
      Acknowledgment.
      Delivered to Mr John Ladd to be sent to Mr Edwd: Shippen for
      the use of Mr John Alford the sum of 65:15.
14   Paid to Mr Hackett for a piece of Linen.
19th Subscribed to pay for the Purchase of a Glebe[147] and Building an
      house of the Missionary of the Church of England to be paid in
      October next.
20   Payed to Wm Peirson for Smith work since last Settlement.
      Received from Henry Chamberlain for a Deed Bond and
      Acknowledgment.
28   Received from Corns Ringo for 2 Deeds to Lawrence Switzer
      from Jere: Trout.
29   Payed to Jane a Spinster for Spining of flax.

September 1761

2   Received from Jno Opdyke by son Thomas for 2 Deeds.
17   Gave to a Charitable Use.
18   Received from Lawrence Low for making a Will.
22   Received from Martin Ryerson fore two Awards.
26   Reconed with Joseph Smith fell in my Debt which I allowed as
      pay for son Tho:s Debt for weaving with money paid.
      Daughter Molly returned from N. York. Expended for Binding
      for Curtains, some necessaries for herself and Pocket Money.

October 1761

7   Received from Jno Pettinger and Jus Cole for a Deed and four
      Bonds.

---

[147] A plot of land belonging or yielding profit to an English parish church or an
ecclesiastical office.

16   Gave to a Charitable Use.
      Molly returned from Mrs Beattys. Expenses.

November 1761

3   Payed to Jacob Mattison for 3 seats; firewood 1s per seat.
6   Payed to Jos: Hollinshead for Cleaning the Clock.
18   Received from Mr Hait on Account of the Lottery (being part of
      the prize money).
      Payed to Mr Hait part of Daughter Molley's ticket being blank.
19   Gave to a Charitable Use.
24   Lent to John Wood to (be returned out of the money when he
      sells his Hogs).
30   Payed to son Daniel the Surveyor Generals Fees for a Return of a
      Resurvey of 3152 ½ Acres of the Great Meadow. Ditto for
      Survey of 109 Acres at Ditto 13/3.
      Payed to Ditto for ½ Oz of Sena.

December 1761

5   John Weycoff paid for a Deed.
9   Lend son Thomas for the Use of the Iron Works in Partnership.
12   Returned back of the above Cash £5.
14   Sent by Dk Zutphen to Luke Ryerson's Daughter Eliz a gold
      Ring and Bible; my gift 00:16:0.

1762

January 1762

[No entries]

February 1762

2d   Received form Ch: Hoff Esqr the sum of £2:6:4 being in full of a Debt of John Ayers against whom I obtained Judgment and Execution.
Received from Charles Stewart 10s for a Deed and _____over to be returned.

9   Lent son George by his Apprentice Abraham Williamson in Cash. About the last of this month Subscribed I think 7(6) to Re Erect Boundbrook Bridge.

March 1762

3   Son George Returned the money Borrowed.
15   John Wood Payed the money being formerly Borrowed.
20   Lent son George twelve pounds Proc.
26   Son George returned paid back part of the money borrowed.
Payed son George Fifty Shillings upon account of Mrs Beatty's share of the Mine.
Payed Ditto for Daughter Mollys share of the Mine.
Then reconed with son George and he paid the Balance in my favor.

April 1762

5   Received of Danl Van Boskirk for a Lease from Derrick Dumont.
12   Received from Nichs: Miskumb for a Deed and proof thereof.
13   Payed Mr Ryerson for half the proof.
Payed son George for Recording of Matth: Kases Deed.
Payed Ditto for Physick from Dr Norton (the old Physick being left behind).
Gave to a Charitable Use (to one who had his mill burn't at the Flat Kill).
Gave to another object of Charity.
14   Payed the Subscription towards the Purchas of a Glebe etc. to the Church.
16   Edward Hunt Payed his last years Rent.

George Morden Payed by Edwd Hunt his last years Rent.

10   Payed Tho: Lowry the Balance of our Accounts (the Money said Lowry is indebted).

29   Received from Peter Foxe for a Deed.

May 1762

1   Received from Jeremiah Lambert for a Deed.
     Received from Simon Wicoff for a Deed, for the half of two Acknowledgments.

3   Received from Son George on Account of a Bill of forty pounds.
     Gave to Mr Mills for an Outset for his wife the sum of £100 Proc.
     Gave to his Spouse our Daughter Mary for a Weding Suit etc.

8   Lent Coenrad Philipse by Bill. Payed back the said money at infra[?].

10   Philip Kuilinger paid for a Deed.

12   Received from Jos: Van Kirk and Elisha Barton for a Deed and other Writings.

15   Received from Henry Winter for Christn Manners Deed and his own.

17   Received from Martin Ryerson for 3 Deeds, for Dk Zutphen et al.

21   Coenrat Philipse Payed the money borrowed as above by Bill.

24th Received from Jno Cole; Corn: Low; Gast Alen and Henry Johnson for Deeds.

June 1762

1   Received from Saml Brugler for a Bond and Interest thereon for 7 Years.

16 or 17 Gave Richard the above money to be divided between him and his bro: Joseph.

23   Payed to Timothy Smith the Balance of Account for Services don at the Great Meadow.

25   Received from Aaron Starke for the last Years Rent.

28   Lent unto Enock McKinsey and Gershom Lee per Bill.

July 1762

5th   Reconed with Dr Viselius. Payed him the balance the whole being
      [an amount].
21   Payed Mr Beatty for 4 oz Elixer Proprils _ sold for 1/6 per oz.
      To Dr Malachy Treat for an opening Electuary.
23   Payed for the Weaving of 39 Ells of Tow Cloath.
24   Son George paid the rent of remainder of the £12 borrowed
      March the 26.
28   Enoch McKinsley paid part of the money borrowed as above.

August 1762

6   Son George Payed in Burlington in the Surveyor Generals Office.
      I paid him back again.
14   Payed for son Thomas to a Weaver.
25   Payed Mr Beatty for some Books formerly sent from England.
27   Payed Mr Hackett in part of Ditching of one side of Daughter
      Molleys Lott.
      Sometime this month son Daniel had by Ger: Lee part of 41£
      lent to En: Mackinely.

September 1762

Little else to be taken notice but same money received for
Writings.

October 1762

7th   Daughter Mary Mills had £1:17:6.
27   Payed ½ years sallary to the Minister for 3 seats and firewood.
28   Gave to a Charitable Use.

November 1762

18   Son Thomas Expended at Phila for a Coat Cloath, 2 pair of stockins and Alm[anac]k.

20   __ Hackett bought a Gown of Damask for Wife.
Received from Morris Creature for a Deed etc; Extra ordinary Services.
Payed on account at Mr Hackett for Tallow and Scraps.

23d   Gave to a Charitable Use.

December 1762

18   Payed to Corns Whitenack for Taylor work by a Deed and Cash.

20   Lent in cash to son George.

21   Debtor to Hugh Hunter since last Settlement on July 1761 for the making of 12 pairs of shoes. His last Balance 18/2 and cash paid. On the 6th of this month signed a Deed of Gift and Conveyance to Aug: Reid and Sarah his wife for the Calf Pasture Containing 500 Acres more or less to Hold to the said Aug: Reed and Sarah his wife their heirs and assigns for ever etc Against the said John Reading and his heairs etc. and aganist his further cites free from all Incumbencies Committed by him or them.

1763

January 1763

9th   Matths Brand paid off a Bond. I kept £6 gave son Tho: the remainder.

14   Bought two Busls of Buckwheat from Tho: Marshall.

26   Reconed with Son George and paid him the Balance of his Account. being _____ the said Account in Proc is Martin Ryerson in part silver, paper, small pa [Paper, Pennsyvania?] Bills.

(I have paid that part of his Uncle Ryersons Account charged for his first Services at the Meadows and got a receipt for which the Account and cash which he paid me makes up and compleats which I lent him last month.)

February 1763

12th	Gave to Mrs Beatty the above Charges of the Cost in Working the Mine.
	Expenses on a Journey to Mrs Beattys.
14	Gave to Ann Post 6s besides paying for the making of her son Jno a pair of shoes.
	The beginning of this month son Geo: paid to Moor Furman for the last Years Gazette.
17	Martin Shifly had ½ a busl of Seed Corn.
14	Tunis Tunisen paid for a Deed.
17	Francis Quick paid for the Acknowledgment of a Deed.
18	Payed half years Support of the Minister John ought to pay.
	Payed Vincent Aaron Runion for dressing of a Deerskin.
16	Maths Brandt had 2 Bls of Rye.
20	Tunis Habbagh paid for a Deed.
21	Isaac Smaley paid for a Deed.
23	Sent to Dl Bray at the Landing for Shingles.
	Gave to son Richard to buy Rum and to pay for lime etc.
	Sent per son Richard to pay Wm Pierson.
25	Cash expended with Mr Low at the Landing per Abraham Smith in Rum, wine etc.
28	William Akers paid for the Recording of a Deed by Pr Moor.
30	Payed to Joseph Reed for 2 Bls of Pork.
	Bought ½ a doz of Knives and Forks.
	Payed to Henry Landis in full of Book Account and Remainder of Ricds Korn.
	Son Tho: expended when he took up the Cattle.
31	Gave Son Richard to pay off a Stubber for one month Service.
	Matths Brandt had 2 Bls of Rye.

March 1763

21 Gave to Son Joseph towards his Loss suffered by Fire in his Provisions.

24 Gave to a Charitable Use.

April 1763

4th Lent Hugh Hunter in Cash.

11 Received of Francis Quick by Tho: Jones the full of Accounts.

13 Expended upon a Journey to the Calf Pasture and home again.

28 Payed Thomas Lowrey the Balance of Accounts being I believe [an amount].

Payed Wm Pearson his Account.

Payed son Tho: for 2 oz of Elixir Proprietaly bought at Phila.

3d The third of this month Edwd Hunt paid towards his Rent £3 and a Bill for £10 more drawn upon Son Daniel by Mr Cowell.

May 1763

2d Martin Shifly paid the remainder of a Bond.

6 Peter Woollever paid for 6 sheep had near 10 years ago at 7s per piece.

Gave to Peggy Carr towards pay for the Doctor in Curing her broken Legg.

14 Payed Dr Creed for some Physick for selfe and wife.

16 Gave to a Charitable Use. Vizt: to a German for use of his son to recover his Sight.

Gave to Mr Mills for the use of his Daughter Mary Half Johannis[?] and Sp. Pistole.

27 Gave to Jacob DeCow [acco]modations of his house and other Expenses when up in the Country.

31 Gave to Mr Mills.

This month Received from son Thomas in Gold and Silver the sum of 10:8:0.

My Account against Son Thomas in cash paid to Sundry Persons amounted to 7:4:2.

John Reading's Diary

June 1763

4   Received from Aaron Starke by his son the last years rent for the
     Calf Pasture.
8   Received from Richd Philips for 2 Arbitration Bonds and Award.
21   Received from George Morden by Martin Shifly for last Years
     Rent

July 1763

Little this month worth taking notice of Excepting some Little
Expenses in a visit to Mr Beatty's with Danl Mills and a little
money Received upon Account of some Writings.

August 1763

6   Gave to son-in-law Aug: Reid a Bill of five pounds upon Wm
     Douglas and Interest thereon for above Two years. He giving me
     a £3 Bill.
     I also returned the _____ back to his wife.
     Sold to John Aller a Cow and Calf for £6 payable before Winter.

September 1763

Nothing of moment to be taken notice of.

October 1763

4th   William Force by Tho: Reading paid his Bill and one Year and
      one Month's Interest for the Same Bill.

November 1763

22d   Payd ½ years Sallary to the Minister for 3 Seats at 4s Each and
      firewood and nine Shillings on son Thos Account.

December 1763

9   Bought at Thos Atkinsons a gown for Sarah Van Sicklen.

13   Lent son Thos in Cash (the 20th returned back the said Sum).
     Son George Received and Paid me the Balance of Mr Byerlys
     Account.
     Payed for Recording the Minute concerning the Land lying near
     the heads of Paulins Kill. The Resurvey made by Mr Ryerson.
     Thomas Lowrey gave me Credit for the Balance of Messrs

31   Coxes's Account and I gave my Receipt for the said sum on the
     same day paid his Account.

1764

January 1764

13   Reconed with Son George and Payed him the Balance of his
     Accounts.

26   Received from Arthur Gray for Writings done in the Family.

February 1764

2d   Payed for a Book son Thos bought (vizt Cambray's Private Thots
     on Relign[148]).
     Bought at Thos Lowrey's 10 Skins of Parchment at 2/9 per skin.

23   Gave to a Charitable Use.

24   Gave to Son John as a help to his loss of Meat by fire.

.

March 1764

---

[148] Fénelon, Francois de Salignac de La Mothe-, 1651-1715, Archbishop of Cambray.
Private thoughts upon religion, in several letters. Written to His Royal Highness the Duke Regent of France. London: English edition printed, 1719.

Son Thomas paid to the Post for my use - Paid the whole for 8 month.

28   George Mordon paid towards his last Years Rent.

April 1764

16   Gave to a Charitable Use 5s. As also to sister Blanda Hall.

19   Reconed with Hugh Hunter for the making of 5 pair of shoes

20   Reconed with son Daniel and paid him for a Calf Skin and Dog Skin.

       Garret Van Campen paid me for Service formerly done (inst Supp ___).

       About the beginning of this month my wife let upon here for one lb of good Wooll per annum 6 sheep for each sheep being instead of those formerly had from Johnston Imlay being 5 Ewes and one whelher) or to Wm Coelbach who is to return them or others in their stead in N[umber] and quality when required. The wool to be delivered at our Dwelling house yearly.

16   Sold to Jos: Roseberry 165 acres on Delaware in Greenwich Sussex County for 65£ Proc: 150 on the first of D[ecembe]r next and 15£ upon interest for 12 months.

May 1764

11th   Received from Martin Ryerson cash due by Bill and Interest.

21   Received from Son Jos: Reading due for a fat Cow sold in Novr 1760.

June 1764

9th   Received from George Morden the Remainder of his last Years Rent.

       Received from Edwd Hunt in Cash for Rent both by son Daniel.

       Payed the Ministers ½ years Sallary etc.

       Payed for some contingent Charges about the Meeting House.

13   Gave to a Charitable Use at Foxe Hill.

14   Payed to Mr Hait for his use 12s and for further Contingent
      Charges of the Meeting House.
26   Received from Wm Douglass _____ part of the Rent for the year
      1763 the Sum of 4:05:0.
      Some time this month John Aller by Jos: Stout paid for a Cow
      and Calf had last Augt my wife agreeing for six pounds and the
      money not mentioned whether light or Proc. John Aller insisted
      that he meant light I asked 10s, .5£ whereof son Thomas had
      10s paid to me.

July 1764

22d   Received from Edwd Hunt in Cash for Rent per Son Daniel.

August 1764

1st   Payed to Wm Norcross for the use of Josiah Furman according
      to subscription the sum of [an amount].
10th Received from Richard Reading for the use of Wm Coelback for
      6 lb of wooll.
13th Gave to Son George upon account of bearing the Expenses of a
      reference at the Great Meadows.
15   Lent to Hy Van Oven upon Bond.
16   Edwd Hunt Payed more Cash for last years Rent.

September 1764

1   Gave to a Charitable Use.
3   Gave to the same purpose.
6   Lent to son Thomas when he went to Easton.
10   William Colebach brought home the 6 sheep which he had upon
      hire having paid for the hire thereof per Richard Reading as
      above.
22   Received from the Douglasses part of the Rent for 1762 per Mr
      Mills.
25   Lent to David Bartron by Bill payable upon Demand.

October 1764

1st   Lent to Martin Ryerson the sum of £1:10.
Gave to a Charitable Use vizt: to Person ransomed from Turkis Slavery.

8   Payed to son Richard for a piece of Linen.

12   Expenses upon a Journey to the Calf Pasture and home again.

24   Received from son Thomas which he had in his hand for the cow sold to Jo Aller.

30   Gave to Son John's Eldest son to pay for a New Saddle.

November 1764

1   Payed to Son Daniel ½ years sallary to Mr Hait.

14   David Bartron paid the £7 of borrowed the 25th of September.

18   Gave to a Charitable Use at the Meeting.

December 1764

18   Bought som fish.
Gave to a Charitable Use.

27   Sent by Mr Brinkerhot to Mr Noel to be Sent to Mr Mills the sum of 54:7:6.
Part of the pay for 165 acres of Land sold to Jos: Reading.

1765

January 1765

Payed to Hugh Hunter in part for work done.
Expended with a Pedlar.

February 1765

7 Lent to Sons Thomas and Daniel one 30s Bill.

25 Payed to Henry Bailey for Taylors work.

March 1765

5th Sent by son George to Mr Hall[149] to pay for Pennsylvania Gazatte to 1765.

11 Reconed with Hugh Hunter paid the Ball.

13 Lent to son Thomas in Cash.

18 George Morden paid by Son George for these years Rent.

13 Son George paid 30s to Franklin and Hall in full for the Pennsylvania Gazette to the Seventh of February.

28th Son Thomas returned the cash borrowed the 13th.

April 1765

10th Son Thomas bought at Burlington a Clock Line cost 0:7:6.

20 Left with Saml Fleming for the Post last years _____ing.

May 1765

8 Payed upon an order from Blanda Hall upon Son Georges supposing not at home.

9 Lent to Hugh Hunter [an amount].

11 Bought a quarter of Veal weighted 12 ½ lb.

16 Accompted with Thomas Lowrey and paid him in full.

17 Gave to a Charitable Use by Nathan Calfore.

24 Gave to a Charitable Use to a Young Man who had lost his arm by a Cannonball.

31 Payed to son Thomas an half years Salary for Mr Hait.

June 1765

---

[149] DAVID HALL (1714-72). Moved from London to Philadelphia in 1744 to become Franklin's shop foremen and in 1748 took over the business as mananging partner. Isaacson, *Benjamin Franklin, An American Life*, 497.

5th   Payed son Richd for Sundrys bought May 23rd and this day a pair of stockins.

July 1765

30th   John Baker paid off a Bond for £6:0 a year and two months Interest.

August 1765

7   Lent to Son Thomas when he went to Phila. Payed it Back.

14th   Bro: Ryerson paid the money borrowed in Jany last Year.

17   Sent by Mr Beatty to buy Cloth and Trimming at Phila.

September 1765

23   Lent John Smith in Cash.

30   Received in Cash for several Writings and Trouble and Services from Christian Harshal.

October 1765

1   Received from Martin Ryerson for Services in Drawing Returns for Land.

5   Received per Son Daniel from Mr Beatty Cloth and Trimming.

18   Sold a Steir to Mr Beatty (to be paid in the Spring of the Year).

November 1765

11   Gave to John Richardson for his relief.

15   John Smith returned the 30s borrowed in Septr 23d.

16   Payed Thos Atkinson Jur on account of Goods bought at the Shop.

18   Payed Wm Hackett for a Bonnet Lining.
        Bought six bottles of Bartrams Ballsamick Elixir.

December 1765

11th To Mr Beatty for salve (Turner Carat) and for some Ointment.

12 Paid for the full of Supplys that have been in the old Meeting House since Mr Haits dismission to this date.

13 Sent the Steir bought as above per his Negro Elijah.

17 Payed Henry Bayley for making a Suit of Cloaths.

26 Bought some fresh Rock Fish - Perch.

1766

January 1766

10th Gave to a Charitable Use to two Lame Provincials

31 Lent to son George the sum of 15.

February 1766

22d Lent to Elizabeth the Daughter of Cathrine Johnson. Bought a quarter of Veal.

22 Received of son George part of the above Sum lent the last month.

April 1766

3 Son Daniel Expended on Trouble and Charges about Barkers Lines. I paid it.

May 1766

2d Received from Thomas Reading of the money paid by Jo Baker on son Georges Account.

| 7 | Expenses at Burlington in answering a Caveat against Barkers Resurvey. |

7   Expenses at Burlington in answering a Caveat against Barkers
     Resurvey.
     Bought a quarter of Veal.
     Bought 500 oz Clams.
20   Lent £3 to Mr Stockton[150] for his opinion per some questions
     proposed.
27   Reconed with son Daniel and paid him the Balance for trouble
     and Charges in Bowlby Resury besides Cash for Expenses for
     Surveying on said Tract and Expenses at Burlington.

June 1766

9th Joseph Roseberry on Account of the Land Sold to him at
     Delaware besides mistake.
13   Tho: Silverthorn paid part of a Bond.
17   Reconed with Dr Vericleus and paid what was due to him to the
     7th of April being 1 shilling over.
20   Gave to Jo Tiesort a dumb man as an act of Charity.
21   Son Thomas bought at Phila and brought home with him 5 Skins
     of Parchment @ 3s per skin.
27   Bought a quarter of Veal weighed 17 lb to be discompted with
     son Thomas.

July 1766

26th Payed Thos Atkinson his account against me and on son Thomas
     Account.
     Payed Jacob Mattison for mending the Chair Wheel.
28th Lent Robert Beatty (the 29th Robert repaid the said 5 shillings).

August 1766

---

[150] JOHN STOCKTON (1701-1758). "For many years one of the presiding judges of
the Court of Common Pleas of the County of Somerset, New Jersey under the Royal
Government. He was instrumental in securing to Princeton the College of New Jersey,
and was a friend and liberal patron of the college." Stockton Family Historical Trust,
http://www.stockton-law.com/genealogy/stockton3.html (August 1, 2010).

16th   Received from Wm Douglass Jur (by George Reading) for Rent
        1767.

29   Joseph Roseberry paid more of the Condsideration money due
        on the Land bought.

30   Paid to the Smith for mending the Iron of the Wing of the Chair.

September 1766

2   Payed William Housell for puting on the Cloath etc on Iron of
        the Wing and Saddle Straps.

12   Lent son Thomas in Cash to pay the Scholemaster.

15   Payed Thomas Lowry his account.

26   Payed Mr Mills the money Jos: Roseberry paid at two Sundry
        times as above.
        Gave Thos Jones to buy one pound of Corot at Phila.

October 1766

Gave son Daniel when he was to go upon Son Richards affairs.
Sent by son George to buy an hankerchief and some Wafers at
Phila.

25   Payed Mr Norcross towards half a Years Salarly to Mr
        Kirkpatrick. [151]

November 1766

8th   Received from Mr Jasper Smith [152] a Release from Tho: Bowlby
        for 53 Acres of Land being lying within a Survey of Saml Barkers

---

[151] WILLIAM KIRKPATRICK (ca. 1737-69). Minister of the Amwell Presbyterian
Church who succeeded Rev. Hait in 1766, but died three years later. Rev. Kirkptrick was
a graduate of Princeton College in 1757 and elected trustee in 1768. Mott, *History of the
Presbyterian Church in Flemington*, 30.

[152] JASPER SMITH (1737-1813). Originally from Maidenhead (Lawrenceville). B.A.
from College of New Jersey in 1758, licensed as an attorney and commissoned as one of
three surrogotes of the Prerogative Court of New Jersey in 1766. Member of the Board
of Trustees Flemington Presbyterian Church 1779-1790. Elected President of the
Trustees in 1792. Lewis D. Cook, "Jasper Smith, Esq. of Lawrenceville", *Genealogical*

on or near Foxe Hill (as is said) for the Release, Whereof I gave to the Said Bowlby £12 Proc and for Acknowledgment of said Release 3s/.

15th   Payed Mr Beatty the Interest of Son John Bond £97:16 Being £4 by myself and £2:18:2 ½ by son John (and in full for a steir).

17th   Corns Anderson paid for a Copy of a Deed of Mortgage in the Loan Office.
Payed John Porter his Credit against me for Shop Goods.

25   Gave to Jos: Hankinson Jur when he went to Mr Beatty's on an Errand.

December 1766

3   Received in full of a Receipt for £19 dated last Jany from son George.

15   Son Thomas Expended for me at Phila in Flannel etc. __ak Powder.

16   Son Thomas paid back the money borrowed in Sepr last.

18   Bought some fresh fish.

1767

January 1767   Thursday

19   Son George Expended for me at Phila in salve 1/6, Half Doz. of Spoons and toward Col Boguets Historical Account of His Expedition against the Ohio Indians[153] etc.

Magazine of New Jersey Vol. 46 (1971) 31-32. Rpt. In *Genealogies of New Jersey Families* (Baltimore, Maryland: Genealogical Publishing Co. Inc.) 1996. 781-782.
[153] *Of The Expedition Against The Ohio Indians, In The Year MDCCLXIV [1764]. Under The Command Of Henry Bouquet, Esq. Colonel Of Foot, And Now Brigadier General In America.* Published, From Authentic Documents, By A Lover Of His Country. Philadelphia, Printed. London, Re-Printed For T. Jefferies, Geographer To His Majesty, At Charing Cross. MDCCLXVI (1768).

John Reading's Diary

February 1767 – Sunday

Received from Rich: Hunt part of the last years Rent.
Son Thomas borrowed the sum of 19s. Returned 7/6.
Received from Edward Hunt part of his years rent 50s Balance.
Tho: Jones returned the Balance of the account for 7/6 to buy 7 lb of Ceral Cort.
Son Thomas bought ½ Ct of Limes.

27 Son Thomas borrowed the sum of 7:0:0.

March 1767 – Sunday

17th John Stole paid for some Writings made some time past
Son Thomas Returned the Money Borrowed as above.
Balance for some things theron as limes a pair of Vamps for Shoes the rest in Cash.

31 Mr Reid paid of a Bond to me from T: Barker, G: Woolf with 2 years interest. __ being £4:5:9.
This day was son George Vendue.

April 1767 – Wednesday

2d Richard Hunt paid by his father the full of the last Years Rent and part of this Year Rent.

10 Thomas Expended at Phila for 2 Sheepskins; 5 ½ lb Tea.
Gave to son Richard at Trenton the remainder of 30s which I lent him.

13 Expended with a Pedlar.

15 Gave to a Charitable Use (to a woman from Scholeys Mountain).

16 Bought from Tho: Lowrey one Gall of Rum.

May 1767 – Friday

2 Expended with a Pedlar.
Gave to two Charitable Uses.

4 Received from Richd Hunt by son Thomas the full of the 2 last year R[ent]. Returning about this Time.

Gave to Caty[154], Richard's wife when intended to go to Germantown.

Of 12 for Alexr Flemings Deed to Son Thomas upon settlement of account the sum of £9:19 together with allowance.

13   Received form Edward Hunt more of this years Rent.

Paid Son Daniel Seven pounds the Interest of almost £100 made his by Exchange of Land with Wm Mills.

20   Son George paid Cash formerly borrowed.

21   Gave to Saml Reading upon Expenses to Trenton.

Sent to Richard at Trenton by Saml Reading.

23   Bought a quarter of Veal.

30   Augustine Reid paid one of his Annual Payments being otherways ordered 12:0:0.

June 1767 - Monday

6   Payed Mr Ryerson for Two Journeys into Sussex County viewing Jno Lawrences Line[155] in two Several places of _____ and 422 Acres of mine.

Lent son George (going to Burlington in[?]onally) to meet the Assembly.

18   Augustine Reid _____ the 12£ to be paid to son Daniel which accordingly done this day.

23   Bought a quarter of Veal.

27   Bought 100 of Clams.

July 1767 – Wednesday

8   Gave to a Charitable Use a Scotch man from New York.

August 1767 – Saturday

---

154 CATHERINE REID, daughter of Col. John Reid and Mary Sands and Richard Reading's wife. Leach, *Memorials*, 51.

155 Line surveyed by John Lawrence in 1743 finally settling the disputed boundary between East and West New Jersey. John P. Snyder. *The Mapping of New Jersey* (New Brunswick, New Jersey: Rutgers University Press, 1973) 38-39.

8   Sent down to Richard by Thos Prior.

13   Payed per Mr Beatty for 1 lb of Ceral 3/6, some Limes with _____
      and the grease of _____.
      This day Mr Beatty and wife set out for New York with Mrs.
      Hackett Sett off for Great Britian.[156]
      Had from the Union Stor two quire of Writing Paper.

September 1767 – Tuesday

1   Reconed with Thomas Lowrey and paid off the Balance.
      Some time about the beginning of this month Payed Son Daniel
      for repairs of the Meeting House etc.
      Gave son Thomas the Balance of account between and Will:
      Disher being [an amount].

13   An acknowledgment of a Deed paid to Mr Ryerson. 3s Still Due.

November 1767 – Wednesday

4th   Paid one years Sallery for Mr. Kirkpatrick.
      Paid on Account of son Thomas for Ditto.

Editor's note: John Reading died on November 5th, 1767.

---

[156] Mrs. Beatty (Ann Reading), her husband, and her sister Mrs. Hackett (Elizabeth Reading) were going to Scotland to find a cure for Mrs. Beatty's breast cancer. She died there the following March, Beatty, *Family of Charles Beatty*, 21.

BIBILOGRAPHY

Allen, William. *An American Biographical and Historical Dictionary*. 2nd ed. Boston: Hyde, 1832.

Beatty, Charles C. *Record of the Family of Charles Beatty*, Steubenville, Ohio, 1873.

Bush, Bernard, compiler. *New Jersey Archives, Third Series, Vol. II, Laws of the Royal Colony of New Jersey 1703-1745*. Trenton, New Jersey: New Jersey State Library, Archives and History Bureau, 1977.

Cassel, Daniel K. *Genea-Biographical History of the Rittenhouse Family*. Philadelphia, Pa. 1893.

Collections of the New Jersey Historical Society Vol IX. Newark, New Jersey: New Jersey Historical Society, 1916.

Cook, Lewis D. "Jasper Smith, Esq. of Lawrenceville", *Genealogical Magazine of New Jersey* Vol. 46 (1971). 31-32. Rpt. In *Genealogies of New Jersey Families*. Baltimore, Maryland: Genealogical Publishing Co. Inc., 1996.

Cox, Rev. Henry Miller. *The Cox Family in America*. Somerville, New Jersey, 1912.

Davis, William W.H. A.M. *History of Bucks County Pennsylvania Vol III*. New York, Chicago: The Lewis Publishing Co., 1905.

DeCou, S. Ella and John Allen DeCou, compilers. *The Genealogy of the DeCou Family*. Trenton, NJ, 1910.

Earle, Alice Morse. *Costume of Colonial Times*. New York, 1894.

Felter, Harvey Wickes, M. D. and John Uri Lloyd, Phr. M., Ph.D. *King's American Dispensatory* Nineteenth Edition. Third revision. In two volumes. Vol. I. Cincinnati: The Ohio Valley Company, 317—321 Race Street. 1905.

Flemming, George D. *Brotherton, New Jersey's First and Only Indian Reservation*. Medford, New Jersey: Plexus Publishing, Inc., 2005.

Bibliography

Fowler, William M., Jr. *Empires at War – The French and Indian War and the Struggle for North America 1754-1763*. New York: Walker & Company, 2005.

Gangaware, Beulah, "Baptisms of Readington Reformed Church 1720-1837, Readington, Hunterdon County, New Jersey.", Typescript digital images, *Raub and More.* http://raub-and-more.com/readingtonbap.

Greenwood, Val D. *The Researcher's Guide to American Genealogy*, 3rd ed. Baltimore, Maryland: Genealogical Publishing Co., Inc., 2000.

Hammond, Stanton D. *Hunterdon County Maps with Name Index*. Genealogical Society of New Jersey, 1965.

"Hude, James". *The Twentieth Century Biographical Dictionary of Notable Americans*, Vol. V. 1904. N. pag.

Hunterdon County Land Drafts, MSC 163 F1, Spruance Library, Bucks County Historical Society, Doylestown, Pennsylvania. 1744 map of Rosemont farms.

Isaacson, Walter. *Benjamin Franklin, An American Life*. New York: Simon & Shuster, 2003.

"Journal of John Reading," *Proceedings of the New Jersey Historical Society 10 (January-October 1915)* 35-46, 90-110, 128-133. Surveying trips in 1715 and 1719. The original journal is held by the New Jersey Historical Society.

Keasbey, Edward Quinton, A.M. LL.B. *The Courts and Lawyers of New Jersey 1661-1912*. New York, 1912.

Kline, Mary-Jo. *A Guide to Documentary Editing*, 2nd ed. Baltimore, Maryland: Johns Hopkins University Press, 1987, 1998.

Kraft, Herbert C. *The Dutch, the Indians, and the Quest for Copper: Pahaquarry and the Old Mine Road*. South Orange, New Jersey: Seton Hall University Museum, 1996.

Bibliography

Leach, Josiah Granville. *Genealogical and Biographical Memorials of the Reading, Howell, Yerkes, Watts, Latham, and Elkins Families.* Philadelphia, 1898.

Lender, Mark E. and James Kirby Martin, editors, *Citizen Soldier: The Revolutionary War Journal of Joseph Bloomfield.* Newark: New Jersey Historical Society, 1982.

Love, John. *Geodaesia: or, the Art of Measuring Land, etc.,* 8th ed. London, 1768.

McCusker, John J. *Money & Exchange in Europe & America, 1600-1775, A Handbook.* Williamsburg, Virginia: Institute of Early American History and Culture, 1978.

Mott, Rev. George S. D.D. *History of the Presbyterian Church in Flemington New Jersey, for a Century.* New York, 1894.

Nelson, William, ed. *Documents Relating to the Colonial History of the State of New Jersey,* Vol. XIX, *1751-1755.* Paterson, N.J.: The Press Printing and Publishing Co., 1897.

Petrie, Alfred G. *Lambertville New Jersey from the beginning as Coryell's Ferry.* Lambertville, New Jersey, 1949.

Pomfret, John E. *The Province of West New Jersey 1609-1702.* Princeton, New Jersey: Princeton University Press, 1956.
---. *The New Jersey Proprietors and Their lands.* Princeton, New Jersey: D. Van Nostrand, 1964.

Rabushka, Alvin. *Taxation in Colonial America.* Princeton, New Jersey: Princeton University Press, 2008.

Reading, David R. "For Love or Loyalty". *The Mount Amwell News,* Fall 2010, 1-2.

Ricord, Frederick W. and William Nelson, eds. *Documents Relating to the Colonial History of New Jersey,* Vol. XV: *Journal of the Governor and Council 1738-1748.* Trenton, New Jersey: The John l. Murphy Publishing Co., 1891. Rpt. PDF NJA1153A, Morristown, NJ: Digital Antiquarria, 2006.

Bibliography

Ringo, David Leer, Jr.. "What Ever Happened to the Ringoes". Hunterdon County Historical Society meeting, Ringoes, New Jersey. October 21, 1967.

Ryerson, Phyllis A. and Thomas A. Ryerson. *The Ryerse-Ryerson Family 1574-1994*. Ingersoll, Ontario: T.A. Ryerson & Son, 1994, 1996.

Snell, James P., compiler. *History of Hunterdon and Somerset Counties, New Jersey*. Philadelphia, Everts & Peck, 1881.

Snell, James P., compiler. *History of Sussex and Warren Counties, New Jersey*. Philadelphia, Everts & Peck, 1881.

Snyder, John P. *The Mapping of New Jersey*. New Brunswick, New Jersey: Rutgers University Press, 1973.

Stevens, Michael E. and Steven B. Burg. *Editing Histroical Documents, A Handbook of Practice,*. Walnut Ceeek, Wisconsin: Altamira Press, 1997.

Stevenson, Dr. John R. "Physicians in the Colonization of New Jersey." *The Jerseyman*, Vol.. 11, No. 4. April 1905.

Stratford, Dorothy A. "John's Reading Diary," *The Genealogical Magazine of New Jersey* 62.1 (January 1987): 1-8; 62.2 (May 1987): 83-88; 62.3 (September 1987): 128-134; 63.1 (January 1988): 40-48; 63.2 (May 1988): 91-96; 63.3 (September 1988): 133-138; 64.1 (January 1989): 19-24; 64.2 (May 1989): 73-80.

Wacker, Peter O. *The Musconetcong Valley of New Jersey, A Historical Geography*. New Brunswick, New Jersey: Rutgers University Press, 1968.

Wheeler ,William Ogden, compiler. *The Ogden family in America, Elizabethtown branch, and their English ancestry*. Philadelphia, Pennsylvania: Lippincott, 1907.

Whitehead, William A., ed. *Documents Relating to the Colonial History of the State of New Jersey*, Vols. II-IX. Newark, New Jersey, 1881-1885.

Vossetter, Elias. "Reminiscences of the Kase Family", 1907. Rpt *Case-ette* No. 2 Summer, 1965.

INDEX

A

Abbit, James, 21
Achenbach
    Barnet, 67
    Jasper, 54
Acker, William, 56, 165
Alback, William, 73
Albertse, Adrian, 4
Albertson, Nicholas, 16, 36
Alburtus, John, 31
Alen, Gaston, 162
Alexander, James, 46
Alford, John, 7, 11, 41, 45, 57, 159
Allen
    David, 117
    William, 7, 39, 54, 58, 65, 120
Allentown, Pa., 143
Aller
    John, 58, 60, 167, 170
    Peter, 41, 154
Allison, John, 26, 89
Allward, Mr., 55
Amboy, N.J., 2, 9, 10, 13, 15, 17, 100, 106, 154
Amwell Presbyterian Meeting House, 48, 114, 134, 141, 155, 169, 170, 174, 180
Amwell Township, N.J., iii, iv, v, x, 3, 4, 7, 8, 36, 48, 53, 62, 68, 79, 86, 105, 111, 120, 176, 183
Anderson
    Cornelius, 89, 177
    John, 13, 93, 105, 106, 108, 125, 141, 146, 158
    William, 8, 10, 25
Anthony, Jacob, 114
Antill, Edward, 13, 15, 17
Aray, Adam, 149
Arrison, John, 24, 34, 143

Ashton, James, 102
Aten. *See* Auten
Atkinson, Thomas, 21, 43, 47, 62, 69, 72, 83, 93, 95, 96, 101, 110, 119, 121, 127, 129, 139, 148, 153, 168
Auten, (var. Aten)
    Adriaen, 27
    Derrick, 153
Ayers, John, 161

B

Backer, Johannes, 29
Bailes, Daniel, 35
Bailey (var. Bayley), Henry, 172, 174
Baird
    Charles, 105
    James, 43, 115, 152
Baker
    John, 173, 174
    Martin, 59, 61, 64, 78
Barber, John, 153
Barclay's Tract, 5
Bardack, William, 126
Barkalow, Yarus, 34, 92, 96
Barker
    Samuel, 176
    Thomas, 178
Barnes, William, 33, 147
Barnet, William, Dr., 136
Barns, Robert, 7
barrack, 98, 99, 151
Bartholomew, Jacob, 144
Barton
    Elisha, 162
    George, 109
Bates
    Daniel, 19, 35, 37, 38
    William, 35
Beam, John, 107
Beatty

Index

Charles, 6, 18, 21, 23, 24, 40, 45,
48, 59, 60, 63, 71, 74, 81, 86, 97,
101, 103, 104, 110, 111, 118,
119, 122, 125, 129, 130, 132,
135, 137, 138, 140, 142, 144,
147, 148, 153, 163, 167, 173,
174, 177, 180, 181
George, 34, 39, 64, 69
Martha (Patty), 138, 139
Mrs (Ann Reading), 138, 142, 153,
157, 160, 161, 165
Robert, 175
Bebe, Hezekiah, 53
Becker, Martin, 63, 80, 85, 88
Beemer (var. Beammer, Bemmer),
Henry, 136, 145, 147
Behtelheimer (var. Behtelsiemer)
Abraham, 55
George, 31
James, 95
Johannes Yerie, 2, 3, 22, 27
John, 82
Belcher, Jonathon, Gov., 17, 29
Bellows, Peter, 150
Bemmer. *See* Beamer
Bennet, Ezekiel, 55
Bennets, the, 144
Bergen County, N.J., 134
Bergh
Christian, 151
Handeel, 25
Bernard
Francis, Gov., 29, 154
Berner, John, 78
Berry, Edward, 108, 109, 115, 116,
117, 121, 125, 128, 133
Bertron
David, 30, 32, 81, 170, 171
Besenberg, Josiah, 62
Bethlehem, N.J., 3, 4, 5, 28, 85
Bethlehem, Pa., 85
Beven, Philip, 36, 37, 38, 67, 82, 94,
97, 105, 115, 116, 125
Bickley, Mrs., 17, 23
Biggs, George, 56, 60, 80, 144
Biles, Mrs, 49, 52
Binder
Johannes Yerie, 12, 16, 24, 33, 35,
41, 46, 48, 49, 53, 60, 63, 73, 74,
81, 82, 85, 86, 98, 102, 103, 104,
114, 115, 116, 117, 118, 119,
120, 128, 129, 130, 131, 132,
135, 137, 138, 141, 143, 144,
145, 150, 151, 152, 153, 154,
156, 158
Philip, 121, 122, 125, 127, 135, 136,
137
Bird, John?, 61
Birket, George, 54
Bishop, William, 16
Black River Village (Chester), N.J., 120
Black River, N.J., 38
Black Tom, 121, 138
Black, William, 32
Blornersfelt, Zachery, 3
Bodine
Cornelius, 114
Frederick, 150
Isaac, 19
John, 114
Bog Meadow, 10
Bogart
Cornelius, 10
Isaac, 20
Boltenhammer, Johannes, 107
Bond, Elija, 40
Bonnell, Abraham, 11, 82, 149
Borts, Johannes, 27
Bossenberg (var. Bussenburg),
Johannes, 5, 6, 8, 20, 40, 75, 96
Bost (var. Boss), Joseph, 9, 26, 28, 49,
57, 106
Botner (var. Butner)
Paulus, 27, 43, 53, 78, 93, 115, 131
Thomas, 16
Bowlby
John, 46
Thomas, 176
Bowman, Cornelius, 3, 50, 108
Bowne, James, 63, 64
Boyce, John, 86
Bradbury, James, 12, 31, 47
Braiden, Robert, 70
Brand, Mrs., 114
Brandenburgers, the, 24
Brandt, Matthias, 115, 116, 117, 121,
125, 126, 128, 134, 164, 165
Branson, William, 73
Bray
Andrew, 19, 146
Daniel, 137, 165
John, 11

Index

Bray's Tract, 19
Breimer, Matthew, 99
Brewer
    Hannah, 130
    Magdalen, 58, 60
    Samual, 68
    William, 63, 65
Brink, Lambert, 122
Brinkerhot, Mr., 171
Bristol, Pa., 7, 34, 36, 53, 59, 71, 72,
    85, 87, 89, 132, 133
Britton, William, 31, 77
Broughton, Mr., 67
Brown
    John, 10
    Thomas, 20, 24
    William, 140
Bruglar, Samuel, 89
Brunswick, N.J., xi, 13, 14, 20, 55, 71,
    74, 79, 84, 87, 90, 105, 106, 108,
    112, 132, 156, 179, 184
Bryant, Ebenezer, 132
Bucks County, Pa., 13, 25, 30, 42, 181,
    182
Burcham, John, 70, 71, 78, 90
Burdsall, Jacob, 64, 74
Burgh, William, 155, 158
Burk, David, 32
Burlington, N.J., ix, 2, 7, 8, 9, 13, 14,
    16, 17, 18, 23, 27, 29, 32, 33, 34, 36,
    40, 41, 46, 47, 52, 53, 54, 58, 59, 62,
    64, 66, 67, 69, 71, 72, 73, 77, 79, 82,
    84, 85, 87, 89, 90, 94, 102, 104, 106,
    109, 112, 115, 118, 124, 133, 135,
    145, 153, 154, 157, 159, 163, 172,
    175, 179
Bussenburg. *See* Bossenberg
Butner. *See* Botner
Buyer, Paul, 87, 106
Byerly, Thomas, 31, 47, 54, 145, 168
Byram
    Eliab, Rev., 68, 70, 77, 80, 89, 94,
      95
    Mrs., 98

C

Cadwalader, Thomas, Dr., 15, 75
Cain, Walter, 42
Calcot

    Nancy, 11, 52, 99, 101
    Robert, 1, 4, 5, 9, 13, 14, 15, 17, 31,
      32, 45, 46, 47, 48, 49, 50, 56, 66,
      67, 70, 91, 92, 93, 94, 96, 97, 98,
      99, 102, 103, 104, 105, 107, 118,
      121, 124, 127, 128, 137
Calf Pasture, 37, 67, 115, 127, 141,
    149, 164, 166, 167, 171
Calfore, Nathan, 172
Calvin, Philip, 79, 82, 84
Camback, William, 158
Campbell, Neil, 38
Canby's Ferry, Pa., 81
Carlin, Daniel, 12
Carman, Jasper, 135
Carmer, Abraham, 29
Carr, Peggy, 166
Carriers, Charles, 104
Case (var. Kase)
    Johann Philip, 154
    John, 118, 148, 155
    Matthew, 148, 161
    Peter, 27, 146
    Philip, 76, 108, 141, 154
    Tunis, 53, 75, 97
    Widow, 141
    William, 31, 105, 120, 140, 148, 154
Casper, John, 101
Chain, James, 11
Chamberlain
    Henry, 159
    Lewis, 27, 129, 137
Chancery, 13
Chandler
    John, 33, 34, 37, 40
    Stephen, 97, 98, 99, 102, 137
Chapman
    Mary, 84
    Philip, 79
Cheek, Joseph, 29
Cherry
    James, 144
    William, 72
Clark, John Wright, 133
Clawson, Josiah, 110, 114, 120, 151
Clayton, William, 130
Clook, John, 16
cloth
    flannel, 52
    fustian, 116
    kersey, 19, 73

linen, 68
mohair, 22
Ozenburg, 68
shalloon, 51
tow, 163
worsted, 51, 79
Coat
 Hester, 80
 John, 34, 57
 Thomas, 21, 35, 60
Coats, William, 158
Cock
 Ashfordby, 108, 114, 139
 David, 151
 Henry, 51, 80
 John, 56, 62, 77, 84, 99, 100, 101,
  105, 108, 110, 117
 Joseph, 27
 Margaret, 33
 Widow, 139
Cockin, John, 99
Coelbach. See Coolbagh, See Coolbagh
Coelbagh. See Coolbagh
Coenover. See Conover
Cogh, Henry, 63
Cohoon, Walter, 11, 37
Coil. See Kuhl
Cole
 Barnet, 61
 John, 159, 162
 Michael, 156
 Tunis, 98, 122, 139
Colebach. See Coolbagh
College of New Jersey (Princeton), 26,
 34, 175
Collin, Daniel, 8
Collins, Thomas, 14, 22, 26, 28, 36, 41
Colluel, William, 157
Colvens, Philip, 66
Colvert, Robert, 38
Connagh, David, 13, 14, 15, 18, 30
Conner, David, 31, 32, 46
Conover (var. Coenover), Paul, 62
Cook
 John, 44
 Peter, 121
 Richard, 124
Coolbagh (var. Coolbogh, Colebach),
 William, 68, 78, 169, 170
Coons, Peter, 93
Corwine

John, 43, 127, 135
 Joseph, 127, 135
Coryell
 Emanuel, 28
 John, 66
 Widow, 53
Cottenham, Mr, 104
Cotts, Coenradt, 133
Cough, Henry, 127
Coul. See Kuhl
Coursen
 Jacob, 53, 92
 John, 28
 Matthew, 19, 33, 35, 76, 84, 99
 Tunis, 108, 109, 114, 118
 Yunis, 122
Cowan, John, 87
Cowell, Mr., 166
Cowley, James, 117
Coxe
 Charles, 63
 Daniel, 3, 74
 Daniel, Col., 74
 John, 3, 5, 55, 68, 74, 85, 120, 126
 Messrs., 5
 William, 3, 12, 53, 71, 74, 77, 117
Coxe's Tract, 36
Creature, Morris, 40, 50, 62, 71, 72, 77,
 87, 164
Creed, Dr., 166
Crook, Richard, 21, 38, 50, 153, 158
Crooks, John, 36
Crosswix (Crosswicks), N.J., 140
Cumberland County, N.J., 44
Cupboard, specification for, 5
Curry, William, 68
Curtis
 Benjamin, 88
 Thomas, 5, 33

D

Dainurs, Dr., 56
Davenport, Mr., 20
Davie, Coenradt, 90
Davis
 Aaron, 55, 90
 Isaac, 34
Davison, William, 89
Dawles, Widow, 29

Index

Deal Berg, John, 2
DeCow
    Hannah, 133
    Isaac, 2, 29, 47, 53, 70
    Issac Jr., 53
    Jacob, 166
    Joseph, 54, 78
    Mrs., 132, 134
Degoes, Peter, 44
Dehart, Doctor, 133
Delamater, Abraham, 18, 49, 50, 83
Delaware River, x, 21, 25
Demot
    Isaac, 131, 142
    Jacob, 131
    Michae1, 40, 142
    Michael, 40, 142
DePue, Arie, 50, 51
Depues, the, 57
Deremus, Thomas, 10, 15, 17, 30
DeRosel, Charles, 28
Dierdorf, Peter, 46, 72, 84, 104, 132, 150
Dildine, Henry, 28, 29, 30, 46, 78
Dilts
    John, 93
    Peter, 63
    Philip, 140, 141
    William, Col., 116
Dimsdale, Robert, Dr., 25, 53
Dirdort, Anthony, 122
Disher, William, 149, 180
Dorland, John, 94
Douglas
    George, 134
    William, 120, 149, 167, 170, 176
Douw, Volkert, 19
Drake
    Abraham, 117, 122, 124
    Abraham, Jr., 124
    Jacob, 124
Dubois, Charles, 51
Dumont, Derrick, 161
Dupue, Benjamin, 127

E

Eastaughs, Mrs, 27
Easton, Pa., 85, 112, 170
Ecbird, John, 114, 115

Edelman, Peter, 125
Edmunds (var. Edmonds), John, 38, 42, 50, 61, 62, 78, 92, 93, 94, 108, 110, 112, 113, 114, 116, 118, 119, 120, 121, 124, 140
Egbert
    John, 119, 126
    Nicholas, 120
Eike (var. Eich, Eyke, Eyck), Yerie, 68
Emery (var. Hemerigh), Conrad, 77, 78
Emley
    Molly, 31, 149
    Samuel, 68
Emmans
    Abraham, 145, 155
    Jerome, 150
    John, 37
Ent, Valentine, 44, 58
Erwine, Jacob, 46, 56, 79
Evans, Thomas, 39
Eveland
    David, 62, 115, 116
    Mary, 118
Everitts, the, 86, 116
Exceen, William, 6, 10, 24
Eyck. *See* Eike
Eyke. *See* Eike

F

Falkenbergen, Christopher, 37, 73, 83
Farmar, Robert, 57
Farnsworth, Henry, 39, 141
Farrow, James, 32, 41, 51, 52, 56
Fetters, David, 81
Fisher, Peter, 62
Flagg, Paul, 88, 102, 105, 111, 112, 116
Fleming
    Alexander, 179
    Samuel, 14, 20, 22, 29, 32, 37, 50, 51, 52, 78, 92, 105, 106, 107, 142, 172
    William, 135
Flocker, William, 5
Flood, Thomas, 78
Foin, Peter, 25
Fonger, William, 20
Force
    Benjamin, 158

William, 2, 6, 15, 22, 27, 33, 35, 39,
    40, 42, 46, 48, 59, 61, 62, 66, 70,
    72, 73, 74, 75, 76, 77, 78, 79, 81,
    82, 88, 92, 93, 95, 98, 100, 105,
    107, 109, 110, 114, 122, 124,
    135, 137, 140, 141, 142, 143,
    145, 146, 167
Ford
    Col., 88
    John, Sheriff, 82, 91
Forst, Henry, 72, 74
Forster, Widow, 8, 24
Forter, John, 38
Foxe
    Gabriel, 63
    Hubert Frederick, 51, 73
    John, 116, 148
    Peter, 62, 122, 158, 162
Foxe Hill (Fairmont), N.J., 62, 169
Francis
    Johannes, 84
    John, 99, 101
    Joseph, 79, 80, 84
Franklin, Benjamin, 2, 19, 21, 27, 172,
    182
Freehold, N.J., 97, 108, 116, 121, 122,
    127, 130, 133, 139, 148, 151, 153
Freeholders, 29, 44, 55, 67, 79, 126
Fulper, Peter, 94
funerals and burials, 4, 13, 48, 94, 138
Furman
    Josiah, 170
    Moore, 54, 64, 89, 115, 117, 132,
        134, 143, 151, 165
    Samuel, 29
Furnis, Samuel, 44

G

Ganoe (var. Genoe)
    Stephen, 24, 41
    William, 71
Gans, Justus, 17, 40, 52
Gardenier
    Andreas, 39, 45, 95
    Arie, 45
Garrison, John, 9, 43, 49, 71
Geerhart, Jacob, 103
Genoe. *See* Ganoe

Germans, 36, 83, 102, 113, 114, 124,
    150, 166
Germantown, N.J., 21, 179
Gever, John, 108
Giles, Richard, 127
Gock, John, 78
Godly, William, 104
Golden, Joseph, 102
Gordon, Charles, 55
Gould, Robert, 97
Graff, Henry, 104, 126
Grandin
    John, 140, 148
    Phillip, 111
Grandins, The, 111
Grave, Henry, 50, 78
Graveyard at Amwell Meeting House,
    107
Graveyard at Buckingham, Pa., 36
Gray
    Abraham, 96
    Arthur, 168
    Jacob, 50, 86, 108, 124
Great Meadows, N.J., 14, 57, 70, 148,
    170
Green
    Richard, 24
    Samuel, 3, 14, 44, 47, 68
Greenwich Township, N.J., 89, 90, 169
Griggs
    Daniel, 41, 105, 111
    Joakim, 147, 151
    John, 51
    Yacom, 147
Grove, Henry, 42
Gulick, John, 119

H

Habbagh. *See* Hoppock
Hackett
    John, 46, 120, 122, 128, 134, 136,
        147, 148, 159, 163, 164
    Mrs. (Elizabeth Reading), 180
    William, 173
Haff
    John, 62
    Lawrence, 68, 73, 103
Hager, Lawrence, 147
Hains, Amos, 44

Hait, Benjamin, Rev., 105, 106, 129,
    137, 157, 160, 170, 171, 172, 174
Hall
    Blandina, 131, 169, 172
    David, 172
    George, 40, 49, 131
    Richard, 63
Hampton, Jonathon, 117, 135, 136
Hancock
    James, 17
    John, 133
Hankinson
    Aaron, 117, 140
    Joseph, 8, 24, 134, 177
Hann, William, 68
Hannah, James, 74, 89, 132, 133
Hardin, Martin, 12
Hardung, Paul, 156
Harkers, James, 30
Harman, Samuel, 151
Harney
    Elizabeth, 6, 29, 33, 42, 50, 61, 63,
        68, 78, 79, 85, 105, 110, 119
    Molly, 29, 35
    Walter, 5, 13, 14, 20, 30
    Widow, 48, 63, 127, 129
Harrington, Edward, 84, 139
Harrison, Samuel, 2
Harshal (var. Harshel), Christian, 50,
    77, 82, 88, 156, 173
Hatton
    George, 60, 70, 75
    Widow, 71, 75
Haughinback, Casper, 44
Haun, Andrew, 109
Hawkins, John, 18, 75, 137, 151
Hay, Peter, 3
Hayes, Mary, 57
Heath
    Andrew, 11
    Richard, 28
    Widow, 28
Hegeman
    Adrian, 4, 66, 78, 88, 104, 105, 107,
        111, 113, 117, 137, 158
    Andrew, 86
    Joseph, 66, 74, 153
    Widow, 125, 155
Heiglut, Nicolas, 21
Helby's Tract, 11
Helt, John, 73, 134, 136, 141

Hemerigh. See Emery
Hendrickse, Tunis, 37, 156
Henry (var. Henery)
    Abraham, 45
    Michael, 9, 20, 30, 56, 59, 67, 74,
        78, 82, 105, 106
    Michael, Jr., 77
    Samuel, 52, 59, 65, 77
    William, 19, 37, 44, 49, 60, 106,
        113, 115, 132
Hepburn, William, 33
Herbert, Mr, 20
Higby, Joseph, 132
Hill
    Jonathon, 19, 144
    Joseph, 31, 51
    Joseph, Jr., 31
Hobbagh. See Hoppock
Hoff
    Charles, 75, 82, 132, 136, 138, 149,
        161
    John, 14, 42, 67
Hoffman
    Henry, 66, 79
    John, 14, 21, 33
    Peter, 31, 76, 147
Hogeland
    Derrick, 26, 28, 42, 57, 62, 70, 86
    John, 28
Holcomb
    Richard, 28
    Samuel, 98
Hollingshead, Joseph, 23, 33, 64, 72,
    82, 160
Hommer, Herbert, 103
Honey, Abraham, 25
Hooper, Robert, 39
Hoppock (var. Hobbagh, Habbagh)
    George, 49
    Joost, 51, 105
    Joseph, 147
    Tunis, 26, 165
Horn, Jeremus, 53, 92
Horner, Peter, 10, 86
Horton, Calab, 32
house construction, 4, 5, 10, 12, 17, 67,
    93, 95, 96, 100, 110, 123, 127, 133,
    134, 139, 159
Housel (var. Housil)
    Jacob, 66, 79
    Johannes, 97, 106

Matthias, 37, 79
William, 57, 85, 110, 176
Howe
Abraham, 31, 80, 96, 101, 106, 120
Robert, 57, 90
Howell
Benjamin, 6, 69, 70, 79, 80, 93, 99
Daniel, 6, 25, 32, 35, 40, 62, 70, 154
John, 70
Joseph, 32, 35, 48, 70, 97, 116, 140, 153
Obadiah, 129, 133
Reading, 154
William, 52
Hude, James, 13
Huff
John, 14
Peter, 139
Hulings
Abraham, 133
Marens, 31
Hull
Johannes, 24, 63
John, 37
Jonathan, 140
Hunlocke
Mr., 23
Mrs., 17, 18
Hunt
Edward, 120, 122, 128, 142, 143, 150, 153, 157, 161, 162, 166, 169, 170, 178, 179
Richard, 178
Thomas, 31, 38, 43, 75, 76, 78
Wilson, 77, 129
Hunter
Alexander, 1
Hugh, 94, 98, 99, 100, 103, 106, 107, 108, 109, 112, 118, 121, 124, 125, 135, 136, 137, 138, 139, 145, 148, 149, 152, 158, 164, 166, 169, 171, 172
William, 145
Hunter's Ferry, Pa., 30
Hunterdon County, N.J., iv, ix, x, xi, xiii, 1, 7, 8, 14, 15, 25, 32, 38, 43, 47, 54, 103, 120, 182, 184
Hurlocker, Henry, 70
Hutchins, James, 30
Hutchinson
Isaac, 60

James, 54

I

Imlay, Johnston, 154, 169
Indians, 15
Indians Fields, 44
Insworth, Robert, 108

J

Jewell
B., 93
John, 4, 78, 92, 138
William, 29, 38
Job, John, 82
Johnson
Benjamin, 87, 137
Cornelius, 11
Elizabeth, 174
Helena, 6, 9
Henry, 162
Jacob, 31, 36
Jacobus, 43
John, 24, 27, 42, 52, 53, 110, 119
Joseph, 85
Samuel, 5, 98
Jones
Catherine, 33
John, 74
Thomas, 151, 166, 176, 178
Juriaensen (var. Yerianse), Michael, 128

K

Kase. *See* Case
Kearney, Philip, 100
Keiner, Adam, 139
Kelse, Philip, 55, 79
Kemble, Peter, 14
Kener, Johannes, 61
Kennedy, Dr., 137
Kershaw, (var. Kurshow), Adrian, 63
King
Jereimiah, 157
Joseph, 11, 52, 59
King's Sawmill, 149
Kinney
Daniel, 8

William, 125
Kinny
    David, 5, 12, 19, 32, 65, 116
    Jacobus, 125, 127
    James, 20
    Mary, 1
    William, 60, 65, 78
Kinsey, James, 145, 159
Kirkbride
    John, 41, 47
    Mahlon, 17, 30, 41, 67, 69, 71, 85,
        89, 94, 96, 126
    Messrs, 10
    Samuel, 142
Kirkpatrick, William, Rev., 176, 180
Kitchen (var. Kitchin)
    Ann, 3
    Joseph, 82
    Samuel, 67, 82, 84, 85, 108
    Thomas, 38
    Widow, 12
Kline
    Harmon, 138
    Herman, 73
    Philip, 88, 89
Kuhl (var. Koel, Koul, Coul, Coil,
    Coel)
    Christian, 27, 38, 52, 78, 88, 106,
        115, 126, 150, 152
    Elenor, 35
    Paul, 22, 141
Kuilinger, Philip, 162

L

Ladd, John, 47, 73, 159
Lake
    Daniel, 39, 146
    John, 150
    Thomas, 48
Lamb
    Michael, 146
    Mr., 38, 43, 75
Lambert
    Jeremiah, 97, 162
    John, 25, 65
    Thomas, 80
Landen, Daniel, 38
Landing at Brunswick, 4, 10, 16, 19,
    20, 45, 47, 50, 55, 59, 65, 66, 72, 78,

82, 84, 87, 91, 96, 99, 106, 114, 115,
    135, 165
Landing at Trenton, 47
Landis, Henry, 12, 42, 70, 110, 133,
    137, 153, 165
Lane
    Cornelius, 62, 65
    Henry, 3, 6, 10, 16, 17, 23, 50, 55,
        60, 72, 73, 101, 104
Laning, Isaac, 83
Lare, Jacob, 100
Large
    Ebenezer, 62
    Robert, 3, 15
Larue
    Abraham, 148
    Daniel, 52
Lauseet, Peter, 18, 59
Laushee, Abraham, 109
Lawrence
    Giles, 20
    John, 18, 56, 139, 159, 179
Layman, Martin, 70
Lebanon, N.J., 53
Lee
    Gershom, 46, 84, 89, 107, 112, 122,
        126, 127, 129, 137, 138, 143,
        144, 151, 158, 163
    Mrs., 1, 5
Leet, Isaac, 81
Leigh, Ichabod, 93
Leonard
    Daniel, 40
    Morgan, 69
    Paul, 120
    Thomas, 26, 32
Lequire, Gerardus, 53
Lesley, George, 9
Lewis, Dr., 80
Light, Isaac, 81
Lindsley, John, Jr., 11
loan office money
    cancellation, 29, 55, 67, 73, 79, 126
    deficiencies, 29, 53, 55, 126, 157
    emission, 44
    sinking fund, 44, 101, 141
    use of, 22, 23, 96
Lodor
    Benjamin, 158
    John, 158
Logan

James, 47
Mr., 19, 63
Thomas, 4
William, 66
Long Valley, N.J., 43, 63
Long, Richard, 28
Lore, Cornelius, 106
Lorecs, Daniel, 109
lottery, 33, 43, 54, 74, 75, 87, 160
Loudoun, John Campbell, 4th Earl of, 132
Louks, John, 45
Louzier (var. Lousier), Antho, 3, 12, 150
Low
  Benjamin, 35, 149
  Cornelius, 55, 63, 94, 162, 165
  Cornelius, Jr., 87
  Lawrence, 37, 112, 113, 159
Lowry, Thomas, 117, 118, 134, 142, 144, 149, 150, 156, 162, 166, 168, 172, 180
Lynns, Joseph, 55

M

M'Kracke, Robert, 121
Magrah. *See* McGray
Malachy, Dr., 163
malthouse, 49
Manners, Christean, 129, 130, 162
Marble Mountain (near Belvidere, N.J.), 11
Mare, Lawrence, 88
Marlatt. *See* Morlatt
Marriot, Thomas, 41, 42, 53, 134
Marshall
  Cathrine, 70
  John, 58
  Thomas, 22, 28, 63, 77, 86, 115, 142, 164
Marshcollock, Sarah, 126, 127
Martin
  David, 55
  James, 1, 5, 34, 39, 40, 75
  Justin, 122
  Thomas, 2, 8, 12, 17, 26, 50, 59, 65, 67, 68, 75, 84, 90, 96, 99, 102, 103, 106, 127
Matthews

Mary, 42
Molly, 48, 54, 71, 78, 89, 99
Mattison
  Aaron, 15
  Jacob, 126, 130, 134, 141, 143, 160, 175
Maurer, Jacob, 27
Maurison, Frederick, 111
Maxwell, Anthony, Dr., 100
McCartee. *See* McKarty
McGray (var. Magrau, Magray, Magrah, McGrau), John, 58, 69, 70, 81
McKane, Dr., 149
McKarty (var. McCartee), William, 116, 131, 139, 140, 149
McKinny
  David, 113, 123
  Mordecai, 114
McKinsey (var. McKinsley), Enoch, 163
McLane the Taylor, 91
McMullen
  Henry, 42, 56
  Sarah, 137
  William, 18
McMurtrie
  Joseph, 45, 48, 57, 80, 89, 90
  Robert, 57, 90
  Thomas, 111
McPherson, Samuel, 157
Meddaugh. *See* Middaugh
medicines
  Balsam Mirablis, 151
  Bartrams Ballsamick Elixir, 173
  Daffy's Elixir, 77
  Elixir Proprietatis, 23, 166
  Jesuits Bark, 40
  Lignum Vita, 133
  Lockyer Pills., 158
Meleck. *See* Melick
Melegh, Josiah, 33
Melford's Tracts, 60
Melick (var. Meleck)
  Frederick, 138
  Godfry, 90
  John, 96, 138
Menusigay, N.J., 149
Mershon, Henry, 157
Metcher, Richard, 72
Middaugh (var. Meddaugh, Middays)

Peter, 2, 115, 118, 119
Teunis, 106
Middlebrook, N.J., 157
Middlesex County, N.J., 15
Middletown, N.J., 88
Miller
    Alexander, 76
    Edward, 23
    John, 147
    Julian, 51
Mills, William, Rev., 156, 162, 166, 170, 171, 176
Milly, Mr., 150
Milner, Edward, 29, 55
Mineral Springs, Pa., 10, 12, 15
Minor, Anna, 49
Miskumb, Nicholas, 161
Moier, Michael, 42
Montgomerie, William, 1, 2, 6, 18, 19, 22, 31, 35, 37, 46, 47, 56, 59, 63, 65, 70, 72, 102, 136
Moor, Peter, 165
Moore
    Michael, 147
    Nathaniel, 44, 79
    Samuel, 113
    Sarah, 18, 22, 34, 37, 46, 49, 54, 57, 60, 63, 66, 84, 90
Moravians, 57, 60, 85, 111
Morden, George, 149, 157, 162, 167, 169, 172
Morlatt (var. Marlatt, Murlat, Mullat)
    Derrick, 74
    John, 73
Morrey, Charles, 18
Morris County, N.J., ix, 34, 47, 50, 62, 71, 72, 77, 82, 87, 93, 111, 123, 140, 146, 164
Morrison, Archibald, 30, 35
Mott, Joseph, 8
Moyer, Michael, 158
Mt. Carmel Tract, 66
Mullat. See Morlatt
Mullen, John, 29, 85
Murlat. See Morlatt
Muskonetcong Hills, 34
Muskonetcong River Valley, N.J., 11, 19, 31, 34, 72, 83, 85, 90, 123

N

Nause, Dr, 20
Neams, Isaac, 91
Negros
    Boy, 111
    Cesar, 48, 60, 85, 122
    Dinah, 149
    Elijah, 174
    Harry, 5
    John, 86
    Peg, 128
    Pigg, 5, 62
    Pompey, 110, 131, 140, 142, 146, 149
    Priamus, 5
    Tab, 6, 7, 92, 96, 97
    Tom, 5
Nevill, Samuel, 100
Nevius, Peter, 151
Newbank, Lottis, 128, 129, 150
Newman, Thomas, 47, 50
Newtown, Pa., 118
Nixson, Patrick, 27, 66, 85
Noel, Mr., 171
Norcross, William, 114, 116, 128, 134, 138, 141, 147, 151, 170
Norton, Dr., 128, 130, 132, 151, 157, 161
Null (var. Newell), Johannes, 37, 110

O

O'Neil, Constantine, 85
Off, Nicolas, 125
Ogden, Robert, 97
Oliphant, Ephraim, 151
Oliver, Samuel, 127
Opdyke (var. Opdick, Opdike, Updike)
    John, 16, 24, 92, 108, 132, 148, 155, 159
    Joshua, 3, 8, 86
Oxley, Henry, 8, 27

P

Pahquanack, N.J., 40
Pahuckqualong (Delaware Water Gap), 95
Pain, Elizabeth, 2

Painter, Philip, 135
Pancoast, Joseph?, 19
Paquaess (Pequest) River, N.J., 9, 32
Parke, John, 28
Parker, Nathaniel, 44, 55, 132, 133
Passion, Francis, 62, 67, 103
Paxton, Edward, 17, 28
Pearl, Samuel, 134
Pearson. *See* Pierson
Peckel, Henry, 157
Pena Gulf Rock, 81
Penns, Messrs, 38
Pennsylvania Gazette, xi, 2, 89, 105,
    115, 123, 132, 143, 151, 165, 172
Pennytown (Pennington), N.J., 4, 6,
    29, 58, 133
Penunganchong, N.J., 21, 25, 30, 31,
    45, 61, 65
Peter, Black, 37, 58, 60, 70
Peter, Henry, 93
Peters, Godfrey, 4, 9, 18, 24, 68
Pettit
    Jonathan, 44
    Nathaniel, 120, 136, 139
Pettys, Joseph, 13
Pharoe, James, 24, 28, 41, 44, 46, 50
Phelps, Philip, 4
Philadelphia, Pa., 6, 7, 15, 18, 19, 21,
    35, 41, 46, 56, 68, 76, 77, 97, 100,
    102, 114, 128, 138, 141, 145, 148,
    150, 154, 166, 172, 173, 176, 177,
    181, 183, 184
Philips
    Indian, 16
    Richard, 167
Philipsburg, N.J., 111
Philipse, Coenrad, 145, 162
Pickel, Josiah, 19
Pidcock, John, 128
Pierson (var. Pearson)
    Mrs., 42
    Robert, 52
    William, 95, 104, 111, 132, 133,
        141, 152, 159, 165
Pittinger, John, 153, 159
Plumly, George, 7
Pockus, Mathias, 41
Pohohatcong, N.J., 10, 11, 16, 19, 34,
    67, 82, 85
Poke, Adam, 22, 37, 41, 143, 147, 150
Poquanoch River, N.J., 40, 97

Poquessing Creek, Pa., 7
Porter
    John, 17, 38, 177
    Richard, 104, 112, 121, 129, 136,
        156
Post
    Ann, 165
    John, 145, 146, 150
post riders, 149, 156
Potts, Ruth, 119
Pound at Delaware, 49
Prall
    Aaron, 43, 65
    Peter, 92, 104, 135
Preston, Christopher, 51
Pricket, 11, 19
Prior, Thomas, 180
Proprietary Right, 12
Pues, William, 45
Pursly's Rock, 81

Q

Quick
    Francis, 7, 27, 125, 165, 166
    Jacob, 23, 79
    John, 4, 8
    Tunis, 11, 12, 40
Quimby
    Isaiah, 51, 94
    Jonathon, 81
    Joshiah, 25

R

Rake, John, 108, 110, 112, 113, 118
Raniel, Justus, 82
Raritan River, 2, 26, 37, 55, 61, 66, 85
Raritan River, bridge over South
    Branch, 140
Rawles, William, 24
Rea, William, 150
Read, Charles, 7, 53, 131, 140, 141,
    143, 144
Reading
    Ann, 21, 48, 108, 138, 153
    Daniel, 9, 10, 38, 45, 46, 47, 50, 64,
        67, 69, 72, 74, 75, 76, 77, 80, 82,
        91, 93, 94, 98, 100, 103, 108,
        111, 112, 113, 119, 131, 133,

Index

137, 138, 142, 144, 146, 149,
155, 158, 160, 163, 166, 169,
170, 171, 173, 174, 175, 176,
179, 180

Elizabeth (Betty), 46, 56, 71, 72,
103, 119, 122, 124, 125

George, 13, 15, 30, 34, 35, 37, 43,
44, 45, 46, 48, 49, 56, 57, 58, 60,
63, 65, 66, 67, 68, 71, 74, 75, 76,
77, 79, 80, 81, 82, 84, 86, 87, 92,
93, 95, 96, 97, 98, 99, 102, 103,
104, 111, 114, 117, 118, 120,
126, 127, 128, 129, 135, 136,
137, 139, 140, 142, 143, 144,
145, 146, 147, 151, 152, 156,
157, 161, 162, 163, 164, 165,
168, 170, 172, 174, 176, 177,
178, 179

John (son), 8, 10, 14, 20, 22, 25, 26,
30, 32, 37, 41, 42, 49, 55, 56, 58,
61, 64, 69, 72, 75, 76, 78, 81, 84,
87, 101, 104, 128, 130, 131, 133,
143, 146, 149, 150, 168, 171,
177

Joseph, 14, 61, 75, 76, 88, 92, 93,
97, 101, 105, 110, 111, 115, 118,
129, 135, 142, 155, 166

Mary (Molly), 61, 111, 116, 122,
129, 131, 133, 135, 136, 141,
148, 149, 150, 151, 152, 157,
159, 160, 161, 163

Richard, 36, 48, 56, 61, 86, 108,
110, 111, 112, 116, 120, 121,
122, 123, 124, 127, 128, 131,
132, 133, 135, 140, 141, 142,
145, 146, 148, 150, 152, 155,
158, 162, 165, 171, 176, 178

Samuel, 48, 179

Sarah, 111, 118, 135, 141, 151

Thomas, 71, 112, 116, 121, 122,
129, 132, 134, 136, 140, 141,
142, 143, 145, 146, 147, 149,
154, 158, 159, 160, 163, 164,
165, 166, 169, 170, 171, 172,
173, 175, 176, 177, 178, 179,
180

Reading, John
alcohol purchased, 8, 13, 21, 22, 23,
31, 39, 42, 48, 49, 51, 57, 63, 65,
66, 92, 102, 110, 112, 116, 119,

126, 129, 130, 137, 138, 139,
165, 178

book binding at Nassau College,
156

books and newspapers purchased,
2, 18, 21, 59, 119, 148, 156

charitable donations, 6, 15, 30, 31,
32, 33, 46, 74, 75, 83, 84, 97,
103, 106, 107, 108, 109, 111,
113, 120, 122, 124, 135, 136,
139, 141, 147, 148, 154, 157,
158, 159, 160, 161, 163, 164,
166, 168, 169, 170, 171, 172,
174, 178, 179

deeding land to daughter Sarah and
husband, 164

division of land for sons Joseph
and Richard, 25

donations, 114

fees for military commissions, 130,
135

loans made, 5, 14, 20, 21, 29, 32,
33, 36, 37, 38, 40, 42, 43, 50, 53,
57, 58, 59, 61, 70, 74, 77, 81, 86,
98, 104, 114, 115, 118, 119, 125,
132, 133, 136, 137, 140, 141,
142, 145, 152, 155, 157, 158,
160, 161, 162, 163, 164, 166,
168, 170, 171, 172, 173, 174,
175, 176, 179

Princeton charter, 32

Privy council attendance, 9, 15, 32,
40, 53, 85, 157

Proprietors council attendance, ix,
x, 9, 17, 33, 60, 62, 67, 69, 77,
100, 145, 183

rent collection, 56, 87, 137, 163,
167, 178

support for Amwell Presbyterian
Church, xii, 86, 107, 112, 116,
120, 160, 163, 167, 174

support to the Dutch Ministry, 69

support to the Lenape Indian
reservation, 154

support to the Ministry, 138

sworn in as temporary Governor,
13

taxes paid, 79, 83, 84, 101, 111,
120, 129, 138, 146, 147, 154

Town meeting attendance, 24

Index

use of the Great Seal of New
    Jersey, 133, 134
Reading, John, Col., ix, x, 40, 121, 179
Readington Township, N.J., 79, 111,
    120, 146
Redman, Joseph, 156
Redrick, Anderson, 77, 84
Reed
    Andrew, 27, 125
    Azariah, 70
    Charles, 16
    Giles, 66
    Joseph, 115, 127, 137, 147, 153,
        165
    Moses, 127
    Richard, 29
Reeder, Joseph, 153
Reid, Augustine, 111, 121, 151, 164,
    167, 179
Remersey, Chal'd, 2
Richardson, John, 173
Ridge, Thomas, 99, 105
Rightinghousen. See Rittenhouse
Riley, (var. Ryely), Patrick, 131
Ringo
    Albartes, 11, 23
    Cornelius, 6, 10, 152, 159
    John, 152
    Philip, 2, 8, 9, 10, 21, 23, 29, 32, 43,
        49, 52, 58, 89
rioters, a matter before the council, 15
Rittenhouse (var. Rightinghousen)
    Hannah, 88
    Isaac, 121
    William, 35, 88, 97, 101
Rivenberg, Peter, 116, 141
roads, commission for laying out, 4
Robbins, John, 4
Robert
    Elizabeth, 9, 40
    Vincent, 10, 14, 19, 22, 23, 24, 27,
        37, 40, 41, 42
Roberts, Richard, 152
Robins, Job, 143
Robinson, 52
Rockefeller, Peter, 4, 9, 22, 39, 53, 54,
    61, 155
Rodman, John, 13
Rogers, Alexander, 156
Romine, Peter, 6, 31, 56, 78, 80, 90
Roseberry, Joseph, 169, 175, 176

Rounsaval
    Benjamin, 30
    Richard, 27
Rouse
    Gideon, 58
    John, 44, 79, 117
    John Jr., 138
Roxbury, N.J., 32, 88, 111
Roxiticus (Mendham), N.J., 76, 80
Royall Oak, 6
Ruckman, Thomas, 158
Ruckmans Plantation, 70
Runk, Jacob, 54, 62, 79
Runyan (var. Rugnion, Runion)
    Thomas, 31
    Vincent Aaron, 165
Rush, Yerie, 72
Rutgers, Margaret, 25
Ryely. See Riley
Ryerson
    Catherine, 67
    Elizabeth, 160
    George, 97
    Luke, xiii, 31, 43, 56, 59, 60, 63, 64,
        65, 68, 69, 94, 97, 122, 124, 126,
        160
    Martin, 4, 8, 11, 12, 15, 18, 19, 24,
        30, 44, 49, 50, 56, 61, 63, 67, 76,
        77, 82, 83, 92, 94, 95, 100, 110,
        115, 123, 128, 131, 137, 140,
        142, 143, 152, 156, 157, 158,
        159, 161, 162, 164, 168, 169,
        171, 173, 179, 180

S

Sacket, Joseph, 43, 59
Saltar, Richard, 130
Savery, Peter, 17
Saxton, George, 33
Scattergood, Joseph, 62
Schamp. See Schomp
Schenck (var. Schank), George, 122,
    136, 148
Schomp (var. Schamp)
    George, 10, 89
    Henry, 127
Schonk. See Schenck
Schooley
    Samuel, 57

Index

William, 26
Scott, Thomas, 19, 30, 77
Seaman, William, 4
Search, Christian, 70, 75
Seberings, Daniel, 59
Seed, Timothy, 65
Selvester, Peter, 132
Sergeant
    Jons, 11, 97
    Mrs., 10
Sever, Coenradt, 27
Severns, Benjamin, 3, 15, 155
Seward, Obidiah, 89
Seyoe, Aaron, 5
Shafer, Casper, 49
Sharp (var. Sharpenstine)
    Christian, 37, 73, 126
    Isaac, 30
    John, 120
    Matthis, 27
    Powel, 116
Shavers
    Casper, 151
    Johannes, 31
Shaw
    Dr., 23
    John, 133
    Robert, 144, 148
Sheply, William, 135, 141
Shifley, Martin, 2, 14, 21, 22, 24, 27,
    28, 36, 41, 48, 50, 51, 52, 53, 55, 58,
    61, 67, 74, 76, 78, 79, 80, 82, 83, 88,
    92, 93, 94, 95, 98, 107, 117, 121,
    130, 131, 134, 135, 136, 140, 142,
    143, 148, 149, 150, 151, 158, 165,
    166, 167
Shippen
    Edward, 7, 41, 48, 159
    Ishmael, 4, 5, 6, 10, 11, 43, 46, 48,
        72, 95, 105, 107, 116, 118, 122,
        125
Shirley, William, (Gov. of
    Massachusetts), 16
Short
    John, 40
    Michael, 8, 27, 40
    Mr., 40
Shuke. See Snook
Shultus
    Peter, 153
    Valentine, 62, 101

Shurt, Michael, 53, 55, 122
Silverthorn
    Thomas, 21, 47, 175
    William, 122
Simons, Hermanus, 16, 19, 41, 52, 102,
    103
Simonse, Simon, 113
Sines, Nichcolas, 27
Skank, Ruloff, 2
Skyhawk, Aaron, 88
slaves and servants
    purchased, 81, 83, 100, 146, 150,
        155
    referenced, 28, 86, 130, 145, 171,
        174
    sold, 149
    trial and punishment, 5
Sleight, Henry, 63
Slover, Abraham, 65
Smalley, Isaac, 165
Smith
    Abraham, 142
    Benjamin, 151
    Christian, 144
    Dr., 78
    Jasper, 176, 181
    John, 41, 49, 50, 55, 75, 77, 84, 173
    Jonathon, 71
    Joseph, 129, 140, 142, 144, 152,
        159
    Matthias, 42
    Ralph, 43, 47, 66
    Richard, 13, 17, 25, 26, 62
    Robert, 77
    Samuel, 99
    Timothy, 162
    Widow, 111
    William, 81
Smok, Peter, 28
Snook (var. Snuke, Shuke)
    Adam, 112, 123, 126, 133, 142
    William, 115
Snowden, William, 6
Snuke. See Snook
Snyder, Hendrick, 99
Society Line, 43, 47, 154
Starke, Aaron, 44, 115, 127, 137, 141,
    149, 158, 162, 167
Stenson. See Stinson
Stephens, Richard, 18
Stevens

Index

Cornelius, 53
John, 106
Stevenson
    Cornell, 86
    Molly, 70
    Samuel, 72
    William, 92
Stewart
    Charles, 161
    Francis, 157
    Henry, 19
    Robert, 37
Stillwell, Jereimiah, 131
Stinson (var. Stenson)
    Archibald, 58, 61, 65, 86
Stires, John, 138
Stockton, John, 175
Stoll
    Henry, 137
    John, 178
Stout
    Benjamin, 1, 4, 5, 9, 16, 19, 22, 32,
        33, 46, 48, 49, 52, 56, 83, 86,
        112, 113, 132, 138, 140, 148,
        151, 152, 153, 158
    David, 24
    Freegift, 44
    James, 51, 76, 133
    Jonathon, 81
    Joseph, 9, 16, 30, 39, 47, 68, 145,
        159, 170
    Richard, 11
    Samuel, 43, 140
Stranzfell, Christian, 154
Suiter
    Jacob Peter, 62
Surveying
    Drafts and Fieldworks, 3, 6, 25, 26,
        66
    use of protractor, 3, 37
Surveyor General's Office, 48, 53, 70,
    71, 78, 82, 89, 92, 105, 115, 124,
    163
Sussex County, N.J., 120, 169, 179
Sutphen, (var. Zutphen)
    Abraham, 75, 106, 107, 115, 150
    Derrick, 42, 54, 70, 76, 158, 160,
        162
    Jacob, 68, 157
Swallow, John, 29
swamps, 3, 59, 60, 65, 87, 138

Swazey
    Amos, 138, 142
    Samuel, 76
Switzer, Lawrence, 159

T

Tarr, Coenradt, 96
Tates, Adam, 67
Taylor
    John, 27
    William, 6, 9
teachers
    school, 11, 12, 20, 49, 65, 133
    singing, 65, 150
Teets, Adam, 21
Tegen, Martin, 58, 59, 60, 65, 122
Templar, William, 89, 90
Ten Eyke
    Andreis, 16
    Jacob, 43
    Tobias, 40, 62, 76, 95
Tenant, Gilbert, sermons, 134
Tenyke, Tenis, 88
Terrat (var. LaTourette), Daniel, 107
Thatcher
    Amos, 59
    Bartholomew, 157
    James, 24
    Jeremiah, 5, 24, 67, 103
    John, 14
    Joseph, 38, 77, 91
    Thomas, 6, 24, 33
Thomas
    John, 115, 116
    Sarah, 8, 10, 24, 27
Tildine. *See* Dildine
Titsworth, John, 175
Titus, Joseph, 124
Tomkins, Samuel, 37, 38, 44
Tomlinson, Francis, 123, 131, 132,
    134, 139
Toy, Timothy, 34, 42, 45
trades
    axel treeing, 52, 93
    blacksmith, 27, 66, 78, 95, 111, 116,
        132, 137, 141, 142, 152, 159
    carpenter, 4
    cooper, 52, 83
    currier, 16, 37, 78, 86, 104, 107

fuller, 73, 107, 158
knitter, 56, 77
mason, 96, 100, 105, 147
painter, 110, 150
shoemaker, 18, 28, 57, 68, 69, 70, 72, 93
spinner, 6, 9, 33, 35, 48, 59, 84
tailor, 16, 66, 68, 124, 129, 139, 164
thatcher, 99
tinker, 91, 121, 122, 144, 146, 148, 149, 152
turner, 93
weaver, 18, 21, 28, 33, 35, 37, 79, 84, 93, 102, 105, 108, 110, 113, 115, 119, 120, 124, 126, 127, 129, 131, 135, 138, 141, 142, 151, 154, 155, 159
well digger, 124, 125, 126, 129
Trapnell, John, 47, 72
Travers, Patrick, 93, 107, 128, 129
Trenton, N.J., iv, 2, 4, 7, 8, 9, 10, 13, 15, 17, 18, 20, 21, 23, 27, 28, 29, 30, 33, 34, 35, 36, 37, 40, 41, 42, 43, 44, 47, 53, 54, 55, 57, 58, 59, 64, 66, 67, 68, 69, 70, 73, 75, 77, 78, 79, 80, 82, 83, 84, 85, 87, 89, 90, 91, 104, 109, 118, 125, 128, 129, 130, 131, 134, 137, 143, 146, 178, 179, 181, 183
Trimmer
Andrew, 24, 67
George, 66
Mathias, 55, 56
Tunis, 91
Uria, 66
Trout, Jeremiah, 159
Tucker, Samuel, 129, 130
Tunisen, Tunis, 165
Turner, Joseph, 54, 55, 65

U

Union Furnace, 85
Updike. *See* Opdyke

V

Valentine the Peddler, 2, 33
Van Brike, B., 84
Van Buskirk (var. Van Boskirk)
Daniel, 161

Michael, 75
Van Camp (var. Van Campen)
Aaron, 139
Abraham, 127
Col., 135
Cornelius, 63
Garret, 63, 93, 115, 169
Van Doren, David, 147
Van Duchren (var. Dusen), Domine, (Dutch Reformed Pastor), 54
Van Duren, Godfrey, 2, 4, 5, 10
Van Este
Jeromus, 4, 23
Johannes, 104
John, 49, 52, 69
Joseph, 158
Van Etta, Thomas, 24
Van Fleet
Garret, 64, 125
William, 156
Van Horn
Abraham, 88
David, 27
Mr., 15
Thomas, 27
Van Kirk, Joseph, 162
Van Maple, Yocham, 38
Van Neste, John, 5, 8
Van Oven, Henry, 170
Van Sickle (var. Van Sicklen)
John, 27, 65
Sarah, 138, 151, 168
Van Stay (var. Van Ste), Henry, 52
Van Wagoner, Dr., 5, 24, 99, 105
Van Wyck (var. Wyke, Weyk)
Theodore, 109, 153
Vanbuskirks, the, 4
Vander Spegel, John, 25
Vanderbilt, Jacob, 83
Vang, John, 98, 99
Vansicklens, the, 62
Vendue, George Reading's, 178
Verity, Jacob, 138
Viesselius, George, Dr., 116, 127, 133, 138, 139, 140, 141, 148, 155, 163, 175
Voorhees (var. Voreheis), William, 11, 104, 108, 113

Index

W

Wachcchiok Brook, 25
Wagoner, Harman, 58
Waldrof, Anthony, 101
Waldron, Francis, 126, 131
Walpack mine, 95, 96, 100, 101, 107, 110, 123, 161, 165
Walpack, N.J., 100
Warford
    Job, 62, 79
    Joseph, 19, 35, 40, 90, 103
Warrell (var. Warnell), Joseph, 52, 53
Washer, John, 122
Waterhouse, 25
Watson
    Dr., 48, 56, 63, 128
    John, 25
weddings, 40, 130, 143
Weeks
    James, 11
    Richard, 11, 12
Welch, William, 147
Weller, Phillip, 4
Wert
    Peter, 132
    William, 50
Wertegen
    William, 23, 31, 49, 79, 113
West, Thomas, 70, 78
Weycoff. See Wyckoff
Whippany, N.J., 40, 80, 88
White, Alexander, 106
Whitenack, Cornelius, 164
Whittaker
    Jacobus, 12, 39, 44
    James, 45
Wickoff. See Wyckoff
Wiggins, William, 103
Williams
    Francis, 68
    Lawrence, 2
    Thomas, 138
    Walter, 37
Williamson
    Abraham, 161
    Cornelius, 30, 55
    James, 106
    John, 12, 39, 42, 155
    Nicholas, 30, 112, 113
Wills

James, 4, 80, 137, 152
John, 18
Willson
    G., 34
    J., 122
    James, 4, 80, 106, 137, 152
Winter, Henry, 31, 76, 146, 162
Wise, Philip, 91
Witt, Dr., 21, 46
Wolf, Jeromus, 33
Wood
    James, 91, 107
    John, 75, 84, 87, 101, 122, 134, 137, 155, 160, 161
    Joseph, 46
    Katy, 153
    William, 108
Woods, Nanny, 94, 98, 99, 105, 106, 113, 115, 118, 121, 124, 126, 128, 129, 131, 133, 138, 145, 146, 148, 151, 152, 154
Woolever
    Jacob, 42, 86, 104
    Peter, 62, 84, 89, 111, 166
Wooley, Edmund, 36, 38
Woolf, G., 178
Woolverton
    Dennis, 11, 31, 62, 134
    Francis, 150
    Joel, 74, 90, 141
    Morris, 93
Wright
    David, 30
    Fretwell, 72
    Jerimiah, 8
    John, 130, 133
    William, 68
Writ Non Est, 82
Writ of Replevin, 130, 131
Wyckoff (var. Wickoff, Weycoff)
    Cornelius, 9, 22, 97, 106, 113, 149, 157
    John, 160
    Nicholas, 83
    Nicolas, 83
    Simon, 162
Wynes, Samuel, 14

Index

Y

Yard
    Benjamin, 68
    John, 4, 15, 23, 33, 102, 105, 132
    Joseph, 22
    William, 4, 8, 17, 47, 54, 55, 133,
        134
Yards, Messrs, 60
Yeager
    Henry, 144
    Peter, 71, 77, 108, 156
    Philip, 58

Yockle, Jacob, 119
Young
    Peter, 29, 52, 82
    Philip, 28, 44
    Thomas, 57
    William, 107
Youngblood
    John, 68, 70, 74
    Margaret, 9, 20

Z

Zutphen. *See* Sutphen